# COMICS AND NATION

**STUDIES IN COMICS AND CARTOONS**

Jared Gardner, Charles Hatfield, and Rebecca Wanzo, Series Editors

# COMICS AND NATION

Power, Pop Culture, and Political
Transformation in Poland

## EWA STAŃCZYK

THE OHIO STATE UNIVERSITY PRESS

COLUMBUS

Library of Congress Cataloging-in-Publication Data
Names: Stańczyk, Ewa, 1981– author.
Title: Comics and nation : power, pop culture, and political transformation in Poland / Ewa Stańczyk.
Other titles: Studies in comics and cartoons.
Description: Columbus : The Ohio State University Press, [2022] | Series: Studies in comics and cartoons | Includes bibliographical references and index. | Summary: "Drawing on dozens of press articles, interviews, and readers' letters, the book discusses how journalists, artists, and audiences used comics to probe the boundaries of national culture and scrutinize the established notions of Polishness"—Provided by publisher.
Identifiers: LCCN 2022014474 | ISBN 9780814214961 (cloth) | ISBN 0814214967 (cloth) | ISBN 9780814282236 (ebook) | ISBN 0814282237 (ebook)
Subjects: LCSH: Comic books, strips, etc.—Poland—History and criticism. | Popular culture and literature—Poland. | Comic books, strips, etc.—Political aspects—Poland. | Comic books, strips, etc.—Social aspects—Poland. | National characteristics, Polish, in literature.
Classification: LCC PN6790.P6 S73 2022 | DDC 741.5/9438—dc23/eng/20220505
LC record available at https://lccn.loc.gov/2022014474
Other identifiers: 9780814258385 (paper) | 0814258387 (paper)

Cover design by Andrew Brozyna
Text composition by Stuart Rodriguez
Type set in Palatino Linotype

*For Jurriaan*

# CONTENTS

# ILLUSTRATIONS

# ACKNOWLEDGMENTS

I started writing about Polish comics nearly a decade ago and I am grateful to all the colleagues and friends who have encouraged me to do so. Thank you especially to José Alaniz, who successfully convinced me that English-speaking readers are interested in Eastern European comics, and to Kees Ribbens, who sparked my interest in approaching comics historically, and whose patient advice and feedback helped me in the writing of this book.

I have benefited enormously from the intellectual community at the University of Amsterdam and, in particular, from the support and inspiring presence of my direct colleagues Michael Kemper, Christian Noack, Artemy Kalinovsky, and Sudha Rajagopalan, in addition to many others. I would also like to express my gratitude to the Faculty of Humanities for awarding me the Aspasia grant in 2019/2020, which enabled me to spend more time on this project.

I am grateful to my research assistant in Poland, Joanna Marczyńska, who helped me obtain additional sources for this book, and who did this swiftly and efficiently. Thank you to Ewa Ciszewska, who had recommended Joanna to me.

At The Ohio State University Press, it has been an honor to work with Ana Jimenez-Moreno, whose guidance and consummate professionalism made this smooth sailing. The two anonymous reviewers provided helpful and detailed feedback that enabled me to fine-tune the specific chapters and improve the manuscript as a whole. I am also grateful to the editors of Studies in Comics and Cartoons series, Jared Gardner, Charles Hatfield, and Rebecca Wanzo, for taking interest in this project, and to the OSU Press Editorial Board for making this book possible.

Some sections of chapter 5 have appeared previously in print: "Women, Feminism and Polish Comic Books: Frąś/Hagedorn's *Totalnie nie nostalgia*" (2017) in *Comics of the New Europe: Reflections and Intersections* (Studies in European Comics and Graphic Novels 7), edited by Martha Kuhlman and José Alaniz, Leuven University Press, 2020, pp. 201–13, ISBN 9789462702127; "Between Personal and Collective Memory: History and Politics in Polish Comics" in *A History of Polish Literature and Culture: New Perspectives on the Twentieth and Twenty-First Centuries,* edited by Przemysław Czapliński, Joanna Niżyńska, and Tamara Trojanowska, Toronto University Press, 2018, pp. 762–73; and "'Long Live Poland!': Representing the Past in Polish Comic Books" in *Modern Language Review,* vol. 109, no. 1, 2014, pp. 186–206. I thank Leuven University Press, in particular, for granting permission to repurpose this work.

Writing this book would have been a whole different experience if it were not for my friends and family. Two Amsterdam-based friends and fellow academics, Diederik Oostdijk and Iwona Guść, provided intellectual stimulation at a time when working from home was the norm, and others, particularly Sławomir Łotysz, Paolino Nappi, and Kasia Błażewska, inspired me from afar. My family, Weronika, Ania, Aluś, and Jacek, have been a constant presence in my life, supporting me in all things great and small.

None of this would be worthwhile without my husband Jurriaan. I dedicate this book to him with all my love and gratitude.

# INTRODUCTION

On May 28, 2001, Poland's major liberal newspaper *Gazeta Wyborcza* (*The Electoral Gazette*) reported on the following incident:

> On Saturday, a dozen or so activists of the association "State-Nation-Independence," the Movement for the Reconstruction of Poland (including its youth section) as well as former prisoners of concentration camps protested outside *Przekrój*'s offices in Kraków against comic book *Maus* and its "anti-Polish" content. Piotr Bikont, *Przekrój*'s deputy editor-in-chief, translated *Maus* into Polish. Bikont watched the protest from his office window and, at one point, put on a pig mask. The protest ended with a ripping of copies of *Maus* and *Przekrój*. (PAP)

*Maus* had been contested in Poland long before its release in April 2001. It was precisely due to Spiegelman's damning portrayal of Poles as pigs that the publishing house Prószyński i S-ka, which had acquired translation rights in 1994, delayed publication for years (see Górski; Chaciński). By the time Spiegelman's graphic memoir was released by a smaller publisher called Post, the book had been steeped in controversy (Łysak 470).

*Maus* arrived in Poland at a time when a much bigger discussion on Polish complicity in the Holocaust had been raging for quite some time. Only one year earlier, Jan Tomasz Gross's groundbreaking and highly controversial book *Sąsiedzi: Historia zagłady żydowskiego mia-steczka* (*Neighbors: The Destruction of the Jewish Community in Jedwabne, Poland*) was published in Poland. The book, which described the Jedwabne pogrom, perpetrated by Christian Poles on their Jewish neighbors in 1941, enraged the national conservative circles as well as triggering a collective soul-searching among the liberal elites.[1] As far as the memory of World War II was concerned, the aforementioned protest was thus not an isolated incident.[2] Like their predecessors elsewhere, the demonstrators in Kraków emphasized the suffering of Christian Poles at the hands of the Nazis, while attempting to challenge archival evidence that spoke of denunciation and murder committed by ethnic Poles on Jews.[3] The Polish publication of *Maus* became part and parcel of this wider debate surrounding contested legacies of anti-Semitism in Poland—before, during, and after World War II.

What made the demonstration in Kraków different was Bikont's donning a pig face mask. Grotesque and highly referential, Bikont's response to the protest not only went to the core of contemporary debates about the Polish-Jewish past but also provided a poignant commentary on the comic book as a highly pliable and complex

---

1. For a collection of translated articles and statements surrounding the Jedwabne controversy, see Polonsky and Michlic, *Neighbors.*

2. The largest such full-scale protest in the first decade after the transformation, often described as the "War of the Crosses," took place in Oświęcim between 1998 and 1999. It lasted fourteen months and was staged by far-right former Solidarity activist Kazimierz Świtoń, who opposed the removal of the "Papal cross" from a Carmelite nuns' convent adjoining the former camp. The cross had been placed on the site of the convent in 1988 to commemorate the mass held by John Paul II in Auschwitz in 1979 (the cross had been part of the original altar design). The controversy, involving former Christian and Jewish inmates, Poland's Jewish community, the government, public intellectuals, and others, triggered wider debates on "competitive suffering," the "ownership" of Auschwitz as a site of collective memory, and other unresolved issues around the memory of Polish Jews. For a book-length discussion around this controversy, see Zubrzycki.

3. Gross's book was based on the newly released records of the August trials that intended to punish "fascist-Hitlerite criminals" and their collaborators between 1944 and 1956. See Kornbluth 9.

medium.[4] Through Bikont's rendition, the Pole-pig persona branched out from the page, becoming a subject of self-reflexive and highly critical performance. The activists appreciated the gravity of the stunt and retaliated. They took the case to court, accusing the publisher of spreading anti-Polish sentiment and of defaming the Polish nation. The judge dismissed the accusations as unsubstantiated, arguing that "the representation of Poles as pigs should be interpreted as part of the author's artistic vision" (Żelazny 2). More specifically, the judge argued that allegories employing animal characters have been used in literature since time immemorial and, even if applied to historical events, they were admissible under the author's creative license (Żelazny 2).

Along with contributing to those polarizing debates about the past, Spiegelman's work revived the stereotypical depiction of the comic book as a product of lowbrow culture unsuitable for portraying serious topics and suffering from excessive commodification. To some conservative observers, *Maus* was an uninvited intruder from across the ocean that posed a danger of polluting both national memory and national culture (Łysak 472–74). Although the ripping of Spiegelman's book in 2001 was most likely an isolated occurrence of comic book destruction in Polish history, the anti-comics sentiment that emerged on the peripheries of this debate was by no means a recent invention. Neither was it limited to this particular comic book. Rather, the received view of the comic as an invader from the Western world, preying on the innocence of its readers, had been present in Poland long before this incident.

The story of *Maus*'s arrival in Poland illustrates a long-standing phenomenon of consumption and interpretation of foreign comics in a new national setting. It speaks to the misunderstandings and frictions that might arise following such a relocation, not only due to the content of the comic but also because of the medium used. In many ways, the story is characteristic of the wider trajectory of comics in Poland. As I show in the course of this monograph, since their appearance in the interwar Second Republic, comics elicited contradictory emotions, from deepest fascination to deepest dislike. They have been both enthusiastically consumed as colorful products of foreign popular culture and abhorred as a supposedly inferior medium that was feared to have a damaging effect on national culture. At dif-

---

4. Bikont recalled his stunt to Spiegelman too. See Spiegelman 123.

ferent points in Polish history, the comic has been seen alternately as an intrinsically alien art form, which would never find a home in Poland, and a deeply coveted symbol of the West to be emulated and incorporated into the native realm. Debates surrounding comics have often gone beyond the comics' mere subject matter. In the course of the twentieth and twenty-first centuries, the medium has become a pretext and a prop with which to tackle wider political, social, and cultural issues.

This book investigates how comics have featured in the 100-year history of the Polish state, from its foundation to the present. It focuses on the various ways in which comics participated in the important moments of political transformation, such as the establishment of the Second Polish Republic in 1918; the transition to Communism after World War II; the opening to the West in the 1970s; the political and economic transformation of 1989; and the memory and autobiographical turns of the 2000s. By concentrating on these transitional moments in Polish history, the book discusses how journalists, readers, artists, and public intellectuals utilized comics to express their fears, hopes, and disillusionment with political, economic, and cultural changes in Poland and beyond. By discussing debates surrounding comics, the book shows how the production of homegrown series and the influx of foreign works enabled commentators to probe the established notions of Polishness and scrutinize the boundaries of national culture. Over the years, the communities and discourses that formed around comics spoke volumes about the political predilections and social proclivities of their respective eras.

In this book, I propose that examining these debates can help us rethink the role of popular culture in nation building, legitimation of power, and citizenship formation, among other processes. More importantly, as I show here, many of these developments were informed by cultural exchange, border crossing, and the reimagination of foreign works, and much of the material gathered in this study reflects on the uncomfortable dynamic between local and imported models, their interdependence, and their dialogical relationship.

## Comics and the Transnational Exchange

Scholars have long been interested in how comics questioned existing political and social structures and how their mass popularity with readers went hand in hand with their marginalization by cultural and political elites (e.g., Cortsen et al. xvii). Studies from a variety of regional contexts show how, over decades, comic books have inspired interpretative communities, enabling "producers, consumers, and critics to explain themselves, and to shape their relations with each other and the world" (Rubenstein 3). Ever since the nineteenth century, the production, distribution, and consumption of comics has been intertwined with important global phenomena, such as technological progress, modernization, and the rise of literacy (Mainardi 130). Throughout the twentieth and twenty-first centuries, the spread and reception of the medium have also been bound up with economic and cultural globalization, US cultural influence, the Americanization of Europe (and other continents), and, at times, also anti-Americanism (Campbell 6). Comics mediated between national cultures and bore witness to wider cross-border exchanges. National debates surrounding comics exposed, and continue to expose, the resulting domestic political cleavages and wider global dynamics. As scholar Juan Meneses argues, many of these debates lay bare a complex mesh of intercultural relations, including the intersection of locality and foreignness that the medium has occupied for nearly two centuries now (61).

From the moment comics gained traction in interwar Poland, be it as imports from Denmark, Belgium, France, or the United States, or as homegrown products, they have been an important site of transculturation. Polish commentators were cognizant of the comics' foreign origins but, like many others, tended to view them as an essentially American creation. These trends reflected wider approaches to comics. According to historian David Kunzle, this was no different for the early historians of the newspaper strip in the US, who had often overlooked its European roots ("Precursors" 159). However, well into the late 1880s, American publishers relied heavily on material imported from Europe. Already in the 1830s, the Swiss Rodolphe Töpffer, later dubbed the "father" of the modern comic strip, inspired numerous artists and imitators alike. Aside from influencing European illustrators, such as the French Charles Amédée de Noé (known as Cham) and Gustave Doré, in the 1840s his pictorial stories spawned plagiaries in Britain and the US, including *The Adventures of Mr. Obadiah Oldbuck,* which was hailed as America's first comic book (Kunzle, *Father* 143, 162, 175–76). In a similar way, the work of German Wilhelm Busch was subject to numerous unauthorized reprints, often in a format that was adapted to the receiving culture (Kunzle, "Precursors" 160–61). His most famous work, *Max and Moritz* (1865), in particular, provided a direct model for *The Katzenjammer Kids,* a strip created by Rudolph Dirks in 1897 for the *New York Journal* (Sheridan 58; Smolderen 112–13).

From the end of the nineteenth century onward, these exchanges were largely reversed and it was European publishers who, in David Kunzle's words, began "to pinch" American strips ("Precursors" 161). It was also during that period that recurring comic strip characters emerged in the US, including Outcault's Yellow Kid (1895) and Opper's Happy Hooligan (1900). Although serials had not been unknown in Europe, to mention the eponymous *Ally Sloper* in Britain (first published in 1867), American artists set a trend. They popularized what Jared Gardner described as a "mass-mediated personality" that "emerges through serial repetition" and, in the process, becomes a trademark in its own right (14). The serial format and the transmedial nature of these characters, who branched out to other sectors of culture and industry, from theater to toys to fashion, provided Europeans with new ways of thinking about serial characters as not only one-dimensional newspaper heroes but also as three-dimensional objects of merchandise.[5] More importantly, in the course of the 1920s and 1930s, European print media saw an eruption of similar protagonists and narratives that were firmly rooted in the local context.

Those transferences intensified in the 1930s with the global spread of Disney comics and the rise of Mickey Mouse magazines in a variety of countries, including France, Italy, Sweden, the Netherlands, Yugoslavia, and Poland, among others (see Becattini). During that period, the transnational exchanges became increasingly multidirectional too. In the late 1920s, modern Franco-Belgian *bandes dessinées* emerged, initiating a long line of recurring comic strip characters that were soon to become widely known and imitated (at least in Europe).[6] Tintin was created in 1929, and Lucky Luke and Asterix followed in 1946 and 1959, respectively (Grove 121–22). But the twentieth century was also a period of growing disillusionment with the medium. In the late 1940s and early 1950s, campaigners in the US and Europe were united in a shared struggle against the highly popular "crime and horror comics." Irrespective of location, their purported

---

5. On the transatlantic reach of the Yellow Kid, see Meyer, *Producing* 2.

6. On the unsuccessful transplantation of Franco-Belgian comics in the North American context, see Gabilliet, "A Disappointing Crossing."

rationale was similar: to protect the children and (highbrow) culture. In the 1980s, some of these uncertainties resurfaced around the influx of Japanese manga when commentators across the globe feared the effects it would have on local cultures.

Such global debates, exchanges, transfers, reiterations, creative reinterpretations, and imitations (including bootlegging) have been inherent to national comic book cultures for nearly two centuries. Today, comics in specific national settings are a testimony to the cultural syncretism and global spread of the medium. The recent transnational turn in history, literary studies, and other disciplines can help us deepen our understanding of some of the above-mentioned exchanges and interactions. While acknowledging the importance of national cultures, the transnational approach emphasizes the entangled nature of various comic book traditions. As some scholars argue, "the multidirectional transactions uncovered by a transnational perspective problematize the foundational role of discrete national units," rendering them "internally multiple as the traces of exchange are discovered *within,* and not merely *between,* national cultures, traditions, and identities" (Denson et al. 3). As the ever-growing body of scholarship in the field shows, examining local comic book cultures from this deeply relational and intertextual perspective helps us enrich the traditional understandings of the medium, while revealing the role of various actors, be it intermediaries, publishers, or artists, in bringing these transactions into existence.

Writing about the global spread of the American comic strip *The Phantom* (launched in 1936), Kevin Patrick demonstrates the importance of local syndicates in translating the American content to foreign audiences and "brokering the international acceptance of American comic strips" (66). Similarly, in their discussion of the transnational comic book Western, Christopher Conway and Antoinette Sol argue that "creators from around the world have re-territorialized frontier stories to make them relevant to the cultural politics of their countries" (24). Jason Bainbridge and Craig Norris claim that Japanese manga, too, has been subject to comparable practices. Aside from its inherent "textual malleability," the funding strategies surrounding manga as well as its production and dissemination by a variety of organizations (including national, multinational, and transnational ones) have contributed to the global spread of the genre (241). Similar dynamics have been at play where the circulation of other genres is concerned, as seen, for example, in the various iterations of American superhero narratives, be it in India, Japan, or the Muslim world (see Davé; Bieloch and Bitar; Meier).

For over a century now, comics in East-Central Europe have been part and parcel of these transnational flows, appropriating and adapting global tropes, formats, and transmedial practices. Discussing interwar Czechoslovakia, Pavel Kořínek shows that comics in the region have been a site of cultural hybridity from the very start, oscillating between the local Central European tradition of humor initiated by Wilhelm Busch and his followers and the American influence that arrived in the region in the early twentieth century (244). Other emerging work in the field emphasizes the intersections, commonalities, and shared roots of past and present works, while pointing to the "proliferation of translations, cross-border exchange among publishing houses, [and] international comics festivals" that have reinvigorated the specific national traditions since 1989 (Kuhlman and Alaniz 10, 14).

## Polish Comics: Shifting the Focus

In the past few decades, Polish scholarship has yielded multiple analyses of major comics and the associated cultural phenomena, written both from diachronic and synchronic perspectives. Works by Adam Rusek, for example, provide a history of newspaper and magazine comic strips from 1919 to the mid-1950s against the wider backdrop of print media in Poland (see *Tarzan*; *Od rozrywki*). Wojciech Obremski and Marcin Krzanicki look at the role of ideology in popular comic series under Communism (see Obremski's *Krótka historia*; Krzanicki's *Komiks w PRL*). Justyna Czaja and Bartłomiej Janicki both focus on historical comics and their educational potential, particularly as didactic tools for teaching national history (see Czaja's *Historia Polski*; Janicki's *Dydaktyczny potencjał*). Various other authors provide useful analyses of specific works, including contemporary ones, as well as furnishing biographies of acclaimed illustrators (Czaja and Traczyk; Jasiński; Jaworski, *Urodzony*). Yet others explore the comic book as a unique medium at the intersection of art and literature as well as investigating its relations with film, among other themes.[7]

---

7. For example, Jerzy Szyłak has written extensively on comics for more than two decades now. Even though his work has rarely looked at the history of Polish comics, he is one of the major scholars and commentators of the genre in Poland,

What this book aims to do differently is to look at Polish comics as something more than merely a national phenomenon. The monograph shows how, in the course of the past century, Polish culture has been exposed to a variety of foreign influences. These have included not only American, Franco-Belgian, and Japanese production, but also other cultures that have often been viewed as peripheral to the comics history and, admittedly, to comics scholarship. As I show in this book, already in the 1930s, the newspaper industry in Poland worked to create its own networks and links that complemented the American and Franco-Belgian offerings. The mutual contacts that Polish stakeholders established with their counterparts in the Nordic states and other Eastern European countries are a case in point.[8] This legacy was revived under state socialism, particularly in the 1970s, when the comics market reopened to partners in Scandinavia as well as establishing stronger links with other socialist states.

Many of the questions that this book attempts to answer deal with how that cultural exchange happened, or was prevented from happening, from 1918 onward. These questions are underpinned by recent scholarship in the history of East-Central Europe. Several of my chapters deal with the Cold War and its legacies, in particular the foreign influence and exchange during that period. In this context, historians have increasingly questioned the idea of an impermeable Iron Curtain and proposed to see it instead as a "semipermeable membrane." Throughout the socialist period, many supposedly "harmless" goods and ideas were still allowed to flow across borders and leave their mark on the socialist societies. In the words of Michael David-Fox, "even Stalinism, one of the most isolationist and autarkic regimes of the twentieth century, was shaped and influenced by border-crossings, borrowings, and constant if often covert and skewed observation of the outside world. In other words, taking the

---

focusing on topics such as the intermediality of comics, pornography, and sexuality in comics and comics and kitsch. See, for example, Szyłak, *Komiks i okolice pornografii, Komiks w kulturze ikonicznej, Komiks i okolice kina,* and *Komiks w szponach miernoty.* This list is by no means complete. For a more extensive listing of scholarly work on the medium, see Misiora 264–67.

8. Discussing comics studies in the Nordic states in 2016, Fredrik Strömberg argued that "on an international level we are most probably on the verge of seeing a comics studies discipline emerge." See Strömberg 150. Yet, as I show in this book, Sweden and Denmark, in particular, were crucial to the growth of comic book culture in Poland (especially in the 1930s).

imagery of the Iron Curtain too literally can obscure an important avenue of historical investigation" (18).

Some of the case studies discussed in this monograph could be seen as examples of such "observing" of (and, at times, even engaging with) the outside world. Although undertaken by the privileged few, be it journalists, publishing industry representatives, or artists, who were allowed to travel abroad and were cognizant of Western fashions, those instances of looking across the border, and sharing with local audiences what was witnessed and experienced, were far from parochial or uninformed. In analyzing these commentaries, particularly those that appeared at the height of Stalinism and later, I am thus reticent to apply blanket terms such as "propaganda." Instead, following recent scholarship on visual culture in the Soviet context, I propose that socialist comics, and more generally the ways in which socialist commentators discussed the medium, were more than mere expressions of state-sponsored propaganda (see, e.g., Etty 6–7). Aside from attempting to adhere to the cultural policy of the state, these actors also expressed their affinity with non-national communities that formed around (and in opposition to) comics elsewhere. The communities in question were medium-specific, rather than nationally bound, and used distinct imagery and symbolic languages. Most of these communities went beyond the Soviet bloc, too, speaking to the porousness of the Iron Curtain and attesting to Poland's connections with the wider world. As historians of the Cold War argued in another context, it would be wrong to assume that socialist states were "inward looking, isolated, and cut off from global trends until the capitalist takeover in the 1980s and 1990s" (Mark et al. 2). This is certainly true for comics.

## Poland and the Global Tradition

It would be easy to dismiss countries like Poland as merely "side streams," to use David Kunzle's phrase, of the global comic book history.[9] "In France there was so much I had to stop looking," Kunzle says famously about the nineteenth-century French comic strip (*History* 1). A similar observation could be made about the twentieth-

---

9. Kunzle used the phrase to describe Austria, Italy, Spain, and Russia as nineteenth-century comic strip cultures that developed on the margins of what went on in Britain, France, and Germany. See *History* 334–47.

century American and Franco-Belgian production. No such thing could ever be said about Poland or other Eastern European states. Nonetheless, Poles have been enthusiastic consumers and producers of comics for over a hundred years now. Sporadically, they have also tried their hand at disseminating homegrown work. Thus, although modest and selective, the exchanges and transfers discussed in this book complicate the traditional binary of "established" and "emerging" comic book cultures and point to the agency of these so-called peripheries.

There are advantages to exploring comic books from this "peripheral" perspective. Not only does such an approach decentralize our understanding of the comics industry in a geographical sense, it also disrupts the centrality of production and diffusion as defining cultural practices that shape that industry. Despite their cyclical grievances about being "invaded" or "flooded" by foreign production, commentators, artists, and readers in Poland have been unabashed by their role as the recipients and emulators of foreign culture. It has been these very actors who, at different points of the past century, have had the agency to select what was to be absorbed into the national fold and what was to be ejected from it. Even if, at times, this receiving and rejecting happened in the rhetorical realm only (as it did at the height of Stalinism and, partly, also later), the comic continued to function as a potent reference point in the cultural imagination. It has been these actors, too, who made the medium into an ever-shifting cultural metaphor: a podium on which civilizations and ideologies were said to clash, a site of national conflict and longing, and a locus of other collective emotions.

## Sources, Methodology, Scope, and Terminology

This book argues for a revision of the national paradigm that has guided many of the studies of Polish comics to date. The chapters in this monograph show how for the past 100 years, Polish commentators, artists, and readers participated in a truly global comic book culture, doing so in myriad ways. My main focus is on how foreign influence of various kinds was received and discussed in Poland. To some extent, I am also interested in how local illustrators and authors responded to that influence in their own work.

The bulk of this study examines public debates surrounding comics. To this end, I sifted through numerous press commentaries on this and related topics. More than 200 newspaper and magazine articles were eventually included in the monograph. The articles span the period of nearly ninety years, from the 1930s to the present, and comprise commentaries by both cultural editors specializing in visual media and literature, and rank and file journalists, assigned to cover a variety of associated topics. The majority of these sources come from the daily and weekly press, but there are also several essays that were published in professional journals, exile magazines, and *samizdat* (underground) press. In addition, the book makes use of memoirs and interviews with comic book creators and publishers, as well as discussing readers' letters.

I have obtained most of my primary material through traditional library research, both online and on-site. Several bibliographic databases guided my research. These included Marek Misiora's *Bibliografia komiksów wydanych w Polsce w latach 1905 (1858)–1999* (*The Bibliography of Comics Published in Poland in 1905 (1858)–1999*), which includes a list of important articles about the medium published in both scholarly journals and popular periodicals over the course of nearly fifty years. Poland's national archive, Archiwum Akt Nowych in Warsaw, contains three folders of newspaper clippings about comics that cover a similar period (1953–2009).[10] The clippings have been consistently annotated with the dates and titles of the main publication, but do not always contain page numbers. I tried to verify the provenance of many of these sources and supplement the missing bibliographical details. Some of the articles and press reports (particularly the anonymous ones), however, proved to be too ephemeral and are not included in the major indexes of periodical content, such as the *Bibliografia Zawartości Czasopism* (*The Index of Polish Periodicals*) and the *Polska Bibliografia Literacka* (*The Polish Literary Index*). In those cases, I provided the title and date of the publication, as indicated by the archival annotations, but left out the page numbers.

Although the work by local artists has been covered extensively in the Polish-language scholarship discussed above, this book also makes reference to major comics magazines, series, and books. Several chapters take a closer look at selected titles but do so predominantly from the point of view of cultural translation and adaptation.

---

10. The folders are a part of the collection of the newspaper clippings of Polish TV Archive (Telewizja Polska S. A.: Zbiór wycinków prasowych) and can be accessed using the following record numbers: 2/2514/0/-/2/695; 2/2514/0/-/2/696; 2/2514/0/-/2/697.

In that sense, the monograph does not aspire to provide a comprehensive history of Polish comics and the comic book industry. Rather, it uses selected works by Polish artists to investigate different aspects of the relationship between comic books' producers, publishers, critics, audiences, the state, and the wider world.

Over the course of the past century, comics have been given different names in Polish. Initially, these terms reflected the subtle transformations of the medium. Later on, under Communism, they alluded to the political and cultural context in which the medium operated, disclosing period-specific animosities. For example, in the interwar period (and earlier), names such as *powieści obrazkowe* (pictorial novels), *historyjki obrazkowe* (pictorial stories), and *historyjki ilustrowane* (illustrated stories) were used. All of these terms described graphic narratives that combined pictures with text placed underneath. With the appearance of comic strips based on animated film, the phrase *filmy rysunkowe* (drawn films) or simply *filmy* (films) was also used and applied to stories that utilized speech balloons. The word *historyjki* (literally "little stories") brings to mind terms from other national contexts, including the Spanish *historietas*: a self-deprecating name that stood in sharp contrast with the mass appeal of the medium. Following World War II and the gradual politicization of comics by Poland's socialist government, the original English-language word "comics" was often used to emphasize the foreign provenance of the medium and the menace it supposedly posed to national culture. Later on, from the mid-1960s onward, a native phrase, *kolorowe zeszyty* (color notebooks), was coined, but it was used interchangeably with the Polonized variant of the word "comics" —*komiks* (singular) and *komiksy* (plural). In this book, I occasionally use some of the Polish terms above to emphasize the specificities of the periods in question. I also apply the more general English terms, including "comics," "comic strip," and "comic book," depending on the context.

## The Book's Outline

This book follows a roughly chronological order, focusing on the turning points in the cultural history of comics in Poland. Chapter 1 takes us to the interwar period. It shows how, with the dissolution of empires at the end of World War I and the formation of the Second Polish Republic in 1918, Poland saw a gradual shift away from the former imperial centers of Vienna, St. Petersburg, and (to a lesser extent) Berlin, turning to other cultural models. The US comics, one of the products of America's fast-growing mass media industry, became a frequent guest in Polish newspapers, as did works from Sweden and Denmark. For the United States, the interbellum was a period of dramatic social and economic change, involving urbanization, the expansion of technology, and the growth of popular culture. Europe participated in these developments too, and it was no different for Poland. As the colorful Disney products arrived in the country in the 1930s, opinions were divided, but it was the enthusiasts who spoke with a louder and more united voice. Thus, already in the interwar period, Poland kept abreast of the latest global developments. This was to stand in sharp contrast with the decades that followed. The Communist period would be marked by a public denunciation of the medium and a state-sponsored forgetting of the interwar cultural transfers.

Chapter 2 discusses the anti-comics campaign of the late 1940s and early 1950s. It shows how, despite the virtual absence of the medium in Stalinist Poland, in the early 1950s the comic became a byword for the imperialist threat. That threat was said to lurk on the pages of American publications, corrupting the youth and educating them into violence. Focusing on public debates surrounding comics, the chapter argues that although the anti-comics discourse has often been read as an offshoot of the wider anti-imperialist campaign, in fact, it marked Poland's participation in a much wider transnational community. Like other anti-comics campaigners across the world, journalists, activists, and intellectuals in Poland joined in in the global struggle in the defense of childhood, highbrow culture, and peace. This attested to the porousness of the Iron Curtain and showed that, often, the interests of Polish public commentators were aligned with those of their counterparts in the nonsocialist world. By following developments in the West, for example the anti-comics campaign led by American psychiatrists like Fredric Wertham, Polish commentators, too, participated in the wider global discussion about comics.

Chapter 3 focuses on the cultural opening of the 1970s, associated with the regime of Edward Gierek, an advocate of "peaceful coexistence" and a Westward-looking *bien pensant*. As the chapter shows, it was during that decade that the Polish comics community underwent an unprecedented growth and saw a renewed period of contact with foreign production and influence. This was the period when Polish "super-protagonists," such as *Kapitan Żbik,* the brave and dapper militia officer, emerged. It was also a time when the Polish comics community was not only at the receiving end but also at the transmitting end. Throughout the 1970s, state-controlled publishing houses were able to test capitalist practices and come into contact with foreign audiences, including the Polish diaspora in the United States and the general reader in Sweden, Denmark, and other states. The 1970s was also a decade in which many liberal-minded intellectuals and comic book artists aligned themselves more closely with Western Europe, the Francophone world in particular, which was increasingly seen as an alternative to the binary world of the earlier years of the Cold War.

Chapter 4 examines the political transition of 1989 as well as the associated transformation from command to market economy. It discusses the disillusionment experienced by intellectuals and comic book artists in the aftermath of the transition. In particular, the chapter argues that the 1990s were seen by many as a period of "cultural invasion" from the West. That invasion was said to mar the hard-won freedom and undermine the value of democracy and the free-market economy. Considering their culture to be flooded by "foreign junk," some of these commentators revived the familiar anti-American sentiment that had marked the Communist era and, once more, hoped that Europe and its "true culture" would come to their rescue.

Chapter 5 provides an insight into the Polish comic book scene from the early 2000s until the present day. It focuses on two important trends that have dominated the domestic production in the past two decades, namely the graphic memoir and the state-funded historical comic book. The former trend can be linked to the emergence of autobiographical stories, many of them produced by women, which record the individual experience and provide a platform for the expression of feminist identities, often vis-à-vis (or in opposition to) the patriarchal state or collective identity. The latter trend marks the recent "memory turn" with its exploration of the national past and the proliferation of state-sanctioned visions of Polish history. While distinct, the two trends show a different reworking of the foreign and native models—the graphic memoir being directly influenced by similar stories produced in the West, the historical comics attempting to revive the traditional educational function of pictorial stories, typical for socialist Poland.

The conclusion brings together the various strands of my argument and challenges the common perception of the medium as marginal to Polish culture. It also emphasizes Poland's participation in global debates and developments (particularly under state socialism) and shows that, over the course of one century, comics have played an important role in creating affective communities of readers, critics, and creators.

CHAPTER 1

# COMICS IN
# INTERWAR POLAND

Between Homegrown Stories and Foreign Imports

Poland's first comic strip appeared in 1919 in a satirical magazine in Lviv. By the mid-1930s, comics were known to the majority of Poles, both children and adults. The 1930s would become the "golden period" of Polish print media, ushering in an unprecedented influx of graphic narratives from abroad as well as stimulating native production. The declaration of the Polish state, the Second Polish Republic, on November 11, 1918, created favorable conditions for the development of culture, education, and press. The March Constitution of 1921 instituted freedom of the media and gave the right to all citizens of Poland, who were in possession of suitable capital, to publish newspapers and magazines (see Faber-Chojnacka 9–10).[1]

By 1931, Poland's population reached 32 million people, with approximately 22 million declaring Polish to be their first language

---

1. It is worth noting that the constitution also allowed legislators to curb those freedoms, for example through censorship and municipally conducted campaigns against all sorts of "unsuitable" content, but this did not necessarily impede the emergence of new outlets.

and many others operating in largely bilingual and trilingual settings.[2] It is estimated that in 1920 more than 1,000 titles, including daily and periodical press, existed throughout the country (Paczkowski, "Prasa" 52). By 1929, this figure grew to 2,329, of which 1,928 publications were in Polish (*Mały Rocznik Statystyczny 1931* 130).[3] Although circulation figures are notoriously unreliable, it can be assumed that toward the end of the 1920s the aggregate number of copies of daily publications printed in Polish, Yiddish, German, Ukrainian, Russian, and other languages came to 1 million, with actual readership numbers being much higher (Paczkowski, "Prasa" 60).

Levels of education improved following the introduction of compulsory schooling in 1919. While in 1921 one third of the population was illiterate, by the early 1930s, this figure dropped to one fifth. Literacy rates were highest in the western regions (Silesia and the Poznań voivodeship) and lowest in the east (Lviv and Vilnius). Illiteracy plagued, in particular, the elderly rural population who had been born prior to the institution of universal schooling.[4] Print media were accessible to everyone who could read, while the illustrated content (be it drawings or photographs) was legible also to those who were illiterate or semi-literate. The press was cheap and varied, ranging from quality to popular dailies and periodical magazines. The cost of daily newspapers and periodicals was fairly low. For example, a popular newspaper cost on average between 5 and 15 groszy, with the average worker's salary coming to around 200 zloty per month (Paczkowski, *Prasa* 144).[5]

The increase in urban population, from just above 6 million in 1921 to nearly 9 million in 1931, as well as the rise of literacy and technological advance, meant that almost overnight a new group of readers

---

2. Other major languages were Ukrainian, Yiddish, Ruthenian, Belarussian, and German. Many among the Jewish and Ukrainian populations, in particular, were bilingual or trilingual. See Stopnicka Heller 68.

3. These figures continued to fluctuate throughout the 1930s, with a significant drop in numbers in the beginning of the decade and gradual growth toward the mid-1930s. For example, in 1932 there were 1,831 titles available in Poland, in 1933 there were 1,855, in 1934 there were 1,859, and in 1935 there were 2,186. See also *Mały Rocznik Statystyczny 1937* 326.

4. The elderly in the western regions were an exception. See Leszczyńska 112–13.

5. There were regional variations, too. Wages were typically the highest in Silesia, followed by the Warsaw, Poznań, and Łódź regions, and lowest in Lviv and Vilnius. See Leszczyńska 103–4.

emerged in Poland.[6] The popular press, with its illustrated content, was the cheapest form of entertainment available to the growing population of urban dwellers, the majority of whom were blue-collar workers. It is no coincidence that many of the large press corporations that specialized in popular titles, including Łódź-based Republika and Katowice's Polonia, sprang up in Poland's large industrial centers.

Alongside entertainment, print media was an important platform of ideological persuasion. Reading newspapers in Polish, particularly in the early days of the Second Republic, was an important patriotic act. With unstable national borders and a multiethnic population, Polish-language print media and illustrated content were mobilized to consolidate the state in the minds and the hearts of the citizens, while winning the readers for a particular political grouping (Kochan 40). Print media were an invitation to modernity, too. Heralding that modernity, comics, as I show below, became a platform for mass communication and cross-border cultural exchange that had a wider European and, to some extent, also transatlantic dimension. This was the first time in the history of the Polish lands that consuming popular culture enabled the mass reader to participate in a wider community that spread beyond the borders of their erstwhile Partitions. This meant a subliminal reorientation, away from the former imperial metropolises of Berlin, Vienna, and St. Petersburg, and toward the fast-growing cultural markets of the United States and other countries.

In this chapter, I discuss the early pictorial stories in Poland, from their arrival in the mid-nineteenth century until the height of their popularity in the 1930s. My main focus is on the latter decade, which saw increased economic stability and a greater variety of pictorial offerings. I focus on graphic narratives by Polish creators as well as those that were imported from abroad. In doing so, I show how from the very beginning the Polish comic book tradition oscillated between American, European, and local influences.

## A Short History of Homegrown Pictorial Stories in Interwar Poland

It has been commonly believed that Poland does not have a rich comic book tradition (see Tylicka; Dunin; Kałużyński, "Polak"). This

---

6. For the exact breakdown of urban versus rural population, see *Pierwszy powszechny spis* 5 and *Drugi powszechny spis* 1.

is only partly true. Pictorial narrative has been known in the Polish lands since at least the mid-nineteenth century. German imports, such as Heinrich Hoffmann's *Der Struwwelpeter* (published as *Złota rószczka*), appeared in Polish already in 1858, thirteen years after the original German version.[7] Homegrown stories for children, which combined text and image, were not rare during that period either: *Gwiazdka Kazia: Podarek na kolendę dla małych dzieci* (*Kazio's Christmas: A Carolling Gift for Small Children*), published in Lviv in 1883, with a text by Władysław Bełza and illustrations by Władysław Witwicki, has often been named a representative example of the genre. Serialized stories for children could be found in the press from the period too, for example *Historya jedynaczka* (*The Story of an Only Child*; 1859), which ran over five issues in the Warsaw *Tygodnik Ilustrowany* (*The Illustrated Weekly*) (see Rusek, *Tarzan* 27–28). Also Wilhelm Busch's duo *Max and Moritz* (1865) made it to Poland; it did not, however, achieve the same popularity as it did in other countries. There is only one recorded edition of the serial, called *Wiś i Wacek* (*Wiś and Wacek*), published in 1905 in Łódź (Dunin 12). At the turn of the century, pictorial narratives began to appear in satirical calendars too, combining illustrations with short poems and dialogues (e.g., Oppman and Sikorski).

Following the establishment of the Polish state in 1918, posters containing short graphic narratives were used as a tool of propaganda, notably during the Polish-Soviet War of 1919–1920. These were modelled on the Soviet *lubok* and contained, on average, five to seven panels with verse that was intended to demonize the enemy, encourage conscription, and incite patriotic sentiment (Leinwand, "Polski plakat" 57, 60–63). The use of *lubok*-infused posters to fight the Red Army was not that surprising. The government was determined to entice the nonethnically Polish populations, including Ukrainians and Belarusians from borderland territories, with the lure of Polishness, or, at the very least, to counter the Bolshevik information campaign. Using the poster was seen as a convenient and efficient way to do so. Although in most cases the stories were written in Polish, in some instances local languages were used to ensure that the ideological content fell on fertile ground (Leinwand, "Polski plakat" 61–62). The poster was a familiar sight in those territories since the Soviets, too, used them for similar purposes, often addressing the

---

7. It was reprinted from the Russian edition.

same national groups (Leinwand, "Bolszewicki plakat" 78–82). Writing about the importance of the poster in the USSR, scholar José Alaniz contended:

> The poster or *plakat* (as advertisement, as public service announcement, as breaking news vehicle) became a major tool for the Bolsheviks to spread information far, wide, and in a form they could control. Capitalizing, as the icon-makers had done, on Russian culture's penchant for the visual, the producers of posters could cast their message more cost-effectively than film, more quickly than newspapers, more lastingly than radio or the telegraph, all while making an emotionally engaged appeal to the eye. Between 1919 and 1922, over 7.5 million posters, postcards, and lubok pictures were distributed, while in 1920 alone the state publishing house Gosizdat released more than 3.2 million copies of 75 different posters. (*Komiks* 34)

It was precisely this tradition that the Polish government was addressing through its posters. This would be one of the very few instances in which the Soviet influence in graphic narrative was adopted in Poland. As I show below, much of the mass visual culture, which laid foundations for the growth of the comic book in Poland, came from elsewhere.

The interwar period brought about an unprecedented growth of satirical press, too, which provided poignant social and political commentary. Between 1918 and 1939 nearly 200 satirical magazines were being published in Poland (Szałek 113). Given the ubiquity of such titles and their penchant for caricature and pictorial humor, they became an ideal outlet for illustrated content of all kinds. Although many satirical magazines were short-lived, they provided fertile ground for the expansion of *historyjki obrazkowe* (pictorial stories), as they came to be known in Poland. Poland's first serial comic strip, *Ogniem i mieczem, czyli przygody szalonego Grzesia* (*With Fire and Sword or the Adventures of Crazy Grześ*), was published in one such magazine, the Lviv-based *Szczutek,* in 1919. Created by Kamil Mackiewicz (illustrations) and Stanisław Wasylewski (script), the serial, described by its authors as *powieść współczesna* (a contemporary novel), consisted of episodes comprising six images with rhymed duplet verse placed underneath. *Ogniem i mieczem* was urgent and relevant. It told a story of a young war volunteer, Grześ, who fought the enemies of the nascent Polish state on several fronts, including Germans in Greater Poland, Ukrainians in Lviv, and Bolsheviks on the eastern frontiers of the country. Aiding Poland's military leaders, Józef Piłsudski and Józef Haller, in consolidating state borders, Grześ was an ultimate national hero figure. The story was popular with readers, becoming one of the few magazine serials of the time to be published in book form, in 1920 (Rusek, *Leksykon* 83–85).

Ideological themes of this kind appeared in other satirical magazines too, including the Upper Silesian monthly *Kocynder* (*kocynder* being a Silesian word for a "friendly rascal"). The magazine was inaugurated in 1920 when the region was still a contested territory between Poland and Weimar Germany. Its most representative serial of the time, *Dzieje Hanysa Kocyndra* (*The Story of Hanys Kocynder*; 1920–1921), portrayed a native Silesian who was enlisted in the Prussian army during World War I, fighting in France, Belgium, and other places, before joining the Polish Legions under the command of Józef Haller and partaking in the various military campaigns aimed at expanding Poland's national borders after 1919. Like his predecessor Grześ, Kocynder also became a local hero figure, as his creators attempted to appeal to real-life war veterans and rally support behind the incorporation of Upper Silesia into Poland. Quite tellingly, the last episode appeared on March 20, 1921, the day when the Upper Silesian plebiscite took place, dividing the territory between Poland and the Weimar Republic (Rusek, *Leksykon* 89).

Alongside satirical magazines, daily newspapers provided another outlet for pictorial stories. The Łódź-based tabloid *Express Ilustrowany* was one of the first ones in the nascent Polish state to publish serials. Between 1923 and 1929 it produced five serialized stories. All of them were drawn by Stanisław Dobrzyński, an experienced illustrator and erstwhile author of the anti-Soviet posters (Rusek, *Tarzan* 28). While the 1920s' print media rendered several other interesting serials, notably the futurist story *Warszawa w roku 2025* (*Warsaw in 2025*; 1924) and *Pan Hillary i jego przygody* (*Mr. Hillary and His Adventures*; 1929), it was the 1930s that were more abundant in domestic production (Rusek, *Leksykon* 178–79, 249–50). This was no different from many other states in Europe, all of which saw the first popular newspaper and magazine serials appear in the 1920s, followed by a further expansion of the medium in the 1930s.[8]

8. For a discussion of Italy, Spain, and France, see Zanettin 869. For Romanian and Czechoslovak cases, respectively, see Precup 240 and Alaniz, "Eastern/Central European Comics" 100–101.

However, what made Poland different from other European states was the size of the country and the lasting cultural, economic, and social legacies of the Partitions. For 123 years, since 1772, the historical lands of Poland had been divided between the Russian, Austrian, and Prussian (later the German) empires. Throughout much of the 1920s, many editors continued to look to their former imperial centers, be it Vienna, Berlin, or St. Petersburg, searching for models to emulate (Paczkowski, *Prasa* 193). At the same time, in the 1920s, the state was in urgent need of economic reform and broadly conceived unification. The material destruction wreaked by World War I and the Polish-Soviet War had been immense. Human losses amounted to more than 1 million people. The trifurcated economies of former Russian, Prussian, and Austrian lands had disparate institutional legacies, tax systems, and laws, and as many as five currencies. There was no unified railway system; infrastructure in the different regions was largely incompatible and in need of modernization (Trenkler and Wolf 201–2). While some of these difficulties were alleviated by 1926, including by the introduction of the Polish zloty in 1924, the economy was still in urgent need of restructuring. It was the Americans—a mix of private, official, and semiofficial actors—who stepped in. According to historian Frank Costigliola, between 1926 and the Wall Street crash of 1929, "Americans poured money into Poland and took the lead in placing her finances in order" (92). Unfazed by Piłsudski's authoritarian tendencies, and at times approving of his strong leadership style, American bankers, financial advisors, and government officials wished to integrate Poland into the world economy, while invigorating capitalism in a nation bordering Bolshevik Russia (Costigliola 99). The bankers' loan of 72 million dollars stabilized the value of the zloty and strengthened Poland's credit position (Costigliola 102, 104). It bolstered Piłsudski's regime, too, and gave the Polish people their first taste of American-style mass consumption (Costigliola 96).

As far as pictorial stories went, the modest output of the 1920s was soon to be outmatched by the plentiful offerings of the 1930s. Even though many press outlets continued to be restricted to one specific region and were therefore virtually unknown in other parts of the country, the strategies of graphic narrative production and dissemination were turning increasingly capitalist. *Przygody bezrobotnego Froncka* (*The Adventures of Unemployed Froncek*) was an illustrative example of that. *Przygody* was published daily between 1932 and 1939 by a Silesian newspaper, *Siedem Groszy*. Drawn by autodidact Franciszek Struzik, it was the longest-running serial in interwar Poland (see Misiora 221). Froncek was a local character, a former miner who had been sacked and was struggling to find proper employment, taking up odd jobs, many of which were illegal.[9] Throughout much of the 1930s Froncek was firmly rooted in Silesian environs, and from the mid-1930s Struzik had been sending his protagonist abroad to make Froncek's adventures even more appealing to the reader. For example, in 1935 Froncek landed in Abyssinia, where he fought the Italian army. In 1936 he went to the Berlin Olympics and, shortly after, to the war-torn Spain (Rusek, *Leksykon,* 18–19). In 1937, he traveled to China to crush the Japanese invasion and, in June 1939, to the Reich to disrupt Nazi activity (Rusek, *Dawny* 199–200).

Such voyages were not exclusive to this particular comic strip. Froncek's Belgian contemporary, Tintin, too, traveled far and wide. Between 1929 and 1939, Tintin's journeys took him to the Soviet Union, Congo, America, Egypt, India, and other places. The similarities did not end there. The same way Tintin was accompanied by a white fox terrier, Snowy, Froncek traveled with dog Ciapek. When Ciapek was first introduced, his coat bore dark spots (*ciapki*), which, nonetheless, disappeared several years into the serial. In the end, Ciapek's fur became completely white and the dog itself came to bear a striking resemblance to Snowy (figure 1.1). Ciapek's function in the plot was often similar to that of Snowy's. As the panel in figure 1.1 shows, he was there to protect his owner and save him from trouble, frequently unbeknownst to Froncek himself, surpassing his master's intelligence and foresight. Similarly, although *The Adventures of Unemployed Froncek* were written from a perspective of a country that possessed no overseas colonies, some of Struzik's representations replicated what one scholar described as Hergé's "racist caricatures" (Hunt 93). The episodes set in Abyssinia, in particular, although sympathetic to the indigenous population, echoed the caricatural portrayals of the black body found in *Tintin in the Congo*.[10]

---

9. Froncek was partly based on Struzik himself, who had worked as a miner prior to becoming an illustrator. For more information on the author, see Rusek, *Dawny* 10.

10. *The Adventures of Unemployed Froncek* was not the only comic strip that imitated Hergé's work. In 1937, the Catholic weekly *Gość Niedzielny* (*The Sunday Guest*) began publishing a strip about an unemployed Silesian miner, Wicek Buła. To escape poverty and unemployment, Buła leaves, in the first episodes, for the Soviet Union, where all he finds is "Judeo-Bolshevik" domination. Aside from emulating the basic idea behind Hergé's *Tintin in the Land of the Soviets* (1929–1930), *The Adventures of Wicek Buła* also echoes the persistent antisemitic and "anti-Bolshevik"

**FIGURE 1.1.** *The Unemployed Froncek, Siedem Groszy,* May 8, 1937

Although the serial was not subject to syndication, and was thus largely unknown outside Silesia, the newspaper turned Froncek into a valuable commodity. His image was used for publicity purposes, being placed on posters and vans that brought the newspaper to distribution points (Rusek, *Leksykon* 20). From early on, the paper involved Froncek in a variety of public outreach activities too. Actors playing the character appeared at local events, such as harvest festivals, the 1st of June Children's Day celebrations, and film screenings (see, e.g., "Bezrobotny Froncek na dożynkach w Wodzisławiu"; "Święto dzieci w Rybniku"; "Bezrobotny Froncek w kinie 'Apollo' w Rybniku"). Froncek impersonators went across Silesia, visiting all towns and villages where *Siedem Groszy* was sold, while community organizations and local elites invited "him" to their events (see "Szukajcie bezrobotnego Froncka," October 23, 1934; "Szukajcie bezrobotnego Froncka," October 29, 1934; "Szukajcie bezrobotnego Froncka," August 3, 1935; "Szukajcie bezrobotnego Froncka," April 16, 1935). Around Saint Nicholas Day (December 6), he traveled around the region with Saint Nicholas, handing out bags of sweets, gingerbread, and other gifts to both children and the elderly (see "Bezrobotny Froncek z Mikołajem"; "Przygody bezrobotnego Froncka"). At Easter he would give out biscuits from the Eryk Vesper gingerbread and chocolate factory in nearby Wełnowiec as well as books to all subscribers (see, e.g., "Podarunki świąteczne Siedmiu Groszy"). These events were said to attract crowds. They were subsequently reported

---

sentiments of interwar Poland. For a detailed discussion of the series, see Rusek, *Leksykon* 256–57.

on in articles, photographs, and regular Froncek strips, published in the newspaper (see, e.g., "W Chorzowie"). In 1937, the Polonia concern that published *Siedem Groszy* commissioned a porcelain factory in the Silesian town of Orzesze to produce porcelain figures depicting Froncek in different outfits and settings (Rusek, *Leksykon* 20).

Froncek was an important element of popular culture in Silesia as well as being an amalgamation of recognizable local traits (such as wit and ingenuity). By contrast, the commercial practices that surrounded the protagonist were fairly innovative and only beginning to gain a foothold in Poland. The newspaper's extensive public engagement and state-of-the-art revenue strategies resembled, no doubt, foreign practices surrounding comics. As scholars have shown, transplanting comic strip characters outside the newspaper medium for publicity purposes was visible in Britain and the United States already toward the end of the nineteenth century. With the rise of mass production at the turn of the century, "cross-textual self-promotion and crossmedia branding" turned celebrated characters into collectible commodities, while attracting diverse (and increasingly mass) readership (Freeman 634, 641). In the words of Christina Meyer, "spilling into different areas of both public and recreational life, into theatres and music halls, into the streets (in the form of posters) and into private households (embodied in purchasable and collectible articles)," popular characters—such as Ally Sloper and the Yellow Kid—unfolded across several contexts and media systems, while influencing and shaping modern consumer culture ("Medial Transgressions" 293–94; see also Meyer, *Producing* 29–35; Sabin, "Ally Sloper").

In a similar way, another well-known protagonist, Buster Brown, featured in the early twentieth-century marketing campaigns of numerous products, such as watches, textiles, harmonicas, coffee, flour, bread, apples, suits, and even pianos. Scholars later credited the character with providing "the crucial link between comic strips and the development of a visual culture of consumption in America" (Gordon 49). By 1936, the Tintin image, too, was used for advertising purposes, and themed merchandise, such as Tintin puzzles and Tintin calendars, was being produced (Assouline 55). Actors posing as Tintin were employed to promote various products and values, including the Belgian colonial project in the Congo (Hunt 92). While Froncek-related giveaways and advertising stints were far more modest, and certainly not as politically engaged, the corporate deals that the newspaper forged with local bookshops, cinemas, and chocolate producers (including the Vesper factory) encouraged the consumption of other products and generated a symbiotic relationship between different branches of business.

*Siedem Groszy* was not the only newspaper to publish domestically produced comic strips and use innovative marketing strategies. Since the early 1930s other dailies, too, began to publish comics on a regular basis. These included *Dzień dobry! (Good Day!), Ilustrowany Kuryer Codzienny (The Illustrated Daily Courier), Kurier Łódzki (The Łódź Courier), Kurier Warszawski (The Warsaw Courier)*, and *Lwowski Ilustrowany Express Poranny (The Lviv Illustrated Morning Express)*, among others. None of these outlets limited themselves to homegrown stories only. Works drawn by artists from Poland were interspersed with foreign comics (which I discuss later on in this chapter). During that decade, some newspapers started supplements for children, too, which included comic strips. Alongside comics, they published other popular content, such as crime and erotic stories. Some of these publications, particularly the popular *Express Ilustrowany* and its sister magazines, were criticized for spreading content that could be seen as potentially corrupting. Throughout the 1930s, campaigners across the country, recruiting from Roman Catholic circles, formed action groups aimed at stopping such publications. While pictorial stories also came under attack, it was predominantly illustrated content published in "adult" magazines (e.g., the mildly erotic *Bocian* in Kraków) and more political (e.g., leftist or otherwise anti-government) satirical content that fell victim to censorship (G. Wrona 100–102, 109; Żynda; Lipiński, *Szpilki* 3 and *Drzewo* 27). Unlike these periodical outlets, comic strips printed in daily press were seen as rather unobtrusive. This mirrored wider international trends, where it was the more violent and pornographic comics that proliferated in the 1940s that triggered the notorious anti-comics campaigns of the late forties and early fifties.

Like the creators of the Silesian *Froncek,* some of the newspapers above also attempted to use pictorial narratives to attract new readers, increase sales figures, and generate additional income. For example, throughout 1934, *Express Ilustrowany,* a newspaper from Łódź with many distribution points across the country, ran a pictorial detective story that included a puzzle contest. The readers were encouraged to assemble the puzzle and return it to the editorial office. The complete puzzle provided an answer to each week's mystery and a promise of a raffle prize (Rusek, *Leksykon* 138). That same year, Warsaw newspaper *Dzień dobry!* copied the idea in their comic strip but used the puzzle to also advertise local businesses, be it laundromats, driving schools, or patisseries. As such, the game not only encouraged regular readership but was also a source of additional revenue from advertisements (Rusek, *Leksykon* 189). Such contests were not rare in the print media of interwar Europe. Although maintaining subscribers was certainly an important factor, they have often been credited with developing and cultivating fan communities that emerged around modern media, including film (Cowan 14).

Little is known about the illustrators who made the interwar comics scene in Poland. There were approximately twenty graphic artists who contributed to the above-mentioned dailies on a regular basis. Some of them, like Stanisław Dobrzyński, Bogdan Nowakowski, Kamil Mackiewicz, and Kazimierz Grus, were fairly well known and made their debuts in satirical magazines before World War I (Rusek, *Tarzan* 45). Mackiewicz, for example, had worked for *Szczutek* and *Mucha* and was the illustrator of the first Polish comic strip, *Ogniem i mieczem, czyli Przygody szalonego Grzesia.* He also illustrated children's books for the flagship Nasza Księgarnia (Our Bookshop) children's book publisher (established in 1921) as well as contributing hunting illustrations to Józef Weyssenhoff's novel *Puszcza* (*Wilderness;* 1915) (see Boguszewska 87; "Ś. p. Kamil Mackiewicz"). Grus had a similar trajectory and was particularly well known for his satirical images that featured personified animals (Witz). Recently, the works by Mackiewicz and Grus, as well as Grus's wife, Maja Berezowska, were included in an exhibition on antisemitic cartoons in interwar Polish print media, shedding new light on their oeuvres. Grus was particularly prolific in this respect. His antisemitic cartoons appeared in many right-wing conservative publications, including *Kurier Poznański* (*The Poznań Courier*), *Wielka Polska* (*The Great Poland*), *Samoobrona Narodu* (*National Self-Defence*), *Pod Pręgierz* (*Under the Pillory*), and other magazines (see Konstantynów 37).

There was also a younger generation of artists active at the time, all of whom emerged after World War I. For example, Karol Ferster (pseudonym Charlie) made his name working for popular *Ilustrowany Kuryer Codzienny* and went on to have a successful career as a magazine illustrator after World War II, drawing predominantly for two weeklies: the satirical leftist *Szpilki* and the progressive cultural magazine *Przekrój* (see "Karol Ferster"). Another newcomer of the time, Marian Walentynowicz, became a celebrated illustrator of comic and children's books, including the highly acclaimed *120 przygód Koziołka Matołka* (*120 Adventures of the Billy Goat*).

*120 przygód Koziołka Matołka,* first published in 1932, has been credited with being the precursor of the Polish comic book. Unlike the works discussed above, it was a series of books, rather than newspaper stories. *Koziołek Matołek* told a story of a dopey little goat who traveled the world searching for the mythical Pacanów, the only place that was said to shoe goats. The four Koziołek Matołek books, published between 1932 and 1934, became instant classics of children's literature in Poland. The story was the brainchild of Kornel Makuszyński (script) and Marian Walentynowicz (drawings). It was most likely inspired by publisher Jan Gebethner, of Warsaw's "Gebethner i Wolff," who was said to follow developments in other countries and who encouraged the two authors to produce a book-length pictorial narrative featuring an animal character (Staroń 356). The first volume was published in November 1932 as part of Gebethner and Wolff's Christmas offer. More than 5,000 copies were printed, all of which sold within weeks. The next album was ready for Easter 1933 and the two remaining ones appeared in 1934. Each volume saw several reissues before the outbreak of World War II (Staroń 360). The Makuszyński-Walentynowicz duo continued to work together, creating new popular stories, including a book about a little monkey, Fiki-Miki (*Małpka Fiki-Miki*), which, alongside *Koziołek Matołek,* was later lauded by some commentators as *the* "national comic book" (Dunin 14).

## Foreign Comics in Interwar Poland

None of the Polish strips discussed above existed in a void. Toward the end of the 1920s, foreign strips also made their way into Polish newspapers. One of the first imports to appear in Poland was the Swedish comic strip *Adamson* by Oscar Jacobsson, which ran in the daily newspaper *Ilustrowany Kuryer Codzienny* for nearly a decade, until 1939.[11] As in the case of nationally produced stories, for foreign imports, too, the 1930s were "the golden period." Beginning in 1931, stories about the Danish pair *Fy og Bi,* or Pat and Patachon, were pub-

---

11. According to one American reviewer from the period, Adamson was so universal that he could just as easily be Irish, French, or American. This might also explain the strip's popularity in Poland. See K. C. K.

lished on a weekly basis by *Express Ilustrowany,* initially as reprints and, from 1933, as Polish adaptations written and drawn by local artist Wacław Drozdowski. Those consisted of twelve panels supplied with dialogues that were placed underneath the image (Ochocki 31). In the summer of 1939, excerpts from *Superman* appeared for the first time in the Warsaw daily *Kurier Codzienny 5 Groszy* (Rusek, *Tarzan* 30, 33).

In the mid-1930s, several illustrated weeklies for children, such as *Karuzela* (*Carousel*), *Wędrowiec* (*The Wanderer*), *Świat Przygód* (*The World of Adventures*), and *Tarzan,* emerged. Despite their attempts to introduce homegrown stories, in the end, most of these publications focused on foreign, predominantly American, content. This included *Popeye* (known in Poland as *Ferdek i Merdek*), *Tarzan, Mandrake the Magician* (known as *Alex, król magików*), *Felix the Cat, Laurel and Hardy* (known as *Flip i Flap*), *Barney Baxter,* and *Brick Bradford.* Popular stories from other countries, such as *Pat and Patachon,* were also published in these magazines (Rusek, *Tarzan* 119). The majority of these publications were addressed to boys, and to attract young female audiences, a bimonthly *Wiosenka* (*Little Spring*) was launched in May 1937. Through *Wiosenka* the young reader was able to acquaint herself with American serials for girls, including *Little Annie Rooney, Tillie the Toiler, Etta Kett,* and *Betty Boop* (Rusek, *Tarzan* 90). Some of these serials were known to them from cinema for several years beforehand, including from Max Fleischer's production *Betty Boop* (Sitkiewicz, *Miki* 12–13). The creators of *Wiosenka* recognized this. In the first issue of the magazine, a short note introducing the story was placed on page 1. The editors asked rhetorically: "Who doesn't know the delightful Betty Boop, the immortal protagonist of Max Fleischer's films?" before adding that "the lovely Betty has now arrived in Warsaw, even though she is not performing in any theatre. [Instead] one can see her every week, as Baśka Figlarka, exclusively in our weekly" ("Kilka słów o Baśce"). It is clear that the magazine editors viewed the graphic narrative as an extension of the animated film and understood they could play the popularity of Fleischer's films to their advantage. In a final word of introduction, they both made a nod to the cinematic origins of the story as well as alluding to the common Polish name for the comic, namely *filmy rysunkowe* (drawn films) or simply *filmy* (films): "Attention! Baśka is winking at us, meaning the film is beginning" ("Kilka słów o Baśce"; see also figure 1.2).

**FIGURE 1.2.** Polonized Betty Boop in girls' magazine *Wiosenka*, May 20, 1937

The illustrated magazines not only made use of animated films that had been transformed into comics; some of the pictorial stories published in these magazines were based on popular comedy films. *Karuzela,* for example, drew some of its illustrated content from comics appearing in the British magazine *Film Fun,* which featured British and American comedians, such as Charlie Chaplin, Jackie Coogan, Abbot and Costello, and George Formby (Rusek, "Od 'Grzesia'" 68–69). In a similar way, *Świat Przygód* made the *Laurel and Hardy* comics into a showpiece of their magazine. Like in *Wiosenka* also here the link between film and graphic narratives was underlined, although in a different manner. The editors actively promoted films featuring the famous comedy duo act and, in collaboration with Metro-Goldwyn-Meyer, established a fan club for young cinemagoers that offered discounts on selected screenings (Rusek, "Od 'Grzesia'" 64). Aside from printing pictorial narratives, such as strips and graphic novelettes, many of the children's magazines included imported crime and adventure stories as well as poems and short stories written in rhyme. The educated sections of society considered them a cheap and popular form of entertainment that was unworthy of serious attention and, at times, even damaging to the intellectual growth of young people. Although there was no concerted effort to ban such publications, they were largely frowned upon by parents, intellectuals, and the Catholic Church alike (Rusek, "Od 'Grzesia'" 75; Rusek, *Tarzan* 101).

Perhaps the only children's publication that was considered acceptable by the various pundits was the short-lived *Gazetka Miki* (*Mickey's Little Paper*), launched in Kraków in 1938.[12] The magazine was modeled on similar publications in other countries. Disney scholar Alberto Becattini described it as "a nice local imitation of the British *Mickey Mouse Weekly*" (290). Indeed, *Gazetka* contained cover art by the British Disney artist Wilfred Haughton and was a blend of imported comics, such as *Snow White, Mickey Mouse, The Three Little Pigs,* and *Pluto,* and prose by Polish authors. The front and back covers, as well as the two central pages, were printed in color (see figure 1.3). The remaining pages were black and white. The latter comprised serialized stories by local writers such as Gustaw Morcinek, Janusz Meissner, Zofia Kossak, Zygmunt Nowakowski, Jan Brzechwa, and Julian Tuwim. There were also games, puzzles, and letters from Mickey Mouse to the readers. Each issue consisted of eight pages,

---

12. The magazine operated only for five months.

**FIGURE 1.3.** Cover page by Wilfred Haughton, *Gazetka Miki*, March 5, 1939

which was a standard format for some of the other Mickey Mouse magazines in Europe, including the early issues of *Topolino* in Italy and *Le Journal de Mickey* in France (Becattini 160, 212).

*Gazetka Miki* was something of an elite magazine. While most children's and youth weeklies, for example *Świat Przygód,* cost around

10 groszy, the price of *Gazetka Miki* was four times as high. This was perhaps the reason why it was often described as a publication for children from "good homes" (Rusek, "Od 'Grzesia'" 73). At the same time, the magazine went beyond the ethnic and political divide of late 1930s Poland. Its first issue was advertised in a variety of print media, including Polish-Jewish dailies, liberal leftist newspapers, and ethno-nationalist press.[13] The names of children who subsequently contributed their drawings to the "reader's corner" reflect that intended demographic, with Polish and Jewish names appearing most often.

*Gazetka*'s ethnically inclusive approach was not that surprising given that its editors, Wanda Wasilewska and Janina Broniewska, were known for their leftist views and political activism. This was also purportedly the reason why the publisher Marek Przeworski did not list the two editors by name, attempting to avoid anticommunist fearmongering by the state and Poland's ethno-nationalist groupings. Most of the other collaborators came from similar political backgrounds; they were engaged in a variety of organizations, such as the Communist Party of Poland, the Polish Socialist Party, and the Human Rights League (Borowkin 42–44).

Like some of the other Polish children's newspapers and magazines of the time, *Gazetka Miki* provided space for interaction with readers.[14] The first issue of the weekly contained a call to readers in which Miki asked them to contribute their own drawings. This was, no doubt, styled on similar editorials that were supposedly written by Mickey, published in the American *Mickey Mouse Magazine* (see, e.g., Kothenschulte et al. 345). The drawings requested by "Miki" were to portray celebrated Disney characters or anything else the readers wished to share. Written in longhand, Miki's letter informed his young admirers that a special section of the magazine will be devoted solely to their contributions. He asked them to post "many

---

13. See, for example, *Chwila*, December 16, 1938, p. 11; *Nowy Dziennik*, December 16, 1938, p. 19; *Czarno na białem*, December 18, 1938, p. 3; and *Dziennik Poznański*, December 16, 1938, p. 3. For a later advertisement in a pro-Sanacja tabloid, see *Dobry Wieczór! Kurjer Czerwony*, March 5, 1939, p. 13.

14. *Mały Przegląd* (*The Little Review*), a children's supplement to the Polish-language Jewish newspaper *Nasz Przegląd* (*Our Review*), in particular, became celebrated for its interactive format whereby letters from readers made up the bulk of the supplement. See Landau-Czajka 13–14.

many drawings" of himself and his cartoon friends, which could then be placed in the readers' corner (see "Kochane Dzieci!").

Young subscribers responded with enthusiasm. In one issue a line drawing by Leon Steinberg that presented Africans hunting lions was published. The picture was accompanied by a note in child's writing that explained the scene as well as sending his best regards to "kochany Miki" (dear Mickey) (see "Kochany Miki!"). Another issue included a sketch by young Lucjan Flis from Chełm Lubelski, which portrayed a cowboy chasing a Native American (see "Kowboj goni indjanina"). There were also images of Miki in a boat, Miki sitting under a palm tree, and Miki going to school (see Untitled drawings by A. Heidrich and others). Many of the drawings revealed true fascination with the American continent that went beyond the usual Disney repertoire. To *Gazetka*'s young readers, this was a continent of "exotic" indigenous people, cowboys, wild nature, and adventure. Although the magazine's creators were largely critical of the supposedly naive and simplistic content of Disney stories (and admittedly of the magazine itself), *Gazetka Miki* was generally well received (Szancer 193–94).

Such positive response was to be expected. After all, Mickey Mouse shorts had been known in Poland already in the early 1930s, while the Mickey Mouse image had been reproduced in a variety of contexts. As in other European countries, Mickey Mouse became a familiar and well-liked character. Renditions of Mickey, drawn by local artists, appeared in children's magazines, accompanied by textual content applauding the protagonist (see Arct.). Daily newspapers and women's fashion monthlies alike advertised Mickey-inspired accessories and garments, such as key rings, baby bibs, and embroidered children's clothing (see Advertisement for bibs "St 2369"; Mary; "Myszka Miki"). Various other outlets, film fortnightlies included, gave enthusiastic praise to both the character and his brilliant creator, as well as reporting on Mickey-related events, from the recording of the protagonist in *The Encyclopaedia Britannica* to his globally celebrated tenth birthday in 1938 (see "Jak mała myszka Miki zdobyła świat"; "Twórca słynnych filmów"; "Silly Symphony"; "Mickey Mouse zamieszczona"; "Myszka Mickey obchodzi we wrześniu").

Disney's protagonist also came to be appropriated by didactic comic strips drawn by local authors. One example was a pictorial story *Miki szuka nafty* (*Mickey Is Looking for Petroleum*; 1933), which ran for six months in the children's weekly *Moje Pisemko* (*My Magazine*). In the story, Miki traveled to Borysław (present-day Boryslav in Ukraine), then Poland's main center of petroleum industry. There Miki fought various groups of criminals before handing them over to the police and settling in Borysław to exploit its oil wells (Rusek, *Leksykon* 162). The story was a clear advertisement for one of interwar Poland's major industrial zones and an attempt at instilling pride in the country's economic achievement. Other publications, too, used Mickey Mouse as a tool of persuasion, for example to encourage children to save money in community savings banks (Rusek, *Leksykon* 162).

To emphasize how well integrated Mickey was in the Polish culture, one story in a children's supplement maintained that the mouse was now firm friends with the Polish goat Koziołek Matołek and even promised to visit the goat's home town Pacanów (see "Przyjęcie w bibliotece"). These examples show that the character had been assimilated into the national fold already in the early 1930s, several years before *Gazetka Miki*'s appearance on the Polish market. This was, of course, part of the global fascination with the character that followed the success of Disney's shorts, and coincided with the international spread of Mickey merchandise and Mickey Mouse Clubs from 1932 onward (Kothenschulte et al. 197, 215). Needless to say, not a single one of these early creations was cognizant of intellectual property rights. This was no different from other European countries at the time. For example, in Spain the Mickey Mouse image was usurped by a variety of stakeholders, from toy producers to orange wholesalers. Admittedly, Disney representatives were rarely interested in applying for trademark protection in specific European states and initially had a relaxed attitude to such transgressions (Bellido and Bowrey 1278).

*Gazetka*'s reach and appeal is well exemplified by Julien Bryan's iconic photograph, taken during the siege of Warsaw in September 1939 (see cover). The image presents two boys engrossed in reading as the city in front lies in ruin. The image, published in *Life* magazine on October 23, formed a part of a longer photo-reportage from the besieged city. It contained nearly twenty images, presenting bombed-out buildings, civilians digging trenches, and children grieving for their family members killed in a German air attack (Bryan).

Nearly four decades later, Polish commentators recalled the interwar comics offerings with nostalgia and praised *Gazetka Miki* for its high production value. They remembered it as one of the most accomplished comics magazines of the period, which "matched the American standards," at least as far as the visual content was concerned (Honsza 7). This was all the more, they argued, since the Polish version did not adhere slavishly to the original but, rather, was adapted to meet the needs of the Polish child (Dunin 16). That much of the magazine drew on the successful *Mickey Mouse Weekly,* including the original Disney material by British artists, was not known or acknowledged by these commentators. Even if tailored to local audiences, the comic book culture continued to be viewed as an essentially American import that was devoid of other influence. The various alterations to the original that had taken place in Europe (for example in Britain), and the resulting syncretism of the end product, tended to be overlooked in Poland.

## Adapting Foreign Comic Strips

*Gazetka Miki* was not the only instance of adapting the content to the local reader. Foreign pictorial stories were often heavily edited to appeal to domestic audiences. In many cases, the original speech balloons were removed and replaced with versed captions, typical for Polish *historyjki obrazkowe.* As we have seen, names were also altered and some of the realities adapted to mimic the Polish setting. For example, Superman, whose name was changed to the Slavonic-sounding Burzan, landed his rocket in the vicinity of the city of Kalisz and was later adopted by an affluent family of Warsaw entrepreneurs (Pieczara and Dziatkiewicz 22). Other characters, too, were Polonized. Betty Boop was renamed as Baśka Figlarka, Felix the Cat as Kotek Bibuś, and Donald Duck as Kaczorek Zadziorek. Henryk Jerzy Chmielewski, the Polish comic book creator who began his career in the late 1950s, remembered his surprise at discovering, during a trip to the United States in 1966, that the familiar *Ferdek i Merdek* he had read in his childhood were, in fact, the American Popeye and his sidekick Wimpy (Chmielewski, *Urodziłem się* 109). To add to the confusion, in interwar Poland, the same character could appear under different names, depending on the newspaper. For example, the Swedish Adamson functioned in Polish interwar press as Mikołaj Doświadczyński, Ildefons Kopytko, Pan Fikalski, Pan Franciszek, Napoleon Kluska, Wojciech Krupka, and Agapit Krupka, the latter of which proved to be the most lasting (Rusek, *Tarzan* 71–74; Rusek, *Leksykon* 8–11). In a similar way, Flash Gordon appeared in one newspaper as Błysk Gordon and in another as Jacek Żegota, where he was also described as a modern Polish knight figure (Pieczara and Dziatkiewicz 22).

At times, the plots would be manipulated and images redone by local illustrators. This was due to a variety of reasons. For example, one Polish journalist remembered how in 1933 the original Danish stencils of Pat and Patachon did not arrive in time to complete the Sunday edition of the Łódź-based *Express Ilustrowany* that ran the serial. The newspaper's chief illustrator, Wacław Drozdowski, was called in and asked to draw a new episode from scratch. He was instructed to stick to the original style to sustain the continuity of the serial. Soon enough, the newspaper relied largely on Drozdowski's work, in addition to using original drawings from Denmark in its sister magazines. It was that delayed delivery that was often credited with the birth of series *Wicek i Wacek,* modeled on Pat and Patachon but set more firmly in the Polish context (Ochocki 21). Drozdowski was said to have a good eye for detail and many of his drawings used the backdrop of familiar streets and courtyards of his native Łódź that would have been recognizable to the reader (Dunin 13). As such, *Wicek i Wacek* also built on the wider tradition of placing the city at the heart of the story, turning the industrial Łódź into a celebrated location and evidencing how the comic strip could play the role of "a genuine medium of urban modernity" (Ahrens and Meteling 6).

Other stories, too, became subject to various alterations. For example, the American serial *Tillie the Toiler,* also printed in *Express Ilustrowany,* had to be reinvented after the staff in Łódź mixed up the original printing plates and was unable to reconstruct the correct order of the story. Despite sounding unthinkable to contemporary readers of comics, such glitches were supposedly commonplace in the popular press and tabloids of the interwar period (Rusek, *Tarzan* 71).

The majority of Polish publishers avoided reprinting speech bubbles, typical for American series, and this was no different for other East-Central European states. According to scholar of Czechoslovak comics Pavel Kořínek, there was cultural stigma attached to speech balloons, which were

> often considered a cheap gimmick, a strange, feeble-minded, "foreign" element that somehow devalued the already unappreciated works of sequential art. On the other hand, the common use of verse in captioned series seemed to elevate these works to the vicinity of poetry for children, with its higher recognition and cultural

acceptance. For these reasons, it was much easier for the captioned series to gain cultural legitimization. When printing foreign comics, it was a common practice in the 1930s and the early 1940s to erase the balloons from the panels and as compensation to add simple rhymes underneath the pictures. (244)

Despite revealing similar distrust toward this format, in Poland, some magazines and newspapers opted for the inclusion of speech balloons in their reprints and adaptations from 1930 on. This coincided roughly with Hergé's first encounter with the speech bubble in 1928, which he subsequently popularized through his Tintin series from 1929 onward (Lye 18–19). In Poland, the children's supplement of the Łódź-based newspaper *Kurier Łódzki* published the Danish series *Peter og Ping* (as *Pan Bujdalski i Kaczorek*) already in 1930, retaining the original speech balloons (Rusek, *Tarzan* 103). From the mid-1930s, this practice became more common, particularly for the Łódź-based press magnate Republika. This included the publication of *Mandrake the Magician* in the *Panorama* supplement in 1936 and of *The Katzenjammer Kids*, published by another outlet in Łódź in 1937 (Rusek, *Tarzan* 71). Many of the children's magazines mentioned before, such as *Gazetka Miki* and *Wiosenka*, used exclusively speech bubbles. Some of the stories, which appeared initially as serials in magazines, were later reprinted as albums (notably the Polonized version of Pat and Patachon, *Wicek i Wacek*), retaining this format. Łódź-based publisher Republika also introduced several self-standing albums imported from the United States in 1937 to 1939, while the J. Przeworski publishing company released small books based on stories about Mickey Mouse and Flash Gordon, among others, all of which used speech balloons (Rusek, "Od szalonego Grzesia" 86). This meant that already in the 1930s Polish audiences, both adults and children, were familiar with American-style comics design. Although local artists preferred to use captions, even in the newly created serialized stories, the Polish reader was accustomed to both formats.

The examples above demonstrate the dynamism of the illustrated press and magazine industry in interwar Poland, particularly where imports from abroad were concerned. Although at times chaotic and erratic, the circulation of foreign comic strips was part of a larger process of cross-border cultural exchange. This exchange was relatively well structured and largely uniform across Europe. As Polish audiences were getting acquainted with American cartoon characters, so did their counterparts in the majority of other European countries, including France, Italy, and Spain (see Zanettin 869). This was no different for other East-Central European states, where weeklies and dailies printed similar foreign content. In Hungary, for example, Mickey Mouse and Betty Boop were also popular, as was Secret Agent X9. Those reprints were subject to comparable alterations, including the rechristening of the original characters, to mention the example of Felix the Cat, who was known to Hungarian audiences as Sicc (Szép 263).

This system of cultural transmission of American products was regulated by the American King Features Syndicate, which dealt with the distribution, licensing, and copyright of press products (Rusek, "Od 'Grzesia'" 71–72). The Stockholm-based Bull's Presstjänst Agency, also known as Bulls Press, acted as the representative for King Features in Poland and some of the other states in the region, including Germany and Czechoslovakia (Scholz, "Comics" 74–75). This form of distribution and licensing was also in place where other "globalized" press products were concerned, from articles written by internationally known figures to illustrated content of all kinds (Sterling 570). The Warsaw office was run by Bulls's Norwegian representative, Einar Wyller, who arrived in Poland in 1936 and remained there until the German invasion in 1939.

According to Kevin Patrick, Swedish publishers were interested in the developments in the US already toward the end of the nineteenth century. With the formation of local European agencies such as Bulls Press (established in Norway in 1929), the transatlantic transfer of cultural products entered a new phase. In Patrick's words, European intermediaries "typically possessed greater local knowledge of domestic media markets and could readily identify and cultivate strategic industry contacts on behalf of their American business partners" (66–67). They did so by promoting new titles, collecting licensing fees, and arranging "the distribution of syndicated content to local clients more cheaply and efficiently than American syndicates could ever hope to from afar" (Patrick 67).

Some of the other European states, too, had designated national agencies that dealt with King Features; these included Paul Winkler's Opera Mundi in France and Guglielmo Emanuel in Italy. Aside from being able to import foreign production, these agencies also possessed rights for the foreign distribution of many domestic comic strips. For example, material syndicated by Opera Mundi appeared in Poland, too, including the French comic strip *Professeur Nimbus* (Baudry and Litaudon 26, fn. 20; "Przygody Profesora Nimbusa"). Comics from other countries were syndicated by their respective national agencies. This included the popular Danish imports that arrived in Poland through the Copenhagen-based Presse-Illustrations-Bureau (PIB) (Rusek, "Od 'Grzesia'" 72; Madsen et al. 17, 154).

Discussing the global spread of American comic strips, Kevin Patrick argues that they were "cheap and in plentiful supply": "By the early 1930s, feature syndicates could already draw upon dozens of series, which had several years' worth of backdated daily and Sunday newspaper episodes that could be supplied to foreign clients at a fraction of their original production cost" (66). Despite the low cost and prevalence of syndicated material, the rules of circulation and dissemination of foreign content were not fully grasped by everyone in 1930s Poland. One journalist of *Ilustrowany Kuryer Codzienny,* a newspaper that regularly reprinted foreign content, including pictorial stories (notably the Swedish *Adamson*), bemoaned the ignorance of his counterparts from other dailies. As it turned out, following a reprint of one internationally circulated article on the first Five Year Plan by Trotsky in *Kuryer* in 1931, another Polish newspaper accused *Kuryer* of lying about having interviewed the famous revolutionary. With a clear air of learned superiority, the *Kuryer* reporter explained that Trotsky wrote his article for "world's largest information agency King Features Syndicate whose European representative, Stockholm-based Bull's Presstjänst, bought it with a right to circulate it in sixty countries" ("Prowincjonalne zmartwienia" 4). Thus, explained the journalist patiently, Trotsky did not have to give interviews or write articles for each country (and newspaper) separately. Rather, the licensing rights held by the American agency meant that each reprint was as good as the "original" article (4).

The example above shows that the issue of copyright and licensing attached to the foreign reprints was still a novelty to many in the newspaper industry. Highly popular dailies, such as *Ilustrowany Kuryer Codzienny,* had a strong advantage over their competitors. The daily was a part of a larger press conglomerate with substantial capital coming from the pockets of several high-profile Jewish entrepreneurs (owners of glass and porcelain factories), solicitors, and bankers, among others (Bańdo 120). In the 1930s, the newspaper was said to reach a circulation of more than 200,000 copies, with an estimated number of 1 million readers a day. Despite being published in Kraków, *Kuryer* was circulated nationally and internationally. In 1935, it was sold across 320 distribution points in Poland and 1,827 points abroad (Bańdo 142). Given the substantial capital behind the newspaper and the high circulation figures, this was an ideal outlet for pictorial stories and foreign content to be published and disseminated to hundreds of thousands of readers.

All of the examples above demonstrate the prominence of foreign comic art in interwar Poland. It is true that some of these pictorial stories were constricted to the so-called *prasa bulwarowa*, tabloid press, which was targeting mass audiences. Similarly, there is no denying that the first illustrated children's magazines comprised content that, at times, could be seen as unsophisticated and overly commercialized. However, intrinsically tied to these developments was a growth of technology, the rise of literacy, and an increased access to print media, particularly among Poland's expanding urban populations. With the March Constitution of 1921, which guaranteed freedom of press, publishing houses outdid each other in providing content that would grab the attention of the reader and increase circulation figures. This reflected the experiences of their colleagues elsewhere. As comics historian Jean-Paul Gabilliet demonstrates, in early twentieth-century America some publishers saw a nearly 20 percent increase in circulation after introducing "funnies" in their newspapers (*Of Comics* 192). While no such reliable statistics exist for Poland, it can be presumed that pictorial stories, those with rhymed captions and speech bubbles alike, had a similar effect.

In that respect, publishers in the nascent Polish state were well equipped to engage in free-market business practices, akin to their counterparts in other European countries and in the United States. Liaising with foreign press syndicates taught local players about the mechanisms and prerequisites behind the cross-border flow of cultural products. This was precisely the time for the comic strip to flourish in Poland. The inflow of American loans in the late 1920s stabilized the currency and supported the growth of economy, which, despite the crisis of the early 1930s, recuperated in the mid-1930s. Popular publications were backed by a secure capital, be it the "textile money" of Łódź fabricants (as was the case with the Republika group, which published *Express Ilustrowany*) or the banking capital of former Austro-Hungarian elites in Kraków (owners of *Ilustrowany Kuryer Codzienny*). It was those better-endowed publishers who had a definite advantage over their competitors.

Needless to say, none of these developments associated with widely defined modernity were limited to Poland. Neither were the popular culture offerings restricted to comics. As I show below, with the wider availability of print and film technology, interwar Europe as a whole experienced a vigorous period of cultural exchange.

## Popular Culture Imports and Consumption

The advance of pictorial stories in Poland, and their gradual transition into full-fledged comics containing speech balloons, was largely stimulated by a budding fascination with other products of American popular culture. Animated film, in particular, became one of the best-loved foreign products in Poland. American films made up the bulk of these imports. Stories seen on-screen were often the same stories that could be read in popular papers and magazines, and more often than not, print media industry went hand in hand with film industry. Already in 1928, animated cartoons from the United States were shown in Polish cinemas, most notably the work of Max Fleischer mentioned above (e.g., *Koko the Clown* and *Betty Boop*). Described as *fleischerówki,* a word deriving from the creator's name, the films were widely popular with young audiences and, as we have seen earlier, fueled the consumption of comics that arrived several years later. In the 1930s, other animated imports from the United States were screened in Polish cinemas, including Paul Terry's *Aesop's Fables* series and MGM's *Happy Harmonies* (Sitkiewicz, *Miki* 12–13).

American cinema, more generally, dominated the Polish market in the late 1920s and early 1930s, not least because of its cutting-edge technology, which became crucial with the advance of sound film. It is estimated that in 1929 alone as many as ninety sound motion pictures were shown in Warsaw. Seventy of them were American productions (J. Toeplitz 115; Thompson 136). This is not that surprising. In the interwar years, American production companies considered Poland the eighth largest market in Europe and did their best to support the process of bringing their products to Polish audiences.[15] For example, Paramount films for the European market would

---

15. Admittedly, there were regional differences in cinemagoing, with Warsaw topping the list (in 1936 there were seventy cinemas in Warsaw), followed by the Silesian (seventy-two cinemas) and Poznań (seventy cinemas) regions. See Sitkiewicz, *Gorączka filmowa* 13.

be initially dubbed in the American studio in Joinville using foreign or Polish émigré voice actors. This was later moved to Germany, but the results were rarely satisfactory. According to one historian of cinema, expatriate actors spoke "heavily-accented Polish" (presumably a reference to their Yiddish accent), and the efforts to synchronize word and image left much to be desired (J. Toeplitz 120). There is a reason why the Polonized version of Disney's first feature cartoon, *Snow White and the Seven Dwarfs*, released in Poland in 1938, turned out to be such a spectacular success. New songs were written for the Polish-language soundtrack and performed by the Polish choir Dana (Zajíček 392). The film was dubbed by native-speaker actors in Warsaw, with famous actress Maria Modzelewska as Snow White. Critics praised the performers for their excellent singing and dialogues as well as the synchronization of word and image (Teler). Although some commentators were resistant to its allure, the film's premiere was undoubtedly one of the major cultural events in interwar Poland.[16]

Such successful productions triggered discussions about the animation film industry in Poland, which was nowhere near its American counterpart. Disney creations were often seen as model examples of the genre, and calls for similar productions by local artists were widely heard (Sitkiewicz, *Polska szkoła* 27). This was no different for other countries or even other studios in the US itself. In Michael Barrier's words:

> Throughout the thirties, while the Disney studio was moving steadily forward, cartoonists at other studios were simply figuring out what they were *not* doing, and as it turned out, they were definitely not making Disney cartoons. Since the Disney cartoons had defined the terms of animation's progress, that could have meant that other studios' cartoons were doomed to perpetual inferiority. (4)

The same could, no doubt, be said about Polish artists who racked their brains trying to produce "the Polish Disney." Indeed, Poland's first, by now lost, animated film, *Przygody Puka* (*The Adventures of Puk*; 1932), directed by Lviv native Jan Jarosz, was said to be inspired by American animations (Sitkiewicz, *Polska szkoła* 41). The later productions of Włodzimierz Kowańko, *Pan Twardowski* (*Mr. Twardowski*;

---

16. For a rare negative review of the film, see "Baj i Disney."

1934) and *Wyprawa myszy na tort* (*The Mouse's Meanderings;* 1938), also bore close similarities to Disney productions (Grącka 102).

As was the case with Fleischer's films, Disney's cinematic works arrived in Poland shortly before their print equivalents. In the United States, the cinematic version of *Snow White* and its comic book adaptation appeared almost simultaneously. The film was released on December 21 and the first installment of the comic was already published one week earlier, in the *Silly Symphonies* comic strip, where it ran for the next few months. In Poland, *Gazetka Miki*, which featured reprints from *Snow White,* was published only on December 15, 1938. By then the film had been in theaters for more than two months, following its premiere on October 5, 1938. Irrespective of the delay, like in other states, in Poland there was a clear synergy between the two media. More specifically, the animated film played an important role of introducing Disney characters to local audiences, while the comic book reasserted their presence within the specific national market. The former role was, of course, focused predominantly on the visual element. After all, *Snow White* and other fairy tales by the Grimm Brothers had been known in Poland since the late nineteenth century (Koryga 5). Polish audiences were familiar with the story not only from book editions but also from theater plays.

In the 1930s, American productions were omnipresent in Europe. Their celebrities were revered in the most unexpected places (including remote Soviet towns) (Parks 19). It was in this context that early debates were initiated over what constituted "national" culture (vis-à-vis American and—even more so—globalized culture) (Ellwood 109). As I will show in the course of this book, after World War II similar questions would emerge around comics in Poland and elsewhere. However, in the 1920s and the 1930s, those concerns were related predominantly to American cinema and the impact it had on national cultures in Europe. For example, in 1920s Britain a clear conflict between the "commercial" and "cultivated" culture emerged. In the words of David W. Ellwood:

What made the conflict between them so difficult . . . was that on every site of their confrontation—language, literature, newspapers, broadcasting, music, and above all, cinema—there was an uninvited guest, one that constantly forced the protagonists to define and redefine what it was they were fighting for. That presence was industrially produced, commercially distributed American mass entertainment, vastly expanded compared to its pre-war life. (107)

The conflict between highbrow and popular culture, visible in Western Europe in particular, was not necessarily a symptom of rampant anti-Americanism. Rather, viewing America as the more advanced "Other," Europe's cultural elites were said to perceive the developments on the other side of the Atlantic as foretelling what Europe herself was to become. This (largely unwelcome) European future was to be marked by rampant commercialization, mechanization, and standardization. This, in turn, was seen as imperiling the "true" European civilization, its morality, and its traditional value systems (Kroes 18, 75–76).

Unlike their Western counterparts, Poland's conservative pundits did not necessarily view the American cultural influence as particularly dangerous or damaging. For the nationalist critic, the threat lay elsewhere. According to historian Eva Plach, the nationalist far right "commonly used a very particular string of words—Jewish, Bolshevik, Masonic, socialist, communist, godless, moral relativist"—to condemn "anything and everything perceived to be too liberal, modern, and 'un-Polish'" (148). Even though modern technology, dances, fashions, and Americanization were also criticized at times, they were hardly at the core of conservative debates about the dangers of modernity (Plach 138).

Thus, if one can speak of the Americanization of interwar Polish culture, then this Americanization was not as pervasive as some contemporary cultural guardians in Western Europe pictured it. The print media provided an interesting barometer with which to measure these developments. It is true that, as with the comics and films, other products of American popular culture were believed to guarantee success with audiences, but this made for a small percentage of the overall content of the average Polish daily. One of Poland's most popular newspapers, *Ilustrowany Kuryer Codzienny,* as well as its sister publications, provide an illustrative example of this. The media conglomerate included snippets of American popular culture in its various supplements and sister magazines. The early 1930s marked the rise in this tendency, but to speak of a full-fledged commercialization would be an exaggeration. For example, in 1931, one of *Kuryer's* sister magazines reprinted a detective story by Rufus King titled *Murder by the Clock* (1929) (see "Nowa porywająca powieść"). A year later, *Kuryer's* prose supplement included excerpts from popular fiction for women, including Elenore Meherin's novel *Chickie* ("Chickie idzie w świat"). In a similar vein, *Kuryer's* cinema insert regularly presented short profiles of emerging American film stars (e.g., Barbara

Stanwyck), discussed advances in film technology (such as attempts at developing a 3D technology), and shared trivia about the private lives of famous screen personalities who made their careers in the United States, including Charlie Chaplin (see, e.g., "Nowe gwiazdy ekranu" and "Film trójwymiarowy"; "Życie sentymentalne Charlie Chaplina"). *Kuryer* also made a skillful use of advertising, including ads of new cinematic productions by American directors (including Frank Borzage's 1929 production *They Had to See Paris,* screened as *Jedynaczka króla nafty,* and Millard Webb's *The Painted Angel,* presented as *Anioł pod szminką*) and plays by American authors that were shown in Polish theatres (e.g., a play by Barry Conners) (see "Anioł pod szminką," "Jedynaczka króla nafty," and "Roxy"). That is not to say that the content of these publications was dominated by news from the United States. Quite the contrary—the film supplement, in particular, struck a good balance between discussing American, European, and domestic news and developments, presenting a relatively comprehensive image of the contemporary cinema industry.[17]

The spread of comics was not only facilitated by the wide availability of American cinema and pulp literature; it was also a direct result of new lifestyle and consumption patterns, particularly among the more affluent sections of society, which veered between foreign and native products. Like its popular culture offerings, *Kuryer*'s advertising also bore witness to these practices. Advertisements for American-made Elizabeth Arden cosmetics appeared in the newspaper side by side with the German Nivea body-care and Chlorodont toothpaste products. British Lipton tea ads would be placed in the same issue as Dr Oetker baking powder announcements. The Polish soap, shampoo, face cream, and powder brand Śnieg Tatrzański (The Snow of Tatra Mountains), of Wacław Falkiewicz from Poznań, was also advertised. The list was completed by Philips light bulbs, an export product of the Netherlands. This kind of advertising content was accompanied by subject matter relating to lifestyle and leisure activities, including fashion, travel—especially the popular spa

17. This style of reporting on American popular culture and its various industries coincided with snippets containing information on American lifestyle. As in the cases discussed above, much of this content was fairly subtle and linked to the promotion of wider values that the newspaper professed. In one 1931 issue of a women's supplement, an article was published about the American county Cook that documented a record high of divorces, most of them due to the abuse perpetrated by the husband. The article was clearly sympathetic toward women who were able to choose this path. See "Jeden rozwód co 55 minut."

**FIGURE 1.4.** *Snow White* cinema poster, Movie Theatre Stylowy, Zamość, Drukarnia Rady Powiatowej, 1939

**FIGURE 1.5.** *Snow White* cinema poster, Movie Theatre Rakieta, Łódź, Z. Szaładajewski, 1938

**FIGURE 1.6.** *Snow White* cinema poster, Cinema Zdrój, Łomża, Drukarnia Diecezjalna, 1939

culture—and photography, as exemplified by Kodak photography competitions.[18]

While it is difficult to assess to what extent the exposure to foreign film, literature, and lifestyle encouraged the consumption of comics, it can be presupposed that there was a subtle link between the two. Growing familiarity with an increasingly globalized culture and an experience of new consumption patterns made Polish audiences better attuned to what America had to offer. To quote posters advertising Walt Disney's *Snow White,* to many in interwar Poland American popular culture was, undeniably, "a miracle of text, color and sound" (see figure 1.4). It was a culture that "transgressed the bounds of human imagination," all the more as it was "spoken and sung in Polish" (see figures 1.4 and 1.5). American culture was thus something that could be nativized while retaining its "natural colors" (see figure 1.6).

---

18. See, for example, a variety of such content in the following issues: *Ilustrowany Kuryer Codzienny,* April 2, 1933; *Ilustrowany Kuryer Codzienny,* August 11, 1933; and *Ilustrowany Kuryer Codzienny,* July 18, 1931.

## Conclusion

The interwar period created a unique milieu in which press and popular culture could develop in Poland. Much of this publishing activity was built on the industrial fortunes that had emerged during the
economic boom of the late nineteenth and early twentieth centuries.
It was this capital that enabled Polish readers to participate in the
wider European and global readership of comics. While there is no
proof that the inclusion of pictorial stories increased readership figures, it was certainly during this period that a strong community of
avid readers, both young and adult, emerged in Poland. This early
"fandom culture," which encompassed cinema too, encouraged local
publishers and authors (erstwhile illustrators for satirical press) to
increasingly engage with the new medium and work hard to surprise
and please their audiences. This was particularly true where offerings
for young readers were concerned. In the words of comics historian
Bradford Wright, the 1930s were "a critical moment in the evolution
of youth culture," marked by an increased independence of young
people that enabled publishers to bypass parents and aim "their
products directly at the tastes of children and adolescents" (26).

There is no denying that much of the domestic output was
inspired by the developments farther afield and facilitated by the
influx of American loans, but Polish and foreign comics existed side
by side, in an interesting symbiosis. Often, Polish illustrators were
able to turn their encounters with foreign work into an exercise in
cultural translation, as the example of Wacław Drozdowski's *Wicek
i Wacek* shows. Although much of this activity was cut short by the
outbreak of World War II, this period of sustained exposure to foreign and local pictorial stories created a good understanding among
readers of what constituted a comic book culture. If one can speak
about the Americanization of Poland during that period, then this
was a largely positive experience, even if restricted to the more affluent sections of the society.

As I show in chapter 2, following the consolidation of Communist
power after 1947, comics came to be vilified and gradually excluded
from the public sphere as a symbol of American capitalism. The experience of interwar exposure to American popular culture and the
market economy was expunged from public discourse to pave the
way for a vicious anti-comics campaign.

CHAPTER 2

# THE (ANTI-)
# AMERICAN DREAM

Comics in Public Debates in the 1950s

Scholars have famously remarked that the twentieth century was "the American century." With the advent of democracy and the victory of capitalism over Communism, the United States emerged from the Cold War "as the only global superpower—not only in military, but also in economic, technological, and even cultural terms" (Krastev 5). It was 9/11 that purportedly marked the arrival of "the anti-American century," which was said to put the previous Cold War animosities into perspective (Krastev). And yet, there is no denying that anti-American sentiment was rampant in much of Europe at different points of the twentieth century, too, be it for economic, cultural, or political reasons (see Isernia; Friedman; Gassert). In Poland, anti-American views emerged around two important moments of political transformation: first during the consolidation of Communist power after World War II, and second, following the collapse of Communism in 1989 and the transition from command to market economy (Delaney and Antoszek 86). In both periods, American popular culture was subject to a concerted attack by the media and public intellectuals. As I show in this and one of the later chapters, the reasons for this were specific for each period in question. What was common, however, was that—in both decades—comic books came to be vilified as part of that wider anti-American campaign.

The aim of this chapter is to discuss how comics featured in the public debates surrounding the United States in 1950s Poland. My main focus is on the period prior to the political "thaw" that ensued in Eastern Europe after Stalin's death (1953) and Khrushchev's Secret Speech denouncing Stalinist methods and the man himself (1956). More specifically, I explore whether the criticism of comics at the height of Stalinism was solely an expression of anti-capitalist sentiment, dictated by Poland's adherence to socialism and its political alliance with the Soviet Union, or whether and to what extent it voiced much wider European, and also American, concerns over comics.

## Americanization, Anti-Americanism, and the Comics

The image of the United States in Poland has been, traditionally, a positive one. Since the late eighteenth century, the memory of two nationalist heroes, Tadeusz Kościuszko and Kazimierz Pułaski, who participated in Polish and American struggles for independence, provided fodder for cultural diplomacy, fostering mutual understanding and knowledge. In the nineteenth century, the outflow of emigrant Poles to America, and the successful lives many of them established there, engendered a (largely romanticized) idea of the United States as the land of promise and opportunity. Following World War I, and in line with his wartime "Fourteen Points," President Woodrow Wilson reasserted his support for Poland at the Paris treaty talks in 1918 and 1919, which led to the recognition of the modern Polish state. Two centuries of mutual contacts, even if at times limited, produced a largely positive image of the US among Polish society, and after 1945 this image became a serious obstacle to the "anti-imperialist" campaign of the Communist government (Lipoński 80–81). It is no secret that to many ordinary Poles, the allure of American capitalism was much greater than the appeal of Soviet-style socialism. If the USSR's domination over East-Central Europe had any characteristics of colonial-like influence, as some scholars have argued, then this was undoubtedly a "reverse-cultural colonization," one that was guided by an overwhelming conviction of Soviet inferiority in comparison to their Eastern European allies (let alone the capitalist West) (Chioni Moore 121).

The Polish government campaign of the early 1950s provided a textbook example of anti-Americanism: It was systemic, the American shortcomings were greatly exaggerated, and its successes were downplayed; US policies and the country's way of life were misrepresented and argued to be malevolent, dangerous, degenerate, and/or ridiculous.[1] Both the oppressed people of the US (including African Americans, Communists, strike organizers, and other minority groups) and the "peace-seeking" countries of the wider world were said to be in danger of that influence (Lipoński 84). This is not to say that all criticism of the US constituted misinformation and was invalid. After all, as we will see below, some of the Polish (and international) critiques of American popular culture originated in the US itself and raised alarm among many others in the non-Communist world. Rather, the incessant repetition of certain negative tropes, biased selection of news, and the tendency to de-emphasize some issues and overemphasize others meant that the reporting was grossly imbalanced and molded to fit ideological needs (London and Anisimov 42).

In the same way that modern comics arrived in interwar Europe from America, so, paradoxically, did the outcry over their objectionable content more than one decade later. The first voices of criticism targeting children's comic magazines appeared in the US in 1940, arguing that comics hampered the child's educational and emotional development. In a much-reprinted newspaper article, literary editor Sterling North bemoaned "Superman heroics, voluptuous females in scanty attire, blazing machine guns, hooded 'justice' and cheap political propaganda" and called for parents and researchers throughout America to unite in a shared struggle against this "poisonous mushroom growth" of the previous years (56).[2] The discussion initiated by North in 1940 gained momentum in the aftermath of World War II.[3] This was associated with the mass spread of the medium; according

---

1. For a useful definition of anti-Americanism, see, for example, Rubin and Rubin ix.

2. The article first appeared as an editorial in *Chicago Daily News* on May 8, 1940. This citation comes from a reprint in *Childhood Education* that same year.

3. In the meantime, already in the early 1940s, education scholars refuted the assumptions made by North, "noting that reading comic books had little impact on [the child's] reading skills, academic achievement, or social adjustment." See Nyberg, "The Comics Code" 25.

to historian Bradford Wright, by the end of that decade nearly 1 billion comic books were printed each year (88–89). With an upsurge in juvenile delinquency, mental health professionals argued that crime comic books "desensitized youngsters to violence," seeking to restrict the supposedly offensive content (Nyberg, "The Comics Code" 26). From the late 1940s, German-born psychiatrist Fredric Wertham embarked on a crusade against the medium, using the experiences of his teenage patients from Harlem, New York City, as evidence supporting his quest. He maintained that "comic-reading was a distinct influencing factor in the case of every single delinquent or disturbed child we studied" (Crist 22).[4] In his best-selling book, *Seduction of the Innocent* (1954), Wertham developed the critique of crime and horror comics, while putting forward ideas about what he described as the child's "mental hygiene" (3). In the opening paragraph of the book, Wertham likened child-rearing to gardening:

> Gardening consists largely in protecting plants from blight and weeds, and the same is true of attending to the growth of children. If a plant fails to grow properly because attacked by a pest, only a poor gardener would look for the cause in that plant alone. The good gardener will think immediately in terms of general precaution and spray the whole field. But with children we act like the bad gardener. We often fail to carry out elementary preventive measures, and we look for the causes in the individual child. (2)

The psychiatrist blamed the publishing industry, comics creators, and the American state as a whole for the proliferation of "blight and weeds" that spoiled the "crop," rather than seeking the cause for delinquency in the individual child.[5] This was in stark contrast to publishers, who were reticent to take responsibility for the impact of crime comics on young readers and who instead emphasized the importance of parental control over what "children read, see on the

---

4. Wertham's mental health clinic, Lafargue Clinic, specialized in treating African American teenagers. His colleagues, including Hilde L. Mosse, were also vocal critics of the "crime comics." For an article reporting on Mosse's public lecture on "The Destructive Effect of Comics on Children," see "Psychiatrist Charges Stalling Tactics on Legislation to Control Comic Books."

5. There was certainly a relationship between the rise of competition among comic book publishers and the increase in violent imagery in their publications (see Wright 83).

screen and hear on the radio" (Loeb). Wertham's proposal was much more radical and, admittedly, more sympathetic both to children and their desperate parents whom he encountered in his clinic. He urged America and the world as a whole "to spray the whole field," that is, to banish crime comics completely and to reform the social environment that was said to breed juvenile delinquency. This, he argued, would be an ultimate exercise in democracy: "I am convinced that in some way or other the democratic process will assert itself and crime comic books will go, and with them all they stand for and all that sustains them" (395). But before this could happen, he maintained, "people will have to learn that it is a distorted idea to think that democracy means giving good and evil equal chance at expression. We must learn that freedom is not something that one can have, but is something that one must do" (395).

Even though Wertham's proposals attracted a lot of criticism in the US, they did not fall on deaf ears. In an attempt to rescue their deteriorating reputation (as well as the abating sales figures), in 1954 publishers formed the Comics Magazine Association of America, a self-censoring body that screened publication content. Its censoring regulation, the Comics Code Authority, drafted that same year, provided comics creators with "do's and don'ts" of the industry, including a ban on stories that glamorized crime and criminals, scenes of excessive violence and bloodshed, and stories containing nudity, sexual perversions, and unrealistic drawings of women, particularly those that exaggerated certain physical qualities. An embargo on specific words, such as "crime," "terror," and "horror," was written into the code regulations.[6]

Many of these points would be taken up by the underground comics scene that emerged in the US in the 1960s. Publishing outside the official system, those artists advocated for a return of pre-code aesthetics, and an unrestricted use of everything that the code prohibited, particularly graphic depictions of sex, violence, and drug abuse (Oxoby). It was those limitations that would shape nonconformist underground comix artists, such as Robert Crumb, Gilbert Shelton, Manuel Rodriquez, and others (Cook 34–37). While adhering to the Comics Code was voluntary, most American publishers did so for decades in an attempt to pander to retailers, advertisers, and concerned parents. Gradually, with the emergence of independent dis-

6. For a full text of the 1954 Code, see Nyberg, *Seal of Approval* 166–68.

tributors, one by one, publishers ceased to observe the Code. With the last publishing houses abandoning it in the 2000s, it was eventually rendered obsolete in 2011 (Nyberg, "The Comics Code" 28–31).

Amy Kiste Nyberg argues that, although many critics dismissed Wertham as "a naïve social scientist," his book pointed to the necessity of rethinking the values that structured American society and spoke to the need to reform that society ("Comic Book Censorship" 51). Similarly, Bart Beaty shows that Wertham was not quite the McCarthyite crusader that some opponents considered him to be (*Fredric Wertham* 6). Neither was he an advocate of cultural censorship (Wright 97). Rather, he was a vocal supporter of liberal values, even if his critique of comics called for a relinquishing of the postwar individualist ideology (*Fredric Wertham* 200). Jared Gardner proposes that, as a Jewish émigré who left Germany in 1934, Wertham did not necessarily derive his views from the value system of the American conservative right, as some commentators might have erroneously presumed. Instead, his assessment of the mass culture was closer to that of the Frankfurt school, being largely informed by his experience of fascism in early 1930s Europe (95–96). He was thus careful not to associate himself with anti-comics campaigners whose activism was underpinned by racism, nativism, and anti-Semitism (Wright 97). More importantly, to echo Beaty, among the many critiques of the medium, Wertham's was "the only sustained work from the postwar period that took comics seriously or treated them as if they were important in any way" (*Fredric Wertham* 198–99).

In many states in Europe and beyond, Wertham became an authority on the corrupting influence of comics, even before *Seduction of the Innocent* was published. His arguments, even if overly simplified and molded to match local agendas, were readily cited in similar anti-comics campaigns that took place in the late 1940s and early 1950s across the world, from Canada to Finland, from West Germany to New Zealand and Australia, from Mexico to Italy and to the Scandinavian states (see Adams; Brannigan; Kauranen; Jovanovic and Koch; Openshaw and Shuker; Rubenstein; Jensen; Meda). Wertham followed these developments carefully and one of the chapters of his *Seduction* is devoted to anti-comics sentiments in Canada, the Netherlands, Britain, France, Sweden, and other states (see 273–94).

Scholars in the Polish context have argued that anti-comics attitudes in socialist Poland were principally anti-imperialist in nature (Zwierzchowski 113; Rusek, "Od szalonego Grzesia" 87). This is only partly true. As I show below, the Polish anti-comics campaign followed a wider transnational tendency to conflate discussions on comics with debates on education and child welfare, which was not limited to Communist sympathizers. By the same token, the propensity to use comics as a pretext to express anti-Americanism was not exclusive to the USSR and its satellite states. On the contrary, the anti-comics campaigns of the early 1950s show that "anti-imperial," anti-capitalist, and anti-American sentiment was present on both sides of the Iron Curtain, including in those states that were officially aligned with the United States. Writing about France, Richard Ivan Jobs emphasized the political and cultural complexities of the local anti-comics campaign:

> The campaign against American comics played itself out amid the hottest moments of the early Cold War: the Berlin Airlift, the war in Korea, McCarthyism, the Rosenberg trial and execution, the rearmament of Germany, the Soviet demonstration of nuclear capabilities and the struggle over the *coca-colonization* of France by American capitalism. Although the strident anti-American sentiment was led by the Communist Party and its fellow travelers who viewed American comics, with their exoneration of the violent individual superhero, as promoting "fascistic themes," centrists and Atlanticists also hoped that France would maintain an independent national policy free from American domination. Thus, although not everyone supporting the measures against comic books could be characterised as anti-American, resistance to the capitalist behemoth and the desire for French hegemony and an independent national identity in the wake of Nazi, and then Allied, invasion and occupation did inform the debates about foreign comics and the practice of cultural consumption. (79–80)

These views were shared by French Catholics, who criticized the "excesses" of comic books (and who in 1949 submitted a bill that demanded control over the import of foreign comics), and by the right wing, who saw the medium as threatening the national spirit (Reitberger and Fuchs 185). According to Jobs, those hostile responses to American comics could be read as an expression of wider concerns that emerged around postwar reconstruction, nation building, consumer culture, and, supposedly, the social safety of youth on both sides of the Iron Curtain (80). That the activities of local Communist

Parties were central to much of this campaigning, also in the West, is understandable. As Martin Barker shows, also in Britain, many activists were left-wing intellectuals who were simultaneously involved in other causes célèbres, including the peace movements and the movement against the Korean War. Despite attempting to draw in wider sections of society, who shared their dislike of comics, the majority of British campaigners were, in principle, members of the Communist Party (see 36, 44–45).

However, despite the similarities between Western and Eastern European anti-comics campaigns, there was one major difference. Poland, unlike France or Britain, saw very few American comics post-1945. Several albums of Disney comics, *Mickey Mouse* and *Snow White,* were published in 1946 and 1948. Excerpts from *Tarzan* and *Donald Duck,* among other stories, were also reprinted in youth magazines prior to the rise of Stalinism in 1949 and later (Misiora 10, 135, 147). While other American cultural products were made available to audiences in the Soviet Union, as well as those in other "friendly regimes" (including popular films that were edited and screened without license with a view to bringing profit to the state), it was not until the political thaw of 1956 and the policy of "peaceful engagement" that, from 1957, the Polish government could purchase in zlotys US media products, such as films, books, music recordings, and other items.[7] In that sense, the critical commentaries on comics that emerged in the Poland of the late 1940s and early 1950s were an exercise in rhetoric. They served no practical purpose, such as rallying behind legislation that would curb the supposedly nefarious influence of comics, as was the case elsewhere. They were largely preemptive too, used to counter putative demands from a society that was generally sympathetic to American culture. And yet, those commentaries spoke volumes about the values that the state and, in particular, state-controlled media wished to impart to Polish citizens. As I will show below, the American "example" was portrayed as a warning. The American way

7. Claire Knight discusses American and West German "trophy films" that were captured by the Red Army in Berlin in 1945 and screened across the USSR between 1947 and 1956. Those films were cost-effective (e.g., no licensing fees were ever paid), and even though they were censored and edited, they attracted millions of viewers and, as such, were very profitable. For example, "The four *Tarzan* films released in 1952 were particularly successful, earning between 38.6 million and 42.9 million ticket sales each, making them top-selling films of the late Stalin period." See Knight 132. On the "peaceful engagement" in Poland and the import of American cultural products post-1956, see Delaney and Antoszek 75–76.

of life was to be avoided rather than coveted by the socialist citizen. But before these criticisms came to dominate public debate on comics in Poland, there was one person who offered a very different view of the medium.

## Aleksander Hertz and the Defense of American Comics (1947)

While the early origins of state-sanctioned anti-Americanism in Poland have been traced to 1947, the year the Truman Doctrine was proclaimed with an aim of containing Soviet geopolitical influence, it was not until 1949 that the "anti-imperialist" discourse emerged full-scale.[8] The period 1944 to 1948 was still relatively liberal where cultural policy was concerned, and so was the media discourse surrounding American popular culture (Jaworski, "Obrócić" 130). In the immediate aftermath of the war, journalists were free to pursue their individual interests and report enthusiastically on foreign trends. This would change, by and large, after 1947, when state directives dictated the importance of praising only those cultural developments and products that fit the socialist ethos (M. Mazur 26). At the same time, despite this relative liberty, in those early postwar years comics rarely featured as the topic of public debate. The terms "comic" and "comics" were fairly unknown to the Polish reader and rarely associated with the native *historyjki obrazkowe* (pictorial stories). It was a curiosity and a niche topic, too, one that was known solely to experts conversant with American culture.

One such expert was Aleksander Hertz, an émigré Polish-Jewish sociologist, based in the US since 1940. Hertz was a prolific writer, best known for his *Problems of Sociology of the Theater* (1938) and *Jews in Polish Culture* (1961) (see "Aleksander Hertz, Author, 87"). After World War II, he was a regular contributor to Polish papers, and after being blacklisted by the government and forbidden to publish in Poland, as were many other exile writers after 1949, he collaborated with the chief Polish exile magazine, the Parisian *Kultura,* headed by Jerzy Giedroyc.[9] Prior to his blacklisting, Hertz wrote an impassioned

---

8. For example, Lipoński argues that the campaign "against the capitalist system was introduced into Poland immediately after the Communist party seized power in Poland in 1947." See Lipoński 81.

9. For a list of boycotted intellectuals, see Strzyżewski 88.

discussion of American comics, "Amerykańskie klechdy obrazkowe" ("The American Pictorial Tales"), for the Marxist weekly literary magazine *Kuźnica.* The article is representative of the wider body of his essayistic work. Like many of his future essays for *Kultura,* this article also provided a sympathetic portrayal of his adopted homeland.[10] More importantly, it was forgiving of what some would see as the shortcomings of the American way of life. In that sense, Hertz's 1947 article was unique. It was, by far, the most thorough and informed discussion of American comics published in socialist Poland, even though similar (i.e., positive) portrayals of the medium began emerging following the liberalization of the 1970s. Hertz's discussion of comics reflected a deep fascination with America and its civilization too. It was written from a position of an outsider who attempts to move past clichés and platitudes to get a deeper understanding of a country that, all too often, was misconstrued or vilified. Only one year later, such a representation of the US would be unthinkable in Poland. Polish journalism would turn to a whole different idiom.

The article was divided in two parts. In part one, Hertz introduced the reader to the main themes and tropes of several comics with interwar origins, such as *Superman, The Little Orphan Annie,* and *The Captain and the Kids.* As well as demonstrating how fundamental comics had been to American culture, Hertz stressed the necessity of taking them seriously and looking for a deeper explanation as to why the medium enjoyed so much popularity in the US ("Amerykańskie klechdy obrazkowe" 5). In part two of the article, published in the next issue of the magazine, Hertz presented the crux of his argument. To him, American comics were a clear expression of national character, which was purportedly rooted in the "typically American" values of goodwill, individualism, optimism, and prosperity. American comics were said to attach great importance to women and children too. Female characters may be romanticized, he admitted, but they were also presented as feminine, sensual, and simply *sexy.*[11] Hertz maintained that American comics were also illustrative of America being a child-loving nation, one that set great store by the welfare of its children. More importantly, the typical hero of the comic book

---

10. For an article in which Hertz warns against simplistic and overly critical assessments of American culture, see Hertz, "Czym jest kultura amerykańska?" For a deeply personal essay on his affinity with the United States and its language, culture, and history, see Hertz, "Refleksje amerykańskie."

11. Hertz used here the English word "sexy" rather than a Polish variant.

was at once a demigod and everyman, the latter enabling the reader to forge a sense of identification with the protagonist ("Amerykańskie klechdy obrazkowe II" 4).

The core of Hertz's argument revolved around the comparison of comics with European folktales. To him, comics were a part of the American folklore, one that belonged, nonetheless, to an industrialized and capitalist civilization ("Amerykańskie klechdy obrazkowe II" 4). Hertz argued that comics arose from peasant culture, being an expression of the wisdom of past storytellers who spun their tales by the fire, at once educating and entertaining their audiences. According to him, "Once the storytellers and their listeners arrived in [the world of] skyscrapers, they brought some of those stories with them. They supplemented them with new values that grew out of sadness and disappointment, and out of the goals and dreams that emerged from the most industrialized and commercialized civilization of the world" ("Amerykańskie klechdy obrazkowe II" 4). Comics, Hertz finally argued, were an expression of conflict between the farming past and the industrialized present.

Irrespective of the validity of Hertz's rural/urban binary, the article was, no doubt, an earnest attempt at demonstrating that there was merit to American popular culture. Alluding to rural community life and oral tradition as the assumed origins of "funnies," Hertz operated with imagery that would be familiar to Polish readers. Here, he revealed himself as a true sociologist of culture. He saw comics as a part of a wider tradition of human communication whose role had always been to teach and to instill positive values. In doing so, he gave roots and meaning to a medium that would soon be faulted with having no history, being excessively commodified, and exerting corrupting influence on those whom it was supposed to educate. In that, he could be compared to the early American apologists of the medium, many of them educators, who, contributing to a debate in the *Journal of Educational Sociology* in December 1944, exonerated comics as an important "social force" and a "major medium of communication and influence" (see, e.g., Matsner Gruenberg; Zorbaugh).[12]

---

12. See also Wright 106–7. Other positive commentaries on the medium appeared over the next few decades after the anti-comics campaign of the early 1950s had drawn to a close. This included apologies for the crime and horror comics. This is how Larry Stark, a former fan of the genre, reminisced about it more than two decades later: "They seemed strangely complex for comic books, with unique twists, fresh approaches and artistic detail unseen of in this field before. In short, they were

In the words of one of Hertz's colleagues in the Parisian *Kultura,* Hertz was a true admirer of American democracy, despite all its faults and shortcomings. Above all, as a Polish-Jewish refugee, he was said to always remain loyal toward the country that had once become his safe heaven and his home (Matejko 174). This generosity toward the United States, paired with an effort to present its culture in all its fascinating complexity, was definitely rare among Polish (and, to some extent, also foreign) commentators of the period.

In his article, Hertz made the first step toward the assimilation of comics into the Polish imaginary. His affectionate term for comics— *komiki*—is the only attempt of the time to give the medium a Polish name. As I show below, throughout the fifties, when the anti-comics campaign was in full swing, press commentators would refuse to Polonize the word. This was a clear way of demarcating the medium as foreign and impossible to naturalize. The alien-sounding inflections of the word and awkward spelling ideas, including *comicsy, comicsów,* and *comicsami,* were meant to suggest that comics would never find home in Poland (Zwierzchowski 114). Although Hertz's discussion of the medium is the only one I could locate in the short period of relatively liberal cultural policy prior to 1949, it is representative of the time, marked by curiosity about and openness to the West. *Kuźnica,* the Marxist weekly in which it was published, was soon to be transformed into a cultural magazine *Nowa Kultura (The New Culture),* which, in the early 1950s, would launch some of the most prominent attacks on the medium.[13] As I show below, the first voices of criticism began appearing already in 1948, coinciding with the growing anti-comics discourse in the US and elsewhere.

## Comics and the Upbringing of Children

The majority of Polish press commentaries on American comics focused on the impact of the medium on American children. Common themes included juvenile delinquency and the perceived decline

---

well written, drawn and laid out. They did have the ability to surprise—to delight and astonish as a matter of fact. . . . They displayed a care and craftsmanship in text and illustration that somehow the comic field had seemed unworthy of before, at least in my experience."

13. For a discussion of the various anti-comics statements by *Nowa Kultura* only, see Zwierzchowski.

in the quality of education and literacy rates in the United States. Those themes were frequently used to criticize other aspects of American culture and society, from the purported "money making" mentality to gender role models. One of the earliest Polish critiques of American comics, written in 1948, incorporated all of the above. There were graphic descriptions of crimes committed by avid comics readers (such as injecting ink into the veins of a schoolmate, raping a three-year-old girl, and drowning a toddler in a bathtub), there was a criticism of the medium's supposed misogyny (the author claimed that comics taught American boys how to treat girls as inferior creatures and "as slaves"), and there was a juxtaposition of the violence and torture, depicted in the comics, with the crimes committed during World War II in Nazi concentration camps. In addition, Wertham's clinical observations found their way into the article. More importantly, the article criticized greedy publishers who were said to pay no heed to the moral upbringing of contemporary youth (see "Zrobiłem to dla dreszczyku emocji").

The article could be seen as a blueprint for many other reports that appeared in the Polish press over the next few years, particularly in the early 1950s. One prominent focus of those articles was the rising juvenile crime rates in the United States attributed to excessive exposure to violent comics and TV series. Polish journalists made a skillful use of American statistics, citing numbers and types of vicious crimes committed in the United States. Statements by American experts in the field of education, who were said to be alarmed by declining literacy rates, and who associated this trend with the growing importance of comics, were also cited (see, e.g., "Nauka nie idzie w las"; "Wychowankowie amerykańskiej 'kultury'"; "'Książki,' których oni nie palą").[14] Quotations from American weeklies, including the non-leftist ones (such as *The Nation*), which bemoaned the rapid spread of comics readership, provided additional fodder for anti-comics sentiment (Jaszuński, "Kultura"). So did the repeated references to Wertham, in which he was presented as the only voice of reason in what was seen as a largely dysfunctional American society (Jaszuński, "Poważnie").

The references to World War II and Nazi crimes were fairly common too. One author writing for *Nowa Kultura,* the weekly that

---

14. See also a Polish reprint from the Soviet *Pravda*: "Szkoła młodocianych zbrodniarzy."

emerged from *Kuźnica* (which only five years earlier published Hertz's eulogy of American comics), described Superman as a close relative of the "Hitlerite Übermenscher" (*Superman—nadczłowiek spokrewniony . . . z hitlerowskimi "Uebermenschami"*) (Arski 2). The author argued that Superman was a "personification of the American version of fascism" and that "Superman's favourite preoccupation was performing lynchings, merciless torture, and destroying everything and everyone who dared to stand in his way" (Arski 2). The Übermensch comparison, and especially the "Hitlerite" connotations, were by no means an invention of this particular editor, despite fitting into the postwar anti-fascist narrative of the USSR and its satellite states. In fact, Wertham himself used those comparisons often, as did many anti-comics campaigners in Europe and beyond.[15] Wertham was often quoted saying that "Hitler was a beginner compared to the comic-book industry" (Nyberg, *Seal of Approval* 63). In *Seduction of the Innocent,* he mentioned Nietzsche's Superhuman, vulgarizing the philosopher's idea, and leaving no doubt that the comparison was meant to be anything but flattering (15). Those comparisons to Nazi ideology were also made by Soviet commentators, most notably writer and journalist Ilya Ehrenburg. Speaking at the World Congress of the Supporters of Peace in Warsaw in 1950, Ehrenburg ominously described Superman as the new embodiment of the fascist Übermensch (see Ehrenburg).

Polish media also strove to place their criticism of comics in the context of wider European or global developments, either by citing the international critiques of the medium or by reporting on the declining morals in those states that had already fallen under the spell of American popular culture. This was another rhetorical strategy aimed at stressing the virtues of socialism and, ultimately, persuading the reader to adopt a similar viewpoint. One newspaper, for example, cited Indian Prime Minister Jawaharlal Nehru's strong condemnation of comics as worthless, and glorifying violence and crime ("Nehru przeciw"). Another provided a bleak report from

---

15. Goran Jovanovic and Ulrich Koch show that even in West Germany in the 1950s, where National Socialism was rarely discussed in public, anti-comics campaigners implied that comics replicated the "Hitlerite" worldview. For example, "several writers observed that the comics' enemies, victims, or malefactors were most often portrayed as Southern Europeans, Latin Americans, Asians, or Jews, whereas the heroes typically were representatives of a Nordic 'master race.'" See Jovanovic and Koch 116–17.

Britain, where comics, imported as part of the Marshall Plan, were said to provide a "stimulus for crime" (Bidwell, "Ponury import"). The latter article, in particular, was an interesting example of Cold War reporting. It was written by George Bidwell, a Briton, who had arrived in Warsaw in 1946 (Bidwell, *Ani chwili* 228). Bidwell married a Polish woman, translator and journalist Anna Krystyna Wirszyłło, and adopted Polish citizenship. He remained in Poland until his death in 1989. During that period, he published more than sixty novels and popular history books, becoming a celebrated author in his adopted homeland.[16] In his article from 1952, "Ponury import z USA" ("Gloomy Import from USA"), Bidwell used contemporary reports on growing crime rates in the United Kingdom to extol the virtues of Polish society, where crime, including juvenile delinquency, was said to have dropped significantly in comparison to the late 1930s. Bidwell's standing as a foreigner criticizing the country of his origin, and its cultural and political links with the United States in particular, was meant to add credence to his reporting. His praise of the achievements of the People's Republic of Poland (in the fields of moral education and crime reduction in particular) was yet another way of stressing the superiority of socialism over capitalism.[17]

Bidwell's article not only replicated the critiques that were widespread among Polish socialist pundits, it also echoed discussions that went on in early 1950s Britain. According to historian of the British anti-comics campaign Martin Barker, some of the local activists saw the American comics as "invading" their country and endangering its traditional ways. This view was shared by politicians of various persuasions. According to one Conservative MP, comics were a "crude and alien" import; in the words of a Labour parliamentarian, they were "not the best of American life, the natural American culture that exists in a million homes in that country, but all that is worst in America" (Barker 26).

Polish reports from Britain were not limited to the daily press. Such thinly veiled attacks on comics, capitalism, and the capitalist publisher in particular appeared in specialist journals too. For

---

16. Bidwell was almost completely unknown in Britain, though, and despite his prolific oeuvre, he is largely forgotten in Poland today. See Semczuk.

17. By no means was this the only article that discussed the supposedly corrupting influence of American troops, stationed in various European states, on other nations. See, for example, Małcużyński for an ideologically rabid discussion of American influence (comics included) in the Allied zone in Italy.

example, in 1953, a journal of Polish librarians published an extensive essay that discussed the alarming situation surrounding comics in Britain. The essay provided a compilation of statements by British anti-comics campaigners that included a nationwide appeal from British librarians calling on their colleagues, parents, teachers, and other members of society to unite in the fight against the corrupting influence of American comics. As well as quoting extensively from librarianship journals in the United Kingdom (and citing the common critiques of the comics' pornographic and violent content), the essay contained a brief reflection on the situation in Poland. While describing the predicament of librarians in Britain as fairly "exotic" since "there was no danger that such 'literature' would trickle into Poland," the author advised his readers to remain vigilant (Piasecki 225). After all, he maintained, "there are many ways in which the saboteur [*dywersant*] can spread the pest [*zaraza*]" (225). To add weight to his argument, he mentioned illegal libraries in the city of Kraków that circulated literature that was said to "cause stupidity" [*literatura ogłupiająca*] as well as being infused with pornographic and morally corrupting content (225). The librarian author finished the essay on an auspicious note, wishing luck to his British colleagues in their struggle against that "disgusting and poisonous instrument of the disappearing world of business, exploitation and crime" (226). He hoped that soon enough they would be able to attract more readers with good books. In other words, he wished them everything that was said to be "the pride and joy of librarians in the countries of the peace camp" (226).

Reports from countries such as Britain were sometimes interspersed with acerbic commentaries on the attempts of the American government to regulate the corrupting influence of comics (e.g., "'Comicsy' i wolność"). Those state-sanctioned efforts were valued much less than the struggles undertaken by specific individuals (such as Wertham) or interest groups in other Western states, including Britain, all of which were presented in a more sympathetic light. Aside from America's own crusade against comics, Polish journalists also followed closely, and eagerly reported on, novelties in the comics publishing market in the United States, but they did so in a way that was either disparaging or overly caustic. This included reports on educational comics about science subjects and on the graphic renditions of the Bible, neither of which appealed to the Polish commentators (see "Atomowe"; "Biblia"). At times, articles on comics were placed side by side with pieces on other capitalist products for children that were seen as equally detrimental to their development. This included the "Giant Atomic Bomb" toy, one of the curiosities of the Cold War toy industry, which was said to "explode" when hitting hard surfaces (see "Przeciw selekcji"; "Wesołe książeczki").

Despite themselves spreading anti-American content, socialist pundits were also ruthless in criticizing corresponding examples of anti-Soviet and anti-Communist propaganda appearing on the other side of the Atlantic Ocean. Thus, some denunciations of the comic book were also aimed at exposing specific enemies of socialism who were said to lurk in the shadows of the capitalist world. One such enemy was the staunchly anti-Communist Catholic Church in America. Senior figures of the church, such as Cardinal Francis Spellman, the archbishop of New York, were said to carry their own ideological work, using comics to disseminate anti-socialist content. Commenting on the American comic book *Is This Tomorrow? America under Communism* (1947)—a showpiece publication of Cold War propaganda, which provided a dystopian vision of America overtaken by Communism—one Polish journalist pledged that nothing will be able to stop "the natural course of history and progress," that is, the triumph of Communism. Not even Cardinal Francis Spellman, who was said to encourage and help disseminate those publications, would bring about the victory of imperialism ("Wesołe książeczki" 8).

There was every reason why Communists in Poland would view Cardinal Spellman as an inconvenient figure. His services in New York were attended by thousands of Catholics. His sermons were deeply political, warning against the rise of "atheistic communism" and calling for the support of "democracy and the American way of life" ("Spellman Warns" 12). Even if geographically distant, the "American Pope," as he was sometimes described, attracted a lot of international attention. In 1956, Spellman allegedly supported American Catholics of German descent in their irredentist aspirations that called for the recovery of the Oder-Neisse Territories, incorporated into Poland in 1945 (Allen 191). Although the cardinal refuted the allegations, he soon became the focus of a smear campaign in Poland that criticized his supposed involvement in the matter ("Situation Report"). Even though sources are fragmented in this regard, Spellman also made at least one appearance in the American-funded Radio Free Europe (RFE) in Munich and was scheduled to revisit RFE in 1961, an invitation that he eventually declined ("NYC-72 December").

There is no doubt that his staunch anti-Communist stance would be considered problematic by the Polish Communist state. After all, it was the only country in the Soviet bloc with a sizable Catholic community and vocal church authorities who would soon emerge as the nucleus of anti-state activity.

I have found no evidence that Spellman was behind the publication of *Is This Tomorrow?* but it is true that the book was published by a religious organization, the Catholic Catechetical Guild Educational Society of St. Paul, Minnesota, whose activities would most likely have been condoned, or even supported, by the hierarchs of the American Catholic Church. The person behind the guild, Father Louis A. Gales, was almost certainly the intended target of this newspaper attack (see Gabilliet, "C'était demain"). The publication was printed in 4 million copies, with a projected readership of 10 million (Clark). As the panel in figure 2.1 exemplifies, the comic presented affecting scenes of roundups, brutality, and concentration camps, all of which were meant to convey the seriousness of the Communist threat. In this particular scene, Communist guards are driving prisoners onto ships and vans to transport them to labor camps in Alaska, which has, by now, been taken over by the Soviets. The prisoners are warned that their elegant clothes will soon wear out due to the severity of the labor that awaits them. This chilling representation was not only meant to equate the Communist threat with Nazi crimes, the memory of which was still very much present in the US (due to American troops participating in the liberation of some of the notorious concentration camps), it also alluded to the widespread stories of the gulags and the inhospitable climate of Siberia and the Russian Far East, which hosted the penal colonies and which devoured many lives over the course of previous decades (figure 2.1).

Despite their ardent critique of *Is This Tomorrow?*, little did the Polish commentators know that alongside his steadfast anti-Communism, Spellman (and Father Gales initially too) also backed the anti-comics campaign, aimed at eradicating the most corrupting examples of the comics medium.[18] At the same time, it is possible that having realized the ability of comic books to capture young minds, Spellman would have been sympathetic to the numerous publications of the guild, which included saints' adventure stories and other illustrated classics, written and drawn in a Catholic spirit.

18. On Spellman's priests criticizing the damaging influence of comics, see "5,000 Youths." On the guild's protests against violent comics in the mid-1940s, see Hajdu 80.

**FIGURE 2.1.** Panel from *Is This Tomorrow? America under Communism* (1947)

Although the anti-Americanism of the Polish media discourse was often pervasive, including personal attacks on anti-Communist campaigners in the United States, cultural editors in Poland were not shy of praising those American initiatives that matched their own ideological agenda. One such initiative was an independent feature film *Mały Uciekinier* (original title *Little Fugitive*; 1953), shown on Polish screens in 1955, which touched upon the theme of comics. The film told a story of a young boy from Brooklyn, named Joey, who escaped home following a child's game during which he believed he had killed his brother. As it later turned out, his brother, inspired by comics stories, staged the incident to trick Joey into believing he was a murderer. According to the author of the review, the film focused on a generation brought up on violent comics and TV series, who could not distinguish good from evil (and reality from fiction) and whose childhoods were, effectively, perverted by those publications. In the mode of Wertham, the reviewer read the film as a tragic story of a young child whose inherent sensitivity and naivety becomes abused by the comics and television industry. He praised the filmmakers for their sympathetic take on the "social issues of their country and a good understanding of the child's environment and psychological make-up" (Grzelecki 4).[19]

---

19. Although other cultural products originating in the US were equally attuned to the social issues of the time, including many EC comics that were critical of racial, ethnic, and religious discrimination, I have found no evidence that Polish commentators of the early 1950s were aware of those publications. For a discussion of this subgenre of EC comics, see Whitted.

Like this film review, the majority of reports and essays discussed above were published in the early 1950s, peaking in 1954, the year that Wertham's *Seduction of the Innocent* first appeared in print. Presenting a negative image of the United States and discussing the corrupting influence of American popular culture on youth both in the United States and in those states that were subject to Marshall Aid (Britain in particular), those articles marked the true advent of the Cold War. Given the fact that American comics were virtually unavailable in Poland (barring a few illegal distribution channels), the public campaign against comics was not underpinned by real moral panic, as was the case with commentators in other states. There were no children to be protected or rescued from the throngs of a comics obsession; neither were there capitalist publishers to fight. And yet, just as in other European states, "the dynamics of nationalism and transnationalism in the comics debate," to use Ralf Kauranen's apt phrase, were also visible in the anti-comics campaign in Poland (220).[20] On the one hand, the references to the potentially damaging influence of comics were largely transnational and visible across the East/West divide. In Poland, they were an expression of a wider anti-American sentiment that the authorities wished to impart to their people for ideological, cultural, and economic reasons. On the other hand, there were some aspects of the anti-comics debate that were strictly regional, being tied to Poland's socialist internationalism. These particular aspects of the debate stemmed from the country's involvement in the movement for peace that the Soviet Union and its friendly regimes were said to safeguard.

## Comics and the Korean War

It is no coincidence that most of the anti-comics reports in Poland emerged in the early 1950s. This was tied to the specific context of rising Cold War tensions, including the Berlin Blockade, the show trials in both the Soviet bloc and the United States (the Slánský and Rosenbergs trials, respectively), and, importantly, the Korean War of 1950 to 1953. The latter context, in particular, featured heavily in the anti-comics campaign. The Korean War was omnipresent in the public

20. Using Finnish anti-comics campaign as a case study, Kauranen shows that the debate was "imported" into Finland from other countries and sustained through a variety of transnational links and inspirations. See Kauranen 220–22.

debate of early 1950s Poland. Following the North Korean People's Army's incursion into the Republic of Korea on June 25, 1950, in the absence of the Soviet delegate, the United Nations Security Council passed several resolutions that approved military intervention in support of the Republic of Korea and against the North Korean Army, which had been backed by the USSR and China.[21] The first American contingent arrived on the Korean peninsula in the beginning of July 1950. From the very start of the war, the Polish press presented the American intervention as a model example of imperialist aggression, following the official Soviet line. In the words of one scholar, North Korea, which had once been a remote and distant country, became overnight a close "companion in battle":

> Korea appeared in almost every speech of the Supporters of Peace Committees, in every article or lesson on the political situation in the world. Exhibitions, manifestations and rallies of support for the people of Korea were organized, as well as demonstrations protesting American aggression. Analytical articles, reportages and news pieces appeared in the press (in "Trybuna Ludu"—from June to December 1950—almost every day); a portrait of Kim Il-Sung hung in many factories. Poems and songs were written, money and clothes were collected for Koreans, resolutions condemning aggression were passed by all officially organized social groups—trade unions, scouts, the Association of Disabled War Veterans, and patriotic priests. (Leszczyński 48)

Despite the widespread anti-imperialist campaign in state media and grassroots support for the Korean people by socialist campaigners, the war also elicited a degree of pro-American sentiment on the part of some sections of Polish society. According to scholar Joanna Witkowska, there were Poles who wholeheartedly supported MacArthur, the commander-in-chief of the United Nations military forces, who also commanded the South Korean army. Many Poles were said to be prepared to go to Korea to join the American forces. Others expressed their support in more subtle ways, for example by taking off their hats as they walked past the American embassy in Warsaw or by wearing sunglasses (a reference to the critical portray-

---

21. Although the USSR denied involvement in the war, it did send medical and material aid to North Korean forces, as well as covertly deploying its pilots and providing planes and military equipment. See Zhang; Weathersby.

als of MacArthur in Polish newspaper cartoons), even in winter, as a sign of solidarity with the United States (J. Witkowska 127).

The authorities were, no doubt, aware that the official anti-American campaign did not efface the pro-American sentiment that had existed in Polish society long before the Communist takeover. But the Korean War was yet another event that was exploited to enforce the idea of the United States as a warmongering nation. In doing so, the authorities hoped to reiterate the notion of the war as a battle between the forces of good and evil, the people of North Korea and the American-led UN troops, respectively. Ultimately, this was meant to boost the image of the "peace-seeking" people's democracies who were said to refrain from military intervention.[22]

One of the most powerful critiques of the American comics, tied to the theme of Korean War, appeared in the marine monthly magazine *Morze* (*The Sea*) in December 1950. The article was written by *Morze*'s correspondent Jacek Welt, who traveled to New York City as a crew member on the MS *Batory* ocean liner. Of all the impressions of America, it was the books, magazines, and newspapers that left the most lasting impression on him. Repeating the common criticisms of comics, including the denunciation of their brutality and supposed "penchant for *Übermensch* mentality," Welt conflated his denunciation of the medium with a description of crimes committed by US-led troops on the civilian population of North Korea. He did not mince his words: "Using degenerate literature and film, the rulers of today's America produce witless conscripts for their army, bloodthirsty murderers of helpless civilians and destroyers of peaceful towns and villages" (10). Placing violent panels from comics next to war photographs from Korea, the author left no doubt as to the crux of his argument: "As I am writing these words, the radio broadcasts the most recent news from Korea. . . . I can see in all clarity the journey undertaken by America from a ten-cent 'superman' to a fascist 'super-criminal'" (11).

Welt's reportage from the United States was a good example of the type of article that a travel writing scholar, Rossitza Guentcheva, described as performing an "authenticating function" (376). As in Guentcheva's examples, which described other socialist travelers to the West, also here the credibility and persuasive power of the trav-

---

elogue hinged on empirical evidence. Welt saw the corrupting publications with his own eyes, the same way he saw the "hostile Atlantic Ocean" and New York's "murky courtyards" and "dirty and putrid squares" (10). In Guentcheva's words, the socialist traveler appeared "capable of uncovering truths about Western society that were invisible to others, even to the indigenous population" (377). Welt's truths were simple: Comics conditioned to violence and turned young men into war criminals. However, in pointing out the supposed faults of American "super-criminals," Welt made a clear distinction between the United States and the "people of Europe who have experienced the bloody ghost of fascism and who knew to bury it under the ruins of Reichstag" (11). To Welt, Europe was far more experienced in recognizing "fascism" and eliminating it from its societies.[23] In stark contrast, America was said to be still learning.

Like Welt, several other commentators made loose connections between comics and the new brand of "fascism" that was allegedly breeding in the United States. American comics were said to enforce a binary worldview whereby the "world of progress and socialism" was presented as a putative aggressor planning an imminent attack on America ("Polityczne wychowanie" 3). The opinion that comics conditioned readers to murder and war appeared in statements of the supporters of peace, too, who emphasized the warmongering mentality of Superman, who was said "to kill Russians" (Ehrenburg 2). Even though those references to the brutalization of American society through comics were fairly widespread at the onset of the Cold War, few journalists cared to elaborate. A Życie Warszawy (Warsaw's Life) correspondent in New York, John Stuart, was a notable exception. In an article published in August 1951, he described in detail how American children were taught civil defense drills in schools (e.g., the "duck and cover" method) and how the ubiquitous atmosphere of impending nuclear attack increased anxiety among schoolchildren. Stuart criticized the apparent militarization of the school environment, too, and described America as a "police state" of "Hitlerite" proportions ("Amerykanie" 3).[24] Most importantly, he linked his discussion to comics and war propaganda, arguing that children were

---

23. Even though Welt made no distinction between the socialist and nonsocialist states of Europe, the implied anti-fascist narrative was strongly reminiscent of the Soviet discourse of World War II.

24. The same article was reprinted in other regional newspapers. See, for example, Stuart, "Koszmar dzieci."

constantly bombarded with violent content that was aimed at inciting hatred. To illustrate his point, he described the cover of one such comic that was said to present an "American GI smashing the head of a North Korean soldier with a rifle butt" ("Amerykanie" 3). In a similar vein, the content of the comic was said to vilify North Koreans as well as making the young reader familiar with the sight of various weapons being used to hurt and murder civilian populations.

The Korean War comic books described by Stuart were a new genre of comics that emerged in the United States in the early 1950s. In the three years of the conflict, more than 100 comics based on the war were published (Wright 114). In the words of one scholar:

> Korean War comic books operated under various pressures and constraints. The basic rule governing popular culture representations of war has been that it encourage, or at least not discourage, military recruitment and retention. By describing military service as an adventurous rite of passage to masculine adulthood, comic books supported the messages preferred by military recruiters. (Rifas 630)

The ability of such comics to increase the appeal of conscription could not, of course, be underestimated.[25] According to Bradford Wright, although some of the titles presented the conflict in a rather ambivalent manner, many still gave "the impression that the Korean War was lots of fun," obscuring the darker side of the conflict (114). Nonetheless, it is difficult to disagree with Stuart's criticism of those publications. For example, scholar Melissa Hilbish argues that some of the Korean War comics presented "the insanity of war on both sides, and the effect it can have in driving men over the edge of reason to become, not soldiers, but killers" (222). In a similar vein, using the case study of Mexico, where such publications were available in translation, historian Anne Rubenstein explains why the Korean War comics caused so much controversy there. They were seen by some as instigating war and fomenting hate toward Communist nations and, as such, going against the values adopted by the government of Mexico (119, 193).

Both the situation in Korea and the anti-comics campaign were also closely followed by the Women's League in Poland. The league

---

25. According to Mia Sostaric, such practices were also present in World War II. For example, publications such as *Captain America* were meant to sell "the war to its readers through engaging readers' sense of patriotism and enthusiasm to contribute to the war." See Sostaric 29.

was part of the wider socialist-Communist network of women's organizations, such as the Women's International Democratic Federation (WIDF), with which it shared the same values, pledging to strive for world peace, democracy, and women's rights. It also vowed to protect family values and children, in particular their right to education, growth, and a war-free existence (Dajnowicz 412). Polish women took part in international events aimed at advancing these shared goals. One such event was the International Conference in Defence of Children, held in Vienna, on April 12–16, 1952. The conference, which was co-sponsored by the WIDF, brought together 600 delegates from various countries. Writing on the eve of the conference, the leader of the Polish Women's League, Alicja Musiałowa, explained that the main purpose of the convention was to discuss the ways of providing, to all children, "access to schooling, medical care, . . . progress, culture and appropriate upbringing" (2). In line with the statements by other socialist women activists of her time, Musiałowa criticized the increased spending on armaments in the United States, which was said to happen at the expense of education. She bemoaned the corrupting influence of television, films, and comics that supposedly glorified violence and poisoned "the soul of the young American generation" (2). In her article, Musiałowa also included a powerful antiwar message, speaking of the terrifying conditions faced by (North) Korean children, who were said to be "the most tragic victims of American imperialists" (2).[26]

One could argue that Musiałowa's text was a classic example of Soviet-style anti-Americanism, all the more typical since it was accompanied by a largely romanticized vision of socialist children who were said to live in peace and happiness. And yet, one of the core themes discussed during the Vienna conference in 1952 was indeed those cultural influences that affected the development of children across the world. It was not surprising, then, that similar opinions about comics and world peace (including in connection to the Korean War) were voiced by women from other countries.[27] Italy was one interesting example. Here it was both leftist and Catholic women who joined forces to develop a legislation that would limit

26. It is worth noting that this was a common motif appearing in Musiałowa's statements, also those that were addressed exclusively to the fellow league members. See B. Nowak 125–26.

27. Delegates from other states joined in their criticism of those developments too. For a discussion of the Finnish participation in the Vienna conference, see Kauranen 224–25.

the corrupting influence of American popular culture, comics, and film in particular (Pojmann 426). Italian women were also part of a WIDF-led commission that traveled to Korea in May 1951 to investigate crimes committed by UN troops on local women and children. They concluded unanimously that "the people of Korea are subjected by American occupants to a merciless and methodical campaign of extermination which is in contradiction not only with the principles of humanity, but also with the rules of warfare as laid down, for instance, in the Hague and the Geneva Conventions" (Pojmann 423).

As seen from those examples, different forms of women's engagement, be it the struggle over the right to education or anti-war activism, could take place under the umbrella of the WIDF. Although leftist and socialist, and thus largely anti-American, the organization provided a platform through which women could voice their concerns about topical issues of the time. Having experienced one destructive war (many of them in active combat or underground resistance roles), women activists saw themselves as particularly skilled at recognizing and opposing mass political violence.

What is striking in many of the commentaries discussed in this section, both those voiced by the politically engaged defenders of peace and the rank-and-file cultural editors, is their bias: Like many other forms of criticism directed at the United States during the Korean War, those articles reveal telling omissions. None of them mentioned, for example, that it was the Communist Korean aggression that started the war. In a similar vein, the actions of the South Korean army were virtually absent from the litany of crimes attributed to the American troops. In that sense, "America" appeared in those reports as a convenient synecdoche with which to describe all perpetrators of war crimes committed in Korea, particularly those executed on helpless civilian populations.[28] This is not to say that those commentators were entirely mistaken in their criticism. Rather, their tendency to overemphasize certain events and actions and deemphasize others painted a largely skewed and imbalanced picture of this first, serious, armed conflict of the Cold War. The suspicion of ulterior motives rarely left the associated debates on the American economic, military, and cultural influence.

---

28. Similar representational strategies were also used in the Polish Film Chronicle, one of the major tools of socialist propaganda. See Rabiński 181–82.

Poland and other Soviet bloc states were not alone in doing so. Some of the Western European states, too, insisted on replicating common misconceptions concerning American involvement in the Korean War, for reasons that were specific to their respective national contexts. Rubin and Rubin argue, for example, that "it was an article of faith to many French intellectuals . . . that South Korea had been encouraged by the United States to attack North Korea in 1950 rather than the other way around" (134).

That misrepresentation and exaggeration were part of the ideological package was clear to many of those commentators. A story told by a Chilean writer, Ariel Dorfman, is representative of that. As Chile underwent its own belated socialist revolution in the early 1970s, Chilean intellectuals too engaged in similar critiques of the US, taking on American popular culture more generally. In 1971, Dorfman and his fellow Marxist scholar from Santiago Armand Mattelart launched an intellectual attack on Disney comics in their book *How to Read Donald Duck*. Providing an informed discussion of Disney works, the two men attempted to shed light on how "capitalist and imperialist values [of a country] are supported by its culture" (Kunzle, "Introduction" 2). Discussing the book more than twenty years later, Dorfman admitted to having "exaggerated the villainy of the United States and the nobleness of Chile" as well as not being "entirely true to the complexity of cultural interchange, the fact that not all mass-media products absorbed from abroad are negative and not everything we produce at home is inspiring" ("Introduction" xi). Dorfman's is one of the very few candid commentaries on the pitfalls of socialist readings of American popular culture and America more generally. In its unembarrassed sincerity, his admission of ideological bias goes to the heart of the Cold War mindset and discourse described above.

## Comics and the American Way of Life

Many of the discussions surrounding comics in Poland came down to how the Polish Communist government wished to define culture and consumption. Eastern Europe's traditional attachment to highbrow culture, and the attempt to convince the socialist citizen that such culture did not exist in the United States, governed much of the official anti-comics debate in Poland. This was reminiscent of Wertham, whose work on comics was, in Bart Beaty's words, "rife with negative comparisons to the type of culture that he personally preferred as a reader and art collector" (*Fredric Wertham* 202). In the Polish case, the criticizing of American mass culture was a skillful balancing act that involved both elusion and exaggeration in an attempt to persuade the socialist citizen that the "American way of life" posed serious dangers to one's morality and intellect.[29] Literature was meant to edify, but only in ways that were regime-friendly, in line with Stalin's famous dictum that writers were the "engineers of the soul." The socialist anti-comics campaign was thus also a struggle against consumer culture and against the possibility that the socialist citizen might wish to be part of that culture in the same way his or her counterparts on the other side of the Iron Curtain were. In the words of two historians, the American-style consumerism that the authorities feared was "driven and mobilized by marketing and corporate strategies" and aimed at stimulating "ever more unquenchable desires" (Bren and Neuburger 5). In contrast, the command economy afforded no space to the consumerist dream since it was bound to expose the deficiencies of the system in place.

The exhibition *Oto Ameryka* (*This Is America*), which opened on December 15, 1952, in Warsaw's Arsenal, was underpinned by those very same ideas. It sought to ridicule American consumer culture and expose "the true face" of American democracy. In the words of Poland's foreign minister, Zygmunt Modzelewski, who inaugurated the exhibition, *Oto Ameryka* was meant to tell the "truth" about the United States, without trying to glamorize or conceal anything (*bez żadnego upiększania, bez żadnej maski*) (cited in Romek 174). According to Modzelewski, the exhibition was nonetheless a story of "two Americas": the America of the warmongers and the America of the oppressed masses (African Americans, Native Americans, the working class, and others), who strove for peace (Romek 174). When the exhibition opened two years later in Kraków, "the two Americas" still comprised "bloodthirsty imperialists" and those who participated in

---

29. That American highbrow culture, literature in particular, was part of the reconstruction of Europe, for example in the form of the Salzburg Seminars (also described as the "Marshall Plan of the mind"), was conveniently omitted. For a discussion of the role played by Americanists (and American literature and culture more specifically) in the intellectual reconstruction of Europe, see, for example, Blaustein 122–71.

the shared struggle for progress and peace (see, e.g., Cybulski 4). The idea of "two Americas," or "the two faces of America," was fairly widespread in the socialist discourse of the time, both in Poland and elsewhere. It was often employed as a convenient metaphor with which to emphasize the social and economic divide between the "capitalist" and the "proletarian" America.[30] It also emphasized the apparent belligerence of the United States and, conversely, the peace-seeking credentials of the socialist world and their supporters.[31] The binary of peace-loving and warmongering nations was to be expected, not only given the wider international context (the Korean War in particular), but also that *Oto Ameryka* was organized by the Polish Committee of the Defenders of Peace, a state-sponsored organization that opposed Western militarism and participation in war ("Oto Ameryka" in *Życie*).

The exhibition was largely biased and one-sided. It overemphasized the ills of American society and the flaws of its political system, without mentioning any of their positive qualities. It presented heartrending images of poverty, homelessness, and civil rights violations (including crimes committed on African Americans by the Ku Klux Klan). The creators of *Oto Ameryka* also accused the American government of bowing to Wall Street bankers and cultivating ruthless capitalism. Further, they denounced the "imperialist aggression" in Korea, screening a documentary film that showed vicious crimes committed by MacArthur-led troops on civilian populations. More importantly, the exhibition compared America's military prowess and intervention in Korea to the actions of Nazi Germany in the occupied territories during World War II. The latter, in particular, was meant to resonate with the Polish population, traumatized by the years of Nazi occupation (Romek 176).

One part of the exhibition was devoted to the American way of life and culture. This is how one socialist commentator described what he saw there:

---

30. The concept structured other representations of America too, including in travel writing. See Guentcheva 365–68.

31. Often the same phrases and comparisons would be used. Parts of Modzelewski's speech mirror, almost verbatim, statements by other socialist peace campaigners. See, for example, a speech by North Korean socialist politician Pak Den-ai, delivered during the Congress of Defenders of Peace in Warsaw in 1950 in which she, too, spoke of the "two Americas." See "Rozszerza się front pokoju."

What kind of culture did American imperialism develop and impose on its society? In painting—anti-humanist formalism; in science—a return to Malthusianism with proposals of methodically destroying "surplus" population; in education—*comics which hamper learning, detective literature . . . with flashy covers spreading pornography,* in everyday life—children's toys in packaging that encourages crime and murder (a small atomic bomb, rubber stick, and a gendarme's hat). (Cybulski 4; my emphasis)

Although the condemnation of comics made only one point in a long line of accusations toward American political, economic, social, and cultural life, it was meant to contribute to a bigger picture of a decadent capitalist country that was on the brink of moral, educational, and intellectual collapse. The creators' intention was to make their audiences realize that Polish reality provided much better conditions for growth, happiness, and a wholesome existence.[32] Seeing the glitzy, brightly colored American publications was meant to make visitors recognize that the locally available "volumes of Balzac, Prus and Tolstoy, modestly bound in brown cardboard jackets," were much better than the "'masterpieces' of American literature whose covers were dripping with blood and poison" ("Oto Ameryka" in *Trybuna*).[33]

Those points were reinforced through the imagery used in the exhibition. Aside from displaying the supposedly scandalizing covers of American publications, one photograph presented a young boy engrossed in reading a "corrupting" comic book. This particular image was subsequently included in the Polish Film Chronicle newsreel released in Polish cinemas on January 14, 1953. The still was accompanied by an alarmist commentary that warned against the "savagery, sadism and pornography" of the works, which sold "the seven deadly sins for [merely] a dollar." As the photo of the young reader of comics appeared on the screen, the commentator summarized the purported goal of these productions: "to bring up future gangsters" so that they can be used in Korea and in Europe. The Pol-

32. This kind of binary rhetoric, which was introduced in an attempt to provide an "all-encompassing" portrayal of the shortcomings of American culture, also appeared in newspaper articles. For a discussion in which comic books are only one aspect of a wider denunciation of the United States and in which Poland is presented as the binary opposition, see Świątecka.

33. The article was written by a journalist who saw the exhibition in Stalinogród (the official name of Katowice between March 9, 1953, and December 20, 1956).

ish pacifists could not be clearer in their interpretation of American comics.

The organizers hoped to spread the message far and wide. The exhibition traveled to many cities across Poland, and in each of them, it attracted crowds. In Warsaw, 320,000 visitors (20 percent of which were organized excursions) were recorded only two months after the exhibition's opening ("320 tys. zwiedzających"). In Kraków, approximately 100,000 people, many of them schoolchildren and workers, visited the exhibition in the first six weeks since its inauguration ("Wystawę 'Oto Ameryka' zwiedziło"). In the northern town of Sopot, *Oto Ameryka* was said to attract hundreds of visitors every day ("Oto Ameryka" in *Dziennik*). It is true that many of them came with trips organized by factories and schools, but, on the whole, the interest was genuine. According to one historian, it was not the anti-American content that attracted the crowds; rather it was the desire to get a taste of "the forbidden fruit" (Romek 177). In the words of an author from Warsaw, "People wanted to see something American—to look, if only for a moment at something made across the Ocean. . . . This was an unhappy love, a totally unrequited love" (Crowley 105). Many coveted the American goods they were supposed to revile and longed to participate in the American dream. Artist Andrzej Dudziński, who saw the exhibition as a nine-year-old in his hometown Sopot, remembered how he and his friends would spend days devising plans to "nick" the chewing gum and Coca-Cola that they saw displayed in a glass cabinet at the exhibition (Papuzińska 51).

The fascination with the exhibits, collected by the creators of *Oto Ameryka,* did not escape the attention of the CIA, who made the following, somewhat triumphant, observation: "The faces of the visitors did not reflect the disgust intended to be evoked by the exhibitions depicting American brutality, lawlessness, dire straits of the unemployed, rule by Wall Street, et cetera. They appeared not to be impressed by the evils portrayed, but rather by the excellent possibilities that life offered in America" (Central Intelligence Agency Archive, "Poland" 10). Polish visitors were said to marvel at what they saw at the exhibition, including the "clever little camera" and the "excellent cloth in that parachute," as well as admiring how "they certainly produce the best" in the United States ("Poland" 10).

In many respects, those positive reactions to the exhibition marked a victory of the American dream over socialist utopia. This is not at all surprising. By the time *Oto Ameryka* opened, many Polish citizens had already developed interest in the United States and the West more generally. They secretly listened to Radio Free Europe, the BBC, and the Voice of America, bought secondhand Western clothes, and listened to Elvis Presley, Ella Fitzgerald, and Louis Armstrong (J. Witkowska 128). More importantly, they felt the desire to partake in the consumerist dream that was taken away from them with the Soviet rejection of the Marshall Plan. In Katherine Verdery's words, "in socialism desire floated free in endless search of goods people saw as their right" (25–26). Although the consumerist dream did not necessarily go hand in hand with political resistance, or even dislike for the socialist government, as Verdery seems to suggests, the consumerist desire certainly did make America look appealing.

Socialist propagandists understood those sentiments better than anyone else and made sure to publicly berate those states and societies who were believed to have chosen to pursue the consumerist dream at the expense of their own freedom. One damning report from Turkey, which described bookshops overflowing with American comic books and crime stories—as well as youngsters who "incessantly chewed gum" and wore gaudy, ostentatious clothes—made it clear what was the price for buying into the American dream. Turks were said to pay for the American comics and chewing gum in soldiers, sent to fight in distant Korea. In the words of that particular commentator, those men knew very little about why they were making that sacrifice (Lipiński, "Polak"). This chilling report from Turkey was meant to serve as a warning against the lure of consumer culture, of which comics were a part. American consumerism came at a price, the article warned, and that price was combat and a potential loss of life.

## Beyond 1956: Concluding Remarks

The American anti-comics campaign began dying out with the introduction of the Comics Code in 1954. The same happened in other countries across the world, as country-specific censorship committees and anti-comics legislations were imposed to control the influx of the supposedly corrupting popular culture (see, e.g., Lent, "The Comics" 30–31). There was a certain "global interconnectedness" to these processes as campaigners, policy makers, and commentators looked across borders to gauge progress made in other states (Lent, "The

Comics" 29). Despite having no actual comics to fight, the ebbs and flows of the anti-American and anti-comics debate in socialist Poland reflected developments in these other states too. Journalists, authors, and cultural editors were in a privileged position of being able to look over the Iron Curtain and report on those developments that supported the official ideological line. As we have seen, the United States and Britain provided ample evidence with which to wage an information war against the West. Few commentators looked for positive counterexamples in the Soviet Union and other bloc states. Demonizing portrayals of the West seemed to have sold better than the prim and proper representations of the USSR and its socialist allies.

The anti-comics campaign overlapped with the heyday of both Stalinism and McCarthyism, and as those declined from mid-1950s onward, so did the resolve to attack comics. The political "thaw" of 1956 eased restrictions on the influx of American goods too. After 1956 the policy of economic aid and "peaceful engagement" was instituted and the Polish government was now allowed to acquire American goods with zloty. Now that the financial obstacle was lifted, and no hard currency was required to partake in American culture, the authorities in Poland purchased films, newspapers, periodicals, books, and translation and stage-production rights. More American authors, such as William Faulkner, Ernest Hemingway, and Norman Mailer, appeared in Polish translation. Even though some of these restrictions were reinstated throughout the 1960s, the government made the first step toward redeeming American culture and easing the anti-American discourse (Delaney and Antoszek 75–76).

Of course, some cultural editors in Poland continued to disapprove of the medium well beyond 1956. Some made passing references to the term "comics," using it as a byword for cultural products that they saw as naive and unsophisticated.[34] Others, such as the Catholic intellectuals around the monthly *Znak* (*The Sign*), picked up the anti-comics debate where the Communists had left it, with several articles mentioning comics as the culprit that perverted reading habits in the United States and West Germany (Garnysz 810; Rogalska 726; Skwarnicki 525). However, these responses were few and far between and not as vehement as before. Some of them, such as the

---

34. For a review of a Warsaw production of *Kiss Me, Kate* from 1957 in which the play is described as a "musical and theatrical comic," see Grodzicki. For a passing remark by a scholar of print media who defines comics as "newspaper films" (*filmy gazetowe*), see Kobylański 45.

*Znak* articles, published toward the end of the 1950s, seemed belated and irrelevant. The tide was turning and the politics of "peaceful engagement" was paying off. Newspapermen were now allowed to admit that there was more to the American publishing market than crime and horror comics.[35] By the mid-1960s, the alien-sounding word "comics," which the media insisted on using throughout the 1950s, would be assimilated into the Polish language. *Komiks,* as it now came to be known, was being slowly reabsorbed into the national fold.

Just as the 1950s was a decade in which the authorities and the media grappled with the (anti)-American dream, the years to come, the 1970s in particular, would be the European decade.

---

35. See, for example, an article that puts into question Poland's isolation prior to 1957. The author cites the numbers of books published every year in other states, including the Western states, and challenges the common idea that the majority of what is produced in the West is comics. See Kaider.

CHAPTER 3

# "POLISH EUROPEANS"

The Opening of the 1970s

The death of Stalin in 1953 and the ensuing political thaw of 1956 had an immense impact on the publishing market in Poland. The authorities gradually abandoned the overt propaganda of the early 1950s. State publishing enterprises moved toward new formats that were meant to appeal to the reader, combining didactic content and attractive design. The regime rehabilitated comics, too, viewing the medium as a useful tool of ideological indoctrination that could be used to spread regime-friendly content. Early examples could be found already in the late 1950s. On October 22, 1957, the youth weekly *Świat Młodych* (*The Youth's World*) published an illustrated story, *Romek i A'Tomek* (*Romek and A'Tomek*), to celebrate the launch of Sputnik 1 by the USSR (see Chmielewski, "Nasycony").[1] Despite its didactic undertone, the series, later renamed as *Tytus, Romek i A'Tomek* (*Tytus, Romek and A'Tomek*), was a great success with young

---

1. The launch of the Sputnik 1 satellite initiated a wider interest in space exploration and science fiction among socialist comics publishers. For a discussion of the East German *Weltraum-Serie* (1958–1962), see Eedy, "Co-Opting."

readers. It ran for more than three decades, becoming one of the best-loved comics in Poland (Misiora 244–47).

Although foreign comic book series were still largely unknown to Polish audiences, local spin-offs were becoming increasingly popular. For example, artist Jerzy Wróblewski drew comic book Westerns already in the late 1950s. These stories were published in daily press and periodical magazines and built on the American tradition of the Western, including stories such as *Lone Ranger* (see Paryz). Also work from abroad was occasionally available in state-controlled youth magazines, which reprinted excerpts from French comic book series as unlicensed translations; this included Morris's highly popular *bande dessinée Lucky Luke,* which appeared in *Na Przełaj* (*Across Country*) from 1962 through 1968 (Rusek, *Leksykon* 26). According to historians Reinhold Reitberger and Wolfgang Fuchs, in the 1960s, selected American strips imported by Bulls Press were making advance into the Soviet bloc states, including Czechoslovakia (182). While I have found no evidence that this was also the case for Poland, it is likely that some of the American reprints appearing in Polish magazines were indeed syndicated by Bulls Press. Foreign comics could also be obtained using illegal channels. During that period, *Tarzan* albums in English, Swedish, and German were said to be available on the black market, having been supposedly produced in Poland for export. Some albums never made it out of the country and, similar to the comic series that were smuggled into Poland, were sold illegally (see Tochman).

This situation was to change in the 1970s, a period some scholars have described as the "golden age" of Polish comics (Rusek, "Od szalonego Grzesia" 90). In this chapter, I demonstrate how the political and cultural liberalization of the 1970s affected comics production in Poland. I discuss the growing visibility of the medium and the attempts to "catch up" with the rest of the world after more than two decades of dismissing comics as naive and unworthy of attention. While discussing the first comics magazine, *Relax,* that emerged during that period, as well as several homegrown comic book series, I examine how cultural editors, readers, and comics creators defined the medium vis-à-vis the liberalizing economy and culture of the 1970s. In doing so, I also pose tentative questions about the ways in which the above-mentioned actors used the medium to define Poland's relationship with the wider world in general, and Europe in particular.

## The Cultural Opening of the 1970s

In the 1970s, under the leadership of Edward Gierek, Poland saw a brief period of cultural, political, and economic liberalization, as well as witnessing a considerable opening to the West.[2] From early on, the first secretary was said to have "struck an acceptable relationship with the intellectuals, students, and middle class" (Central Intelligence Agency Archive, "Gierek's Poland" 6). Artists were given more liberty "to work as they pleased," provided they could fit into the institutionalized system of culture and refrain from voicing political criticism or challenging so-called fraternal alliances (P. Piotrowski 11). The stagnated cultural climate of the 1960s was temporarily lifted (Ligarski 64). The government made attempts to bolster links with Western European states, too, as seen during Gierek's visit to France, which culminated in the signing of a ten-year "friendship and cooperation" agreement (see "Polsko-francuska"; Lewis). The strengthening of those bilateral ties, which focused predominantly on trade, also invigorated the Polish art scene.

Already in the 1960s, cultural editors, more so than other members of society, were able to keep abreast of developments in France, Belgium, and the United States. There was a concerted attempt at breaking the silence around comics too. Cultural magazines published articles that discussed both the global origins of the medium and the more recent developments, genres, and titles, as well as striving to offer an instructive historical examination of the cross-pollinations of word and image (see, e.g., Banach; Łysiak, "Anatomia"). Some commentators were willing to recognize both the need for domestic comics production and the growing importance of the medium worldwide (Łukasiewicz, "Batman"; Lubelski). At the same time, despite the lessening of the overt anti-American rhetoric, comics were still seen as a foreign product that was largely irrelevant to Polish cultural reality. They were presented as either a curiosity typical for faraway cultures, including Communist China, or a niche product unsuitable for an educated reader (Isaak; "Dla dzieci i niepiśmiennych"; Kossak).

---

2. Gierek was known to have a penchant for French culture in particular. He spent more than twenty years in the West, first as a child and young man in France, and subsequently working as a miner in Belgium for more than ten years. Several other politicians around Gierek had ties with France too. See Bromke 13.

Given the scarcity of the local production, the majority of magazine and newspaper articles from that period were bound to focus on the comic book abroad.[3] Some magazine contributors commented reluctantly on the commercial successes of foreign series in the West, including the best-selling *Tintin* and *Asterix* series ("Comicsy, pasja"). Those who were granted the privilege of foreign travel admitted to bringing supplies of comics albums home, while marveling at their supposed ability to "train the imagination, wit and intellect of the masses" (Ziemilski 5).[4] Already then, the state exercised a degree of permissiveness toward such practices, as long as the consumption of those publications did not lead to challenging the political system in place. Comics series from France or Belgium were specifically tolerated and seen as valuable examples of pop culture. It was precisely those early encounters with foreign works in the 1960s that laid the groundwork for the "golden era" of comics in the 1970s.

Throughout much of the 1970s, daily papers and periodical magazines were able to showcase snippets of Western culture, including comic book culture, and discuss other cultural developments that, particularly in the late 1940s and throughout the 1950s, would have been considered imperialist in nature and, as such, detrimental to socialist morals (Rusek, "Krótka historia" 35). This was the case with one of Poland's best-selling weeklies, *Przekrój* (*Cross-Section*), which carved out an unusual position in the state-controlled media landscape. Priding itself in being "a window onto the world" (*okno na świat*), *Przekrój* educated the society on foreign travel, fashion, music, and literature (K. Wrona 222). Its reporters were given more opportunity to travel abroad. They attended international events, including the International Congress of Comics in Lucca, and wrote home to their readers about new French, American, and Italian comic book publications they saw there (Skarżyński, "O Międzynarodowym"; Lovell). It was during such events that Western and Eastern European illustrators and animation artists were able to come together

---

3. One notable exception is a short press note on a new Polish newspaper comic, *Kawalerią na okręty* by Władysław Dybczyński, published by *Tygodnik Polski* in 1969. See "Morski komiks."

4. The quote comes from an article by columnist, writer, and sociologist Andrzej Ziemilski, who recalled a trip to a scholarly conference in Switzerland where, through his hosts, he came into contact with comic books and magazines, such as *Tintin, Spirou,* and others. His generous hosts gave him a farewell gift of thirty different titles, which he eagerly accepted and brought back to Poland with him.

and share their work, too. In one report from what he described as an Italian "comics paradise," illustrator Jerzy Skarżyński marveled at the growing sophistication of the medium, as exemplified by the rich offerings of publishers showcasing their products in Lucca. He reported on discussion panels and film screenings during which animations from Poland, the USSR, Switzerland, Britain, the United States, and Japan were presented side by side (Skarżyński, "Z komiksowego"). Even though such encounters with Western culture were available to the selected few, popular magazines brought it closer to the mass reader. This included occasional reprints of excerpts from famous works and interviews with internationally renowned artists as well as translations of articles by Italian, French, and Austrian scholars (see Goscinny; Goscinny and Sempé; Leydi; Schmölzer). Increasingly, articles by local authors, too, discussed new trends from abroad, including the emerging underground comix scene in the US (Łysiak, "Przejrzyj"). Reports on film adaptations of foreign comic books, such as the animated feature films based on *Astérix*, were also discussed in mainstream press (see, e.g., "Astérix").

In the 1970s, comic art flourished under state tutelage, which, in an attempt to attract the young reader, combined Western visual influences with familiar content. Some of the Polish characters bore striking resemblance to their French, and even American, predecessors. *Kajko i Kokosz* (*Kajko and Kokosz*), the creation of Janusz Christa, was the most conspicuous example. First published in 1972 in a local newspaper in Gdańsk, the series gained nationwide popularity later on in the 1970s.[5] It was set in the early Middle Ages, but the manner, habits, and daily lives of the two characters alluded to the realities of socialist Poland (Malinowski; Rusek, *Leksykon* 108). Both the historical setting and the format of the series echoed the French *Asterix*. At the visual level, the small and slender Kajko and the hefty Kokosz were a spitting image of Asterix and Obelix, respectively, a comparison that the artist often denied (Marciniak, "Koniec świata przygody" 32).

Following a transferral of the series to the highly popular *Świat Młodych*, Christa's *komiks* became one of the best-loved and longest-running comics stories of the 1970s and 1980s. Christa was not an exception—such borrowings were not exclusive to the 1970s, nor

5. The series emerged from an earlier serial called *Kajtek i Koko* (*Kajtek and Koko*) on which Christa had worked since 1958. For a letter to a national magazine in which a local fan of Janusz Christa's stories asks for more national exposure for the *Kajtek i Koko* series, see Kałucki. For a response from the artist, see Christa, "Kajtek."

were they only typical of Poland. As José Alaniz shows, even in the anti-Western climate of the 1960s USSR, Soviet comic characters, such as Ivan Semenov's Petia Ryzhik, would still bear resemblance to their counterparts from across the Iron Curtain, including Hergé's *Tintin* (*Komiks* 65). Despite the fairly regimented character of popular culture under socialism, Polish illustrators continued to flirt with Western comic art also in the 1980s, as shown by the case of a Lucky Luke look-alike, the Polish cowboy named Binio Bill (Rusek, *Leksykon* 26; Paryz).

While Kajko and Kokosz provided a clear example of visual appropriation that was fairly literal, other borrowings went further, also attempting a reinterpretation of foreign comic art. *Inżynier Nowak* (*Engineer Nowak*; 1974–1976), drawn by Andrzej Mleczko for *Przekrój*, was a Kraków-based counterpart of Superman. Mleczko endowed him with superhuman physical and intellectual abilities as well as high levels of compassion and civic responsibility. Although short-lived and less known than *Kajko i Kokosz* (also because of its more serious themes that were less appealing to the young reader), Mleczko's series toyed with Western and Polish graphic narrative traditions in a truly postmodern manner. In one of the episodes, Nowak was presented side by side with the Polish Robin Hood, Janosik (as drawn in a 1973 comic story by Mleczko's *Przekrój* colleague Jerzy Skarżyński) as well as a variety of foreign characters, such as Superman, Simon Templar of *The Saint,* and Zorro. Several panels showed Nowak serving cheesecake to Superman and the others and enquiring about the weather in their respective locations. Dressed in their usual attires, including the iconic Superman suit, the characters were also shown indulging in Polish delicacies, such as vodka and sausage. Mleczko's explicit references to these American and British characters were both a spoof on famous graphic narratives and their improbable plots, and a witty commentary on the possibilities of the medium, including its ability to permeate the Iron Curtain (Rusek, *Leksykon* 93–94). More importantly, the series was a candid reflection on the eclectic nature of comic art in Poland, which built on the Western mass culture, while attempting to appeal to the cultural sensibilities of domestic audiences (figure 3.1).

By the mid-1970s, there was a consensus among critics that comics could no longer be ignored: They were said to be an important means of contemporary cultural communication; they appealed to the young and taught them how to tell stories and appreciate culture (see, e.g.,

**FIGURE 3.1.** Superheroes visit Inżynier Nowak, *Przekrój* 51 (1974)

Gębski). While admitting that domestic production was falling behind developments in France, Belgium, and other countries, commentators reflected wistfully on the lost time and opportunities that needed to be recuperated. As put enigmatically by one editor, "toward the end of the 1940s our country struggled with other issues," and comics, as a medium that did not respond to the concerns of the time, "simply died out" (Łukasiewicz, "Porucznik" 6). Some contemporary enthusiasts of the medium blamed the publishers of the time for continuing to remain dismissive about comics. According to one journalist, publishers were embarrassed to publish graphic narratives; "one talks about comics with a sheepish smile," the journalist maintained (Zientek 8). Others attempted to restore the link between the "now" of the 1970s and the successful comics magazines of the interbellum, marveling at the richness of the past offerings and praising interwar titles such as *Karuzela, Świat Przygód,* and *Gazetka Miki* (see Honsza;

Dunin; Łukasiewicz, "Batman" 32). These commentators proposed that to make the Polish comic book scene thrive, more valuable products needed to be imported and the knowledge about recent European and global developments expanded. More importantly, the existing "parochialism" (*zaściankowość*) of the Polish comic book had to be tackled (Dunin 17; Żółkiewski 6). Despite their dissatisfaction with the status quo, these commentators were also clear about what models they would rather not see repeated in Poland. This included American and Italian comics with supposedly fascist content, as well as work that incited war and racial hatred (Łysiak, "Monarchia komiksu" and "Monarchia komiksu II"; Pilot).

## *Kapitan Żbik*: Poland's First Super-Detective

The highly popular comic series *Kapitan Żbik* (*Captain Żbik*) was no doubt underpinned by the considerations above. Żbik was Poland's first full-fledged superhero. The serial was an attempt to catch up with the West and to develop Poland's own model of comic book. First appearing in 1968, *Kapitan Żbik* had an enormous impact on the perception of *komiks* in Poland (see Birek). Published by the highly successful Sport i Turystyka, the largest publisher of sports literature in socialist Poland, it was infused with regime-friendly content and fulfilled the kind of didactic function that the authorities wished to impart to the comic book. According to one journalist, who wrote about the series in 1973 at the height of its popularity, Żbik albums revealed that—if supplied with relevant content—comics could play an important educational role ("10 tys.").

Telling a story of a brave and handsome militia (*milicja*) officer, the series was undoubtedly aimed at educating the youth and, even more so, at boosting the social capital of the Polish police. The story was thought out by experienced police officers. According to Żbik's creator, law graduate and militia officer lieutenant colonel Władysław Krupka, who wrote thirty-six out of fifty-three scripts, the series had supposedly nothing to do with politics, as some of the latter-day commentators presumed. Rather, in Krupka's words, its main aim was to show the "difficult and interesting work" of Polish police officers (Tochman 12).

The appeal was undoubtedly there. Żbik was not a rank-and-file militiaman, neither was he a part of the special militia forces employed in riot control, both of whom were unpopular with the people. He was a detective, a Polish James Bond, who worked on criminal cases, many of which involved international crime networks. No wonder why one of the series' main illustrators, Grzegorz Rosiński, rejected the "propagandist" interpretation of the series, widespread in post-1989 Poland. To his mind, Żbik was simply chasing villains (Rosiński, "Impresjonista"). The captain was unequivocally good, too. Like Bond, he was handsome and popular with the ladies (Wojtczuk). Krupka wanted his character to be, above all, an excellent detective, one who uses his intellect and deductive skills to solve criminal cases, as opposed to employing physical force. This was meant to distinguish Żbik from what Krupka saw as the main characteristics of the protagonists of comic series in the West (Krupka).

As one comic book publisher recalled, at a time when *komiks* was still foreign, like "Coca-Cola, horror, chewing gum and jeans," Żbik was "ours," speaking to Polish sensibilities and reflecting the realities of the time (Tochman 12). The series was said to satiate the hunger for comic art as well as mobilizing the youth who organized their own "Żbik teams" (known as *drużyny żbikowe*) that were aimed at implementing the values promoted by the series (see "10 tys."; Pawlas). More importantly, the series became home to some of Poland's most talented illustrators, including Grzegorz Rosiński, Jerzy Wróblewski, and Bogusław Polch, all of whom found an influential patron in the state.

Aside from fighting crime, Żbik was there to teach about safety, instill civic responsibility and good manners, and answer questions about his profession. Some of the early albums contained illustrated one-page columns that came before the regular Żbik episode. Most of these columns focused on safety regulations. For example, albums 5 and 7 featured stories on road and fire safety, respectively (Rosiński and Bryczkowski, "Jak chodzić?"; Wiśniewski and Doński, "Przestrzeganie"). Episode 8 contained a story dissuading readers from ice-skating and sleighing close to busy roads or on rivers where unstable ice could form (Rosiński and Szczepański, "Pamiętaj!"). In yet another album, the authors cautioned the youth to stay away from unexploded ordnance and report any sightings of such material at the closest militia station (Sobala et al., "Niewypały").

With time, those rather stilted and prescriptive panels on safety came to be replaced with letters to readers. Krupka recalls receiving numerous letters to which he initially responded on behalf of the fictional Jan Żbik. As the series progressed and gained more popularity, the amount of mail increased too. People confided in Żbik and asked his advice. Starstruck women wrote to him, asking him out. Even Krupka's secretaries found it difficult to keep up with the volume of letters. The popularity of the series was so great that the circulation figures quickly rose to 200,000 copies per album, with some of the installments going to second print (Krupka 53). Krupka understood that high circulation figures provided him with a rare opportunity to reach a considerable number of readers and push through important educational content. The letters were to provide a platform on which such content could be showcased (53–54).

In his letters, the captain recalled his daily life and the stories shared with him by colleagues. The letters were meant to serve the youngest members of the public. They were aimed at protecting them from danger, correcting behaviors that could be seen as antisocial, and encouraging them to perform random acts of kindness. The first letter in a series recalled, using first-person narrative, Żbik's motivations to become a police officer. He told his readers an "authentic" story from his childhood. The story described Żbik's encounter with a former SS officer looking for lost wartime documents in a forest near his village, in the formerly German region of Silesia. Encountering the SS man during a stroll in the woods, the young Żbik found himself in grave danger. He was rescued by a local policeman who had been following the criminal. It was as a result of that formative experience that the young Jan had decided to join, one day, the police force (Rosiński and Krupka, Letter in *Kapitan Żbik* 10). The letter made a skillful use of the anti-fascist narrative that marked the immediate post–World War II period, the purported time of Żbik's adolescence, as well as eulogizing the important role of local police in enforcing the law and protecting the most vulnerable members of society (and, possibly, reinstating order in the formerly German territories, which were rife with crime in the early postwar years). To many readers, this supposedly autobiographical story was also an implicit admission that Żbik was, indeed, a real person.

Other letters, too, made a good use of the first-person voice. One group of letters revolved around public disorder and antisocial behavior. For example, in episode 11, the protagonist recalled a scene he was said to have witnessed on public transport where an elderly woman was not given a seat by a group of youths. He used this experience to remind young people to show more respect for the elderly (Rosiński and Krupka, Letter in *Kapitan Żbik* 11). Elsewhere, he recalled an attack perpetrated by a group of youths on two young women in which he personally intervened. He asked his readers to be equally responsive, and depending on their strength and abilities, to defend those who might be in need (Polch and Krupka, Letter in *Kapitan Żbik* 17). Żbik also encouraged his readers to look after common spaces, such as public lawns that were being perennially destroyed by antisocial individuals, and fight against collective vices, such as alcohol abuse. The latter letter was particularly alarming, discussing the social impact of alcohol abuse and asking young readers to get involved in anti-alcohol campaigns (Wróblewski and Krupka, Letter in *Kapitan Żbik* 50 and Letter in *Kapitan Żbik* 52). Another group of letters contained safety advice, similar to the one-page stories that appeared in the early episodes of the series. In one letter, Żbik warned his readers against stray and forest animals that might carry rabies, and asked young people to remain alert (Rosiński and Krupka, Letter in *Kapitan Żbik* 13). Elsewhere, as the summer was approaching, he reminded them of water safety regulations (Polch and Krupka, Letter in *Kapitan Żbik* 23). In yet another album, he tried to dissuade the readers from playing with weapons by recalling a "real-life" situation he witnessed in which a teenage boy was hurt (Wróblewski and Krupka, Letter in *Kapitan Żbik* 30).

Aside from educating his readers on socially acceptable behaviors and safety rules, Krupka also responded to their queries on behalf of the fictional Żbik. In their letters, readers asked Żbik about his profession, including entry criteria to police academy. "Żbik" entertained those requests willingly, repeatedly emphasizing how demanding the job was (Polch and Krupka, Letter in *Kapitan Żbik* 32; Wróblewski, Gabiński, and Bednarczyk, Letter in *Kapitan Żbik* 41). Elsewhere, he discussed the specificities of the profession, including technical equipment used by the police to analyze and document crimes (Rosiński, Kłodzińska, and Tomaszewski, Letter in *Kapitan Żbik* 16). Above all, he shared his achievements with readers, most notably the long-awaited promotion to the rank of major in 1978, ten years into the series (Wróblewski and Krupka, Letter in *Kapitan Żbik* 47). The latter was accompanied by congratulations from the publisher as well as a portrait of a smiling Żbik in uniform with updated rank insignia on his shoulder: two stripes and a star (figure 3.2).

Readers responded to the series with enthusiasm. This was not only due to the personal tone of the letters but also owing to the

*Z okazji nominacji kapitana Jana Żbika do stopnia majora, kierownictwo oraz zespół redakcyjny Wydawnictwa „Sport i Turystyka" składają Mu serdeczne gratulacje i życzenia dalszych sukcesów w pracy zawodowej oraz pomyślności w życiu osobistym.*

DRODZY PRZYJACIELE!

Jak zdążyliście się już zorientować z zamieszczonych powyżej gratulacji Wydawnictwa „Sport i Turystyka", za które serdecznie dziękuję, zostałem mianowany do stopnia majora.

Wręczenie nominacji miało – tak jak zawsze u nas przy takich okazjach – uroczysty charakter. Były życzenia i gratulacje od przełożonych, koleżanek i kolegów.

Gdy przy kawie w gronie współpracowników snuliśmy refleksje o wspólnie przepracowanych latach, o wspólnie prowadzonych akcjach i sprawach, mój przełożony zapytał mnie: „a co słychać u Waszych młodych przyjaciół, towarzyszu majorze? Czy nadal będziecie z nimi korespondować i popularyzować na łamach „Kolorowych zeszytów" naszą trudną i odpowiedzialną służbę?"

Pytając mnie o to pułkownik wiedział i tak, co mu odpowiem. Nie musiałem go nawet przekonywać, że ponad dziesięcioletnia więź z Wami, Drodzy Przyjaciele, tysiące Waszych listów, w których okazujecie mnie i moim kolegom – funkcjonariuszom MO – tyle sympatii, zobowiązuje do dalszej z Wami współpracy.

Moi Drodzy, piszecie w swoich listach m.in. o nowopowstałych w wielu szkołach drużynach Młodzieżowej Służby Ruchu, o akcjach społecznych prowadzonych w szkołach i drużynach harcerskich. Tego rodzaju listy czytam z wielką uwagą i przyznam, że sprawiają mi zawsze ogromną radość. Pragnę, abyście od najmłodszych lat czuli się potrzebni innym, bowiem praca społeczna daje wiele satysfakcji i uczy życia w kolektywie.

Otrzymałem też niedawno list od Waszego kolegi z Andrychowa. Opisał on w bardzo serdecznych słowach sylwetkę dzielnicowego – opiekuna szkolnej drużyny Młodzieżowej Służby Ruchu, który zawsze służy radą i pomocą młodzieży. Ten list ucieszył mnie bardzo.

Moi Drodzy! W przyszłym roku obchodzona będzie XXXV Rocznica powołania organów Milicji Obywatelskiej. Wiem, że wiele szkół w Polsce nosi imię funkcjonariuszy MO poległych w walce o Polskę Ludową. Wiem, że młodzież szkolna opiekuje się ich grobami oraz miejscami, w których znajdują się pomniki lub tablice pamiątkowe. Proszę Was: zbierajcie materiały o tych wydarzeniach i piszcie o tym do mnie.

Chciałbym serdecznie podziękować Małgosi N. z Sufczyna k/Dębna, która na kilka miesięcy przed moją nominacją, napisała do mnie: „Życzę Panu serdecznie, aby zmienił Pan cztery gwiazdki na jedną gwiazdkę i dwie belki – myślę, że to się spełni niedługo". Takich i podobnej treści listów otrzymałem od Was wiele. Dziękuję za nie Wam wszystkim.

Serdecznie Was pozdrawiam
mjr JAN ŻBIK

P.S. Zamieszczone powyżej zdjęcie dedykuję wszystkim swoim Przyjaciołom.

**FIGURE 3.2.** Żbik's letter to readers in which he announces his promotion, *Kapitan Żbik 47. Granatowa cortina* (Sport i Turystyka, 1978)

attractiveness of the plot itself, which contained a good mix of both the foreign and the familiar. Distant locations, such as the Bulgarian resort of Golden Sands, the Romanian capital of Bucharest, and the GDR metropolis of East Berlin, were intertwined with Polish villages, towns, and cities, including the most remote ones, such as Wólka Mała in the east of the country (see Rosiński and Krupka, *Kapitan Żbik 11*; Sobala and Krupka, *Kapitan Żbik 20*). Locations on the other side of the Iron Curtain were mentioned too, but mostly as the breeding ground for crime (such as robbery and money laundering) that, from time to time, spilled over into Poland (see Wróblewski and Milc, *Kapitan Żbik* 22). The specific episodes thus provided an insight into a variety of offenses, from smuggling diamonds, espionage, and illegal trading in currency, to more "everyday" forms of lawbreaking, such as stealing and violence committed by *gitowcy*, members of a youth subculture widespread in 1970s Poland (Rusek, *Leksykon* 121).[6] According to one scholar, the social commentary provided by the episode on *gitowcy*, in particular, was rather unusual in comparison to the usual content of the series. This would suggest that the Polish militia saw the subculture as fairly dangerous, at least as far as its impact on the safety of young people was concerned (Marciniak, "Śmierć"). Press articles from the period confirm this interpretation. Initially, the subculture was seen as typical for the capital city. With time, alarming reports of crimes committed outside of Warsaw began to appear too, many of which involved acts of thuggery, committed on secondary school pupils (see, e.g., Teneta).

There is no doubt that Żbik could be an appealing character. In the words of Polish comics historian Adam Rusek, the captain

> led a lonely life in a small, modestly furnished apartment. He had a weakness for elegant clothes: initially he wore a uniform, later on— impeccably-cut suits. For fieldwork in the countryside, he put on the turtleneck, fashionable at the time. At home he wore a stylish dressing gown. Although single and childless himself, Żbik liked to meet young people: he was active in a model building group, he visited schools, [and] scouting camps. . . . This was precisely Żbik's main task: to educate the youth and to encourage them to work with the militia. (*Leksykon* 122)

Interviewed several decades after the series was first published, its creator, Krupka, expressed regret over making Żbik into such a one-dimensional character (Krupka 55). After all, Żbik had no vices. He did not curse, drink, or smoke. He was equally as concerned for the young and the elderly as he was for the environment and wild animals (some of the cases he worked on focused on poaching). More

---

6. For an episode on *gitowcy*, who steal from and attack students in one of Warsaw's schools, see Wróblewski, Falkowska, and Seidler, *Kapitan Żbik 39*.

importantly, he had no wife, girlfriend, or children, which made his female readers all the more receptive to his charm (Tochman).

However, not everyone was seduced by the series. Even more so, not everyone fell for Żbik's "Polishness" and his supposed anchoring in the local context. One disgruntled journalist found the series so infused with foreign content that he used it as a scapegoat to make a wider stand against the medium as a whole. He described the series as trying to pander to "Polish Europeans" who were said to experience an inferiority complex stemming from an insufficient supply of comic art in the country. The author went on to lament over the plot of many of the episodes, which were supposedly far from educational. To make things worse, he argued, the setting of some of the episodes could not be more alien to Polish readers, featuring luxurious villas, lavish dinner parties (where foreign liquors were in abundance), and hard currency (dollars) (see "Dziwne tropy").

The criticism that journalists and state actors alike directed at the series was not limited to the content. Bogusław Polch, one of Żbik's illustrators, recalls how he was often berated for making his character look excessively well-groomed (and therefore foreign-looking): "I drew him as a handsome man in a suit. He wore a polka dot tie and had big sideburns. The critics decided he was too 'queer' (pedalski), as they described it" (Wolski 16). Polch was also reprimanded for once equipping his protagonist with an American Colt as opposed to a Soviet TT (Wolski).

Looking at the various iterations of the character, one has to agree: Żbik was not an ordinary Pole. He was drawn consistently as an attractive man who, irrespective of the illustrator, exuded an air of elegance and desirability. His ebony black hair, impeccable haircut, and slick sideburns made him stand out, while simple accessories, such as dark sunglasses, added glamour to the all-too-familiar militia uniform. The cover in figure 3.3 is illustrative of that. Not only does it portray the suave Żbik on his way to Jaworzyna, where he is about to get acquainted with a new case, but it is also representative of the "glamorous" police work that he did. The caption on top describes the details of a high-profile robbery in a suburban villa in Silesia, involving stolen dollars and other valuables. Needless to say, the commentators above were not wrong: Such realities would have been alien to most socialist readers.

According to comics scholar Tomasz Żaglewski, many of those criticisms alluded to what remained largely unsaid: that *Kapitan*

**FIGURE 3.3.** Żbik at work, *Kapitan Żbik 24: Wąż z rubinowym oczkiem* II (Sport i Turystyka, 1972)

*Żbik* might have echoed the American superheroes and replicated some of the storylines appearing in superhero narratives (115–16). This is also the view of Mateusz Szlachtycz, a Żbik fan and author of a book on the brave captain: Although lacking superpowers, Żbik was immersed in the world of technological progress, which was unknown to the majority of Poles, using modern computing devices and night-vision goggles and taking impromptu flights in a helicopter (128). While I am not convinced that Żbik should be interpreted as a specifically Polish superhero iteration, it is true that his persona could be linked to Western-style narratives, detective novels in particular. In fact, some of the scripts were based on existing crime novels and short stories, which—although set in the context of socialist Poland—were largely derivative of their foreign counterparts. In addition, two of the regular scriptwriters for the series, Anna Kłodzińska and Ryszard Doński, were crime story writers (see Rusek, *Leksykon* 121).

According to Mikołaj Kunicki, such nods to Western narratives, including the early James Bond films, could be found in Polish television series too, for instance in the popular production *Stawka większa niż życie* (*Playing for High Stakes*; 1967–1968) (47). What is more, by the end of the 1960s, Polish audiences would also have been familiar with the genre of mystery spy drama, including the British production *The Saint*, which was broadcast on Polish television from 1969 onward (45). There is no doubt that Żbik's impeccable clothing and brilliantine-styled hair echoed the cinematic renditions of James Bond and Simon Templar, notably those by Sean Connery and Roger Moore. Thus, the commentators who criticized the series for not being Polish enough certainly had a point. And yet, according to one of the scriptwriters, Zbigniew Bryczkowski, who defended those borrowings, Western models could also be utilized in a productive manner. In particular, they could be used to instill positive values in society, such as respect for the law. This fit in with Krupka's original intentions and the wider political agenda of the Polish state (Szlachtycz 129).

Little did those pundits know that the creators' wish to engender socially responsible citizens, and even whole fan communities, harked back to earlier models that had also been present in the American context. According to scholars Christopher Conway and Antoinette Sol, already toward the end of the 1940s the heroes of popular comic book Westerns (including Roy Rogers and Hopalong Cassidy) spurred their own "ideologically charged fan clubs" that "called for cleanliness, neatness, obedience to parents, courage, safety, Christian values, and patriotism" (8). It was precisely those values and standards that allowed the publisher Dell Comics to evade censorship after the Comics Code was introduced. That later Roy Rogers and other stories introduced anti-Communist plots and reinforced Cold War stereotypes only added to their legitimacy (Conway and Sol).

In the case of *Kapitan Żbik,* it was not only that whiff of something distinctly un-Polish that attracted criticism. Many commentators disliked the series on strictly aesthetic grounds and for reasons that were unrelated to official state ideology. For example, some commented on its crude drawing style. A poet and an important figure of anti-Communist opposition, Stanisław Barańczak, ridiculed the characters' disproportionately long and narrow faces and "equine jaws" (*końskie szczęki*) ("Kapitan" 41). Journalist Anna Borkowska thought the color palette was devised by a "crazed color-blind person" (*oszalały daltonista*), while the dialogues were wooden to the point of sounding farcical (28). Similarly, Maciej Łukasiewicz bewailed *Żbik*'s schematic plots, which were said to push the youth into "intellectual idleness" ("Porucznik" 10).

Only on the surface were those debates solely about *Kapitan Żbik* and its merits. Rather, due to its immense popularity with readers, the series was used to reignite the time-honored discussion on the value and utility of comics. As we have seen above, the two main topics that featured in this discussion were the struggle between domestic and foreign cultural models and, more importantly, the social profitability of comic art. Many of the negative portrayals of the series were firmly rooted in a conservative view of culture that assumed comics were an inherently foreign transplant that could not put down roots in Poland. "Polak nie pasuje do komiksów" (Poles and comics do not go together), one prominent film critic would say in 1985 (Kałużynski, "Polak"). This was a view that many among the cultural elites, irrespective of their political leanings, held much earlier and promoted among the wider public. Both influential cultural editors and anti-Communist intellectuals of the 1970s had often distinctly conservative tastes. Their traditionalist attitudes toward Western culture, and popular culture in particular, were not limited to comic art. Other cultural imports were affected, too, most notably rock and roll. Using the example of music journalism, Michael Rowland shows that those who criticized the popular influences of the late 1960s and early 1970s had little knowledge of and training in how to read these new cultural products.[7] The same could be said about comic book criticism. Many of those who were commissioned to write about the medium in the 1970s (and, arguably, in other periods too) worked with film, literature, art, and television. As such,

---

7. Looking at two *Przekrój* journalists, Lucjan Kydryński and Marek Garztecki, Rowland shows the generational difference between the two and the different styles of reporting on rock and roll that stemmed from their divergent training and musical tastes, Kydryński writing regularly about jazz, classical music, and cabaret, and Garztecki being involved in the pop-rock culture from the start. See Rowland 16–17.

they had little interest in *komiks* and were often ill-disposed toward the medium, presenting it as derivative and inferior to other forms of artistic expression.

That is not to say that *Kapitan Żbik* was a masterpiece. It was not. But the series was well received by those for whom it was intended— young people—as the above-cited circulation figures prove. The series also turned out to be a true generational experience for many growing up in the 1970s and 1980s, as nostalgic accounts, written by former Żbik fans in adulthood, show (see Szlachtycz; Tochman). Others, unmoved by the dapper militiaman and the colorful locations to which the series took them, had to be won over with arguments about the utilitarian value of the series.

## *Relax*: Poland's First Comics Magazine

All of the developments above, in particular the growing popularity of the *Kapitan Żbik* series, laid foundations for the establishment of Poland's first comic magazine, *Relax,* in 1976. Two years earlier, in 1974, the National Publishing Agency (Krajowa Agencja Wydawnicza, KAW) was created as part of the Workers' Publishing Cooperative "Press-Book-Movement" (Robotnicza Spółdzielnia Wydawnicza "Prasa—Książka—Ruch," RSW). RSW was a state enterprise, controlled by the Polish United Workers' Party (Polska Zjednoczona Partia Robotnicza, PZPR), and KAW was one of its offshoots, specializing in art, tourism, postcards, vinyl records, and other high-demand and high-profit products. It was KAW that was to become the publisher of *Relax*. These changes in state publishing stemmed from wider administrative reforms, undertaken by the Gierek government, that increased the number of voivodeships, which, in turn, limited the influence of local party committees and led to a greater centralization. Despite the increased control by the PZPR, the reforms brought about a greater aligning of the publishing market with the economic goals of the state. Underperforming periodicals were liquidated and replaced with outlets that offered a promise of greater revenue (Pokorna-Ignatowicz 45–46). As a result, in the 1970s, state publishing in Poland grew to be the largest of all in East-Central Europe, constituting the main source of income for the party (Pokorna-Ignatowicz 7).

Comics historian Adam Rusek argued that it was most likely financial considerations that provided incentive for the foundation of *Relax*. In the newly established KAW, geared toward generating high income, a special department of periodical publications was created, which included a section of illustrated magazines. It was in that section that, from 1974, plans were made to create Poland's first comics magazine (Rusek, "Magazyn" 77).

The first issue of *Relax* was published in July 1976. Grzegorz Rosiński, one of the illustrators for *Kapitan Żbik,* and later on of the Franco-Belgian fantasy series *Thorgal,* became the artistic director of the magazine. Journalist Henryk Kurta was nominated its editor-in-chief. It was Rosiński's ambition to make *Relax* into a main outlet for artists from all over Eastern Europe. More importantly, he wanted to create a magazine worthy of the Francophone *Pilote* and *Spirou.* This was not to be realized. Aside from occasional comics by Czech Kája Saudek (who was admittedly known for his "Western" style of drawing) and the Hungarian duo Tibor Horváth and Imre Sebök, as well as one-off appearances by others, such as the Belgian Charles Degotte and the Yugoslav Velizar Dinić, the magazine was not able to attract foreign artists, mostly for financial reasons. Till the end, it remained a publication that showcased mostly Polish illustrators.

The editors set a high bar for the magazine, branding it as a publication that was meant to appeal to adults, young adults, and children. As such, *Relax* had an uneasy task of bridging the interests of different age groups ("Listy," *Relax,* vol. 4). The readers were demanding, to say the least. Letters sent to the magazine suggest that *Relax* audiences, both young and old, engaged in an ongoing conversation with the editors, commented on their choices, evaluated the quality of specific pieces, and made requests. The editors responded both to enthusiastic and critical letters, and jokingly commented that it was difficult to please everyone ("Listy," *Relax,* vol. 3). The letters shed light on the readers' expectations and tastes, too. While the majority responded well to the new stories devised by *Relax*'s collaborating artists, some wanted to see new episodes of familiar series, including the foreign ones. A letter from a reader in Warsaw is representative of that. Writing in response to the very first issue, he contended candidly:

> I liked the first issue of *Relax* even though it was not perfect. I think that the illustrated story *Maślok Śmierdzirobótka* was chaotically drawn,

even though the content was not the worst. The rest of the issue was to my liking.

I suggest that a series about Red Indians [Native Americans] is printed. One about their dress, traditions and tragic history. I also think that excerpts of comics such as *Lucky Luke*, *Asterix* and *Kajko and Kokosz* should appear [in the magazine]. There should be graphic stories about space and the history of its exploration. (Smolak 2)

The letter pointed to the eclectic tastes of *Relax* readers, which, in this case, combined Polish and foreign (mostly French) titles as well as various genres, from the comic book Western to science fiction. There is no doubt that the editors would have liked to indulge their audiences. They assured their readers they were doing their best but also stressed that accommodating everyone's wishes was not always possible (Smolak). They were genuine in offering their apologies, but most readers remained in the dark about the financial, political, and artistic considerations behind those editorial decisions.

There were several reasons why foreign comic art did not appear on the pages of *Relax*. First of all, the licensing costs were too high and *Relax* could not afford it. Second, the limited page count and deepening shortages of paper meant that the new issues were quickly filled with comic art that had been commissioned already by the magazine. This included homegrown stories that quickly became *Relax*'s priority. Third, the magazine was often forced to juggle between the wish to satisfy their readers, their own ambitions to promote new illustrators, and the demands of the party, which insisted on including regime-friendly content (Rusek, "Magazyn" 82–86).

Requests for French and American comic art became so common that the editors actively tried to dissuade their readers from hankering after foreign content. Following yet another letter in which Batman, Superman, and Tarzan stories, as well as *komiksy* about Native Americans, were requested, the magazine reasoned with their readers in the following way: "If you think about it more deeply, you'll conclude that new and [hitherto] unknown stories are more interesting" ("Listy," *Relax*, vol. 7). This reasoning was understandable, and it was not only the financial and political considerations, mentioned above, that were at play here. *Relax* had a good base of homegrown illustrators, most notably Grzegorz Rosiński, Janusz Christa, and Jerzy Wróblewski, and it was, no doubt, the editors' ambition to strengthen the local comic art scene and build a strong following around established

Polish artists (see, e.g., Chęcińska). *Relax* also sought out and promoted new talents. This aim was, to a large extent, achieved. Almost every active comic book illustrator passed through the magazine at one point or another (Gmyz).

And yet, the readers could not be blamed for voicing those wishes. After all, in the introduction to the second issue, editor-in-chief Henryk Kurta provided an interesting overview of American, French, and Belgian comic book series as well as discussing film adaptations based on those stories. Kurta listed many iconic characters populating foreign series that made it to the big screen, including Mickey Mouse, Tarzan, Asterix, Superman, Batman, Tintin, and Barbarella (Kurta). He was unaware, perhaps, that even a brief mention of those series might whet the appetite of his readers and send a signal that those stories, too, were yet to appear in *Relax*. This was, obviously, not the case.

Kurta made no secret of his preference for Western European comic art. His assessment of Superman and Batman as "causing stupidity" (*ogłupiający*) was particularly damning. While praising the technical side of the American superhero films, most likely the live-action TV versions (*Superman*, 1952–1958, and *Batman*, 1966–1968), Kurta contended that "in westerns or Superman adventures the 'good cause' prevails not because it is good but because its proponents shoot better and faster, and have bigger fists. This is symbolic for the wider international politics of the north American state" (Kurta 2). It is not clear to what extent this was Kurta's personal opinion or the view of the censors, but it is likely that he was in earnest about his criticism of the artistic value of those stories. After all, the perceived view of American pop culture as shallow and excessively commodified was not exclusive to the early years of the Cold War. As we will see, in Poland, such views persisted throughout decades and were still present in the 1990s when ideological concerns were no longer at stake.[8] Neither, as the previous chapter showed, were they typical for the Soviet bloc, being widespread in France, Britain, and other countries. Irrespective of the artistic merits of American superhero narratives, the article echoed the ongoing attempts by socialist states to decouple Western Europe from the United States. In this particu-

---

8. For example, in 1990 journalist Elżbieta Chęcińska wrote: "Europe is defending itself from Americanization. Quite rightly. The excess of Walt Disney can be nauseating. Can we be successful in defending ourselves? I doubt it." See Chęcińska.

lar case, Kurta's mindset was aligned thus with the goals of political elites, even if these parallels were most likely accidental.

At the same time, there is no doubt that Kurta was a true Francophile. Like Gierek, he was born in France, and like many other Eastern European intellectuals, he saw French culture as the apotheosis of intellectual freedom and sophistication. Throughout his text, Kurta was explicit about those sympathies. His assessment of Francophone comic art (in particular *Asterix, Lucky Luke,* and *Tintin*) as subtler and wittier than its American counterpart was illustrative of that. More importantly, while praising the universality of the *Asterix* series, Kurta expressed hope that also the Polish reader would, one day, be able to get acquainted with "this wonderful satire about the weaknesses (and strengths) of the nations that make the [European] continent *of which we also are a part*" (2; my emphasis). He ended his article on a rather pessimistic note: "This [the publication of the series in Poland] is still far in the future" (2). Kurta's prediction turned out to be accurate. The first album of *Asterix* was to be published in Polish only twenty-five years later, in 1992, three years after the disintegration of the Eastern Bloc.

The passage above shows once more how *komiks,* as art that was imported from elsewhere, enabled Polish intellectuals to define their relationship with the wider world. In Kurta's discussion, the "true" Europe and its culture were close, albeit unattainable. Europe, and its culture, was where Polish people organically belonged. This sense of belonging and organic attachment to Europe could not, however, be fully realized. A similar sentiment was shared by many other intellectuals at the time. According to editor, writer, and former member of anti-Communist opposition Adam Michnik, for intellectuals in pre-1989 Poland (and elsewhere in East-Central Europe too), "Europe was the West, to which we naturally belonged, even if we were forcibly exiled from it by Soviet dictate. Europe was a light on the western horizon, a hope that our country, too, might one day become free" (128). This romanticized view of Western Europe as the symbol of freedoms, for which East-Central Europeans longed, also featured in Milan Kundera's famous essay "The Tragedy of Central Europe." According to Kundera, "Europe" was a goal in its own right, powerful enough to begin revolutions.[9]

---

9. Nonetheless, for both Michnik and Kundera, the Europe they had desired was imperfect, too. The "real" Europe took the privilege of Europeanness for granted. In Kundera's own words, little did those behind the Iron Curtain realize

Over the years, opinions on *Relax* have been divided. Some of them, particularly those from the 1970s, when the magazine was still running, are tinged with the traditional dislike of the *komiks*. One such response came from Bohdan Czeszko, a writer, veteran of the Warsaw Uprising, recipient of the Order of Builders of People's Poland, and member of PZPR. In his 1978 article for a literary magazine, *Nowe Książki* (*New Books*), Czeszko provided a pointed commentary on *Relax*:

> The issues that I have flipped through contain comics on various topics. There is a story about the defense of Warsaw in 1939, [one] about the mission of Richard Sorge, [another] about the White Fang (based on London), and finally a serial story about two brave proto-Poles called Kajko and Kokosz, who are accompanied by a very willful mini-dragon Miluś. The latter is clearly a knockoff of the well-known French comics about Gall Asterix. . . . There is a maundering space travel series about cosmonauts who can get to any planet using their spiritual powers. There they experience adventures that have obviously nothing to do with the science fiction of [Stanisław] Lem, whose work I can't stop praising, even though I don't have to do it. There are also didactic stories for the young about how you are not supposed to boat on the lakes of Masuria in a hollow trough. . . . There is also a story about how to deal with inferiority complex. (43)

Czeszko's acerbic commentary on *Relax* was an accurate analysis of the uneven quality of the magazine. In particular, it spoke to the (often confounding) heterogeneity of its offerings, which was supposed to accommodate the different age groups. At the same time, Czeszko made no secret of his own skepticism toward comics, more generally, and of his rather conservative literary taste. This was despite his involvement as a scriptwriter in the popular TV series *Podziemny front* (*The Underground Front*; 1965), which told the story of Polish leftist fighters during World War II, and which was made into a well-read comic book series in the period 1969 to 1972. Czeszko's perspective on *Relax* was, then, a perspective of an accomplished scriptwriter. This was also how he saw *komiks*—as a derivative genre

---

that "in Europe itself Europe was no longer experienced as a value" (38). The subtle, witty, and sophisticated culture, for which many in Eastern Europe longed, "no longer existed as a realm in which supreme values were enacted" (36).

of film and television, in which the script was of primary importance. Not surprisingly, in Czeszko's assessment, many of the stories published in *Relax* were based on naive and sterile scripts that were supposedly devoid of wit and constituted "an absurd babble" (43–44). This was perhaps the reason why Czeszko suspected that many of *Relax*'s stories were castoffs that never made it to the big screen.

Reading Czeszko's commentary more than forty years later, one cannot help but respond with an oft-cited statement by author and critic Douglas Wolk:

> Comics are not prose. Comics are not movies. They are not a text-driven medium with added pictures; they are not the visual equivalent of prose narrative or a static version of a film. They are their own thing: a medium with its own devices, its own innovators, its own clichés, its own genres and traps and liberties. (14)

Despite revealing a clear misunderstanding of the medium, assessments like the one by Czeszko were still, most likely, a blow to the editors. These were all the more damning coming from an author aligned with the PZPR, for whom *Relax* was supposed to generate revenue. The lack of good scripts was indeed a constant worry, to the extent that well-known illustrators, such as the Czech Kája Saudek, had to be turned down because the editors were unable to provide them with suitable scripts (Rusek, "Magazyn" 82). The criticisms voiced by Czeszko were, thus, not unknown to the editors. What made matters worse was that similar opinions were expressed by those on the other side of the political divide, although for completely different reasons.

In 1978, a *drugi obieg* (samizdat/underground) journal, *Zapis* (*Record*), published an essay by Stanisław Barańczak in which he provided a highly critical assessment of the magazine. Like many other literary essays written by Barańczak during that period, this one was also an attack on state-sponsored publications, many of which prioritized ideological concerns over artistic quality. Barańczak mocked *Relax* in its entirety, from its illustrations, to its scripts, to its onomatopoeias. He attacked individual artists, too, in particular Christa and Rosiński, repeating the well-known accusations of plagiarism, directed at Christa's *Kajko i Kokosz* series, and criticizing the latter artist for improbable scripts and crude drawings. More importantly, he belabored propagandistic stories about national history, which were administered by the state, and which stood for *Relax*'s connections with the authorities (Barańczak, "Blurp!").

Many of the points raised by Barańczak contributed to the popular opinion of Polish *komiks* as tainted by associations with the party. This reputation followed *Relax* well into the late 1980s and early 1990s. One columnist described the magazine as a "primitive and unsuccessful" exploration of the comic art (Śpiewak 23). Another claimed it was the only noteworthy publication of the time, before adding that its quality, nonetheless, deteriorated due to the influx of substandard and prescriptive stories that were enforced from above (Zdrzynicki). According to comics scholar Jerzy Szyłak, the quality of the magazine was indeed uneven, ranging from first-rate drawings by artists such as Grzegorz Rosiński to poorly illustrated propagandistic pieces. Still, he credits *Relax* with being critical to the development of a Polish *komiks* community and fandom (Szyłak, *Komiks: świat przerysowany* 137).

Circulation figures attest to that: The magazine began with a circulation of 100,000 copies; one year later, the number rose to 300,000 copies (Rusek, "Magazyn" 80). At the height of the magazine's popularity in 1978, when the essays by Czeszko and Barańczak were published, 400,000 copies of the magazine were printed (Czeszko 42). Even the otherwise unsympathetic Barańczak admitted that *Relax* was "omnipresent in the city" — on trams, in trains, and in doctors' waiting rooms ("Blurp!" 95). More importantly, *Relax* was read not only in Poland but also in other states in the region, including Czechoslovakia and the USSR.[10]

Despite its popularity with readers, *Relax* was discontinued in the early 1980s. The deepening economic crisis of the second half of the 1970s resulted in budget cuts, during which culture was badly hit. The associated paper shortages meant that the magazine was published irregularly, particularly toward the end of the 1970s and in the early 1980s (see "Komiks po polsku"). Some claim that this was the reason why *Relax* did not survive beyond 1981, when only two issues of the magazine were published (in comparison to ten issues in 1977), but other factors have been mentioned, too, including the necessity

---

10. Although the magazine was not officially distributed outside of Poland, readers from other countries were able to obtain copies of *Relax* during trips to the country or using other informal channels. Sometimes readers from the Soviet Union and other satellite states would write letters to the editors asking if they could be sent missing copies of the magazine. See "Listy, listy. Poszukuję Relaxu."

to make compromises with party bureaucrats who were said to exert increasing influence on the content and artistic vision of the magazine (Rusek, "Magazyn" 81–82, 85–86).

As the discussion above suggests, *Relax* enabled artists and audiences to probe the limits of the supposed liberalization of the state-sponsored publishing market of the 1970s. Readers' requests for American, French, and Belgian art not only put the supposed cultural openness to question but also exposed financial considerations that made *Relax*'s offerings lag behind its Western European counterparts. The magazine provided, thus, an implicit commentary on state influence over culture while furnishing a story of economic underperformance under socialism. The people behind *Relax*, too, were an interesting mix of individuals. Some, like the artistic director Rosiński (who was Poland's most popular illustrator of the 1970s), succeeded in practicing their professions both within the state-mandated system of culture and beyond. Aside from undertaking commissioned work for state publishing agencies, he was engaged already in collaborations with artists in Belgium, most notably Jean van Hamme, with whom he worked on the *Thorgal* series and later on also on *Le Grand Pouvoir du Chninkel* (*The Great Powers of Chninkel*; 1986–1987). Recalling this period many years later, Rosiński described his Polish works, produced under state tutelage, as an important lesson in drawing that allowed him to grow as a professional illustrator (Rosiński, "Komiks spod znaku").

As the events of 1981 showed, Kurta, the editor-in-chief, was sincere in his Francophilia. After the imposition of martial law in Poland on December 13, 1981, which was meant to crush growing political opposition and restore the dictate of the party, both Kurta and Rosiński defected. They went to Francophone Belgium. Kurta became a contributor to several Belgian newspapers as well as teaching in the College of Europe in Bruges. Rosiński continued the collaboration with his *Thorgal* coauthor Jean van Hamme. *Relax* closed down, but both men helped satiate some of the hunger for comics that had emerged in socialist Poland.

## Poland's First Foreign Exports

The 1970s was not only a decade in which Western influences in Polish comics were being debated and, to some extent, also negotiated in the homegrown graphic narratives. Neither was it only a period of experiments in the making of the first local comics magazine. It was also a time when Polish illustrators and publishers produced their first exports that were to reach audiences on the other side of the Iron Curtain. *Legendarna Historia Polski* (*The Legends of Polish History*), first published in 1974, was one such export. The idea for the series emerged from the Kosciuszko Foundation in the United States, who wished to use comics to educate young Polish Americans about the land of their ancestors. The bilingual Polish-English albums were aimed at presenting the legendary beginnings of the nation as well as facilitating Polish language acquisition. The series was thus designed to fulfil the utilitarian and educational purpose that Poland's cultural savants long wished to see realized in comic art. There were no capitalist luxuries nor American-style narratives in there, no fashionable Western clothing nor well-groomed men. Instead, the characters originated from traditional Polish legends, while the scripts were largely based on medieval chronicles (Janicki, "Rzetelność" 31).

The series fit in with the larger institutional mission of the Kosciuszko Foundation. Since its creation in 1925, the organization set out to promote "intellectual and cultural relations between Poland and the United States" (Mizwa 628). In the immediate period after World War II, it extended aid to hundreds of Polish scholars, supported the restocking of Polish libraries as well as taking on a more general task of "keeping the torch of liberty alight" behind the Iron Curtain ("The Kosciuszko Foundation" 26). Both then and now, the foundation has offered scholarships to Polish academics and students, as well as supporting American students of Polish ancestry (see "The Kościuszko Foundation Exchange"). Its annual ball, organized until this day, has provided, over the years, an opportunity to enlarge endowment for scholarly exchanges, cultural programs, and other projects (see "Polka Ball"; "23rd Ball"; "700 Attend").

The funding for *Legendarna Historia Polski* came from the May Horanczyk Estate in Chicago and the Alfred Jurzykowski Fund in New York. The state publishing house Sport i Turystyka (Sport and Tourism), the largest comic book publisher in Poland in the 1970s, was responsible for practical matters, such as the recruiting of staff and production process. Scriptwriter Barbara Seidler and illustrator Grzegorz Rosiński were hired to write and draw the three albums (Rusek, *Leksykon* 146). The choice of Rosiński was obvious. He was one of the most sought-after illustrators in Poland and had a growing reputation as one of *Kapitan Żbik*'s best artists. Seidler made a name for herself as a journalist for the weekly *Życie Literackie* (*The Literary Life*), reporting on court and criminal cases. She was not new to comics either, having written scripts for several *Żbik* episodes (Ciborska 486). In her reporting from the courtroom, Seidler was known for being thorough, providing in-depth analyses of the case at hand, as well as being sensitive to Polish realities. According to author Mariusz Szczygieł, her work as a reporter went further than just relaying criminal cases. She was an excellent writer, too, who provided a perceptive commentary on the mentalities of the time (610).

The series consisted of three albums: *O smoku wawelskim i królewnie Wandzie* (*Queen Wanda and the Wawel Dragon*; 1974), *Opowieść o Popielu i myszach* (*King Popiel and the Mice*; 1976), and *O Piaście Kołodzieju* (*The Legend of King Piast*; 1977). The three episodes were based on medieval chronicles by Wincenty Kadłubek and Gall Anonim, respectively (Janicki, "Rzetelność"). The very first album, published in 20,000 copies, was prepared exclusively for the American market (see R. W.). One year later, four different versions with English-, German-, French-, and Russian-Polish scripts, were published with the Polish reader in mind. The same order of publication followed for part 2 and part 3 of the series. The only difference was that the editions that were prepared for the American market were of a much higher quality—printed in a larger format, with more solid binding, and on better paper (Rusek, *Leksykon* 147). The Polish-American press praised the idea behind the comics and endorsed them as useful resources for language learning, alongside traditional textbooks. Each album cost one dollar and was available for purchase at the offices of the foundation (see "Nowe publikacje").

Polish media, too, responded with enthusiasm. Writer and art historian Waldemar Łysiak thought the series heralded the emancipation and ennobling of Polish comic art. After all, it did both: educate the youngest readers on Polish history and enhance their language skills through the use of simple bilingual scripts and evocative drawings (Łysiak, "Bajthriller"). It was not only Łysiak, but other commentators, too, who marveled at how useful the series was in "smuggling in" (*przemycać*) educational content, which many of the earlier *komiksy* were supposedly lacking (R. W.). The series was also praised for bringing the Polish language closer to the diaspora. Dictionaries supplied at the front and back covers of each album were to facilitate the reading of bilingual captions and speech bubbles (Pawlas). The principle of the series is in line with more recent research by second-language-acquisition scholars who have shown that comics can be a useful tool with which to introduce students to colloquial language, stimulate informal communicative situations in the classroom, and bring in elements of history and culture into the curriculum (see, e.g., Hajduk-Gawron).

To contemporary commentators, the series was also an expression of what French sociologist Jean Cazeneuve described as "exploring the full potential of comics" (A. L. 8). Quoting Cazeneuve, Polish journalists proposed that the best way of fighting the alleged dangers of comics was to take them seriously and to use them for one's own purposes. Comics should not be rejected or left to fester (the French sociologist supposedly argued); rather, a sensible way of allowing for comics and literature to coexist peacefully had to be devised. Sport i Turystyka was said to have found that sweet spot (A. L.). Even though not all critics were persuaded, they were willing to admit that "comics do not have to be for idiots [only]" (Maciejewski 6). What all of the observations above confirmed was that to uninvolved commentators (neither comics creators nor their fans), comics could only be rehabilitated if they served practical purposes. Educating the youth was one such purpose that expedited the magnanimity of the literary critic. If the educational element was missing, the medium was either forced into obscurity or treated as the proverbial whipping boy.[11]

Although the series was designed to wow Polish-American audiences, it went largely unnoticed in the United States, with the exception of a few cursory mentions in the diaspora newspapers (see, e.g., "Podręczniki"). The planned follow-up to the series, a comic book on the Polish-American hero Tadeusz Kościuszko, never materialized.[12] Nonetheless, Poland's first foreign export product turned out to be an immense commercial success with domestic audiences. Throughout the 1970s, the series also became popular in the USSR. To respond to the demand in the Soviet Union, Sport i Turystyka published a

---

11. This is how many proponents of the medium described the negative attitudes toward comic art in the 1970s. For example, Maciej Łukasiewicz argued that comics led a "hidden life" (życie utajone); Maciej Parowski described it as "chłopiec do bicia" (whipping boy, scapegoat). See Łukasiewicz, "Pismo"; Parowski.

12. The planned comic book on Tadeusz Kościuszko was mentioned in an article from 1976. It was supposed to be published the following year in 20,000 copies. See R. W.

single-language Russian version of the albums in 1976, 1977, and 1979, aimed exclusively at the Soviet market (Rusek, *Leksykon* 148).

Encouraged by these successes, the publisher decided to carry on with new albums about Polish history. This was a strictly commercial enterprise that continued without any foreign involvement. Throughout the 1980s, a series of four albums, entitled *Początki państwa polskiego* (*The Origins of Poland*), was published. These recalled the history of Polish kings, from Boleslaw the Wry-Mouthed (c. 1107–1138) to Casimir the Great (1333–1370). The series repeated the format of *Legendarna Historia Polski* and, aside from fulfilling the usual educational function of facilitating foreign-language acquisition, it also contributed to charity: 5 percent of the sales was to be donated to a children's fund (see Skonka). By 1987, the total number of copies for all editions and their reprints was estimated at 2 million (Rusek, *Leksykon* 148).

This was not the only foreign endeavor for Sport i Turystyka. Around the same time, in the early 1970s, comic book *Kapitan Kloss* (*Captain Kloss*), based on the popular TV series *Stawka większa niż życie,* was published in Sweden, Denmark, Norway, and Finland, in addition to appearing in Czechoslovakia. In 1975, it also came out in Yugoslavia but without the involvement from Sport i Turystyka. Instead, the Zagreb-based Vjesnik took on the publication; three years later several albums were published by Dnevnik in Novi Sad (Rusek, *Leksykon* 117).

The original television series, which told a story of a Polish double agent, Hans Kloss/Stanisław Kolicki, in Nazi-occupied Poland, had been sold to several countries, attracting wide following everywhere it traveled. As one scholar has noted, despite its World War II setting, the TV series emulated "the glamour of the early James Bond films," showcasing fast vehicles, expensive drinks, and beautiful women—all in an attempt to outstrip the Western mystery spy thrillers (Kunicki 46–47). The resulting comic book, too, fashioned Captain Kloss into a local Bond. The cover of the first album introduced the protagonist (drawn as the TV series actor Stanisław Mikulski) by his code name Agent J-23, while presenting his perfectly cut military uniform and beautifully styled hair. It presented Kloss in action, as any other adventure narrative would, driving an oversized motorcycle (figure 3.4).

The connection with the Scandinavian markets emerged from the popularity of *Stawka większa niż życie* with local television audiences.

**FIGURE 3.4.** *Kapitan Kloss: Agent J-23* (Sport i Turystyka, 1971)

Alfred Górny, the erstwhile director of Sport i Turystyka, who struck the publishing deal with the Swedes, recalled how during a meeting with a Swedish publisher he was told how popular *Stawka większa niż życie* was with local viewers. Górny offered that he would print the series as a comic book, specifically for the Swedish market. The deal was successful. In three years, twenty issues were published in Sweden, in addition to approximately ten albums in each of the other Scandinavian states. In total, Sport i Turystyka sold 1.5 million copies in the four Nordic countries and in Czechoslovakia, earning the publisher "a great deal of hard currency" (Górny 36).

The case of *Captain Kloss* shows how socialist publishers used the leverage of successful television series to market comic books to publishing companies outside the socialist world. Despite being a state enterprise, which had focused almost entirely on the Polish market, they adopted proactive entrepreneurial practices. Such practices could happen under the umbrella of wider economic transformation, instituted by the Gierek regime, which was aimed at stimulating links with Western economies, often with a view to developing and modernizing certain sectors of Polish industry.[13] More generally, based on their experience with *Kapitan Żbik,* Poland's first long-running comics series, Sport i Turystyka gained a good understanding of the appeal of the comic book. The publishing house had experience in printing high numbers of albums too, which could be utilized in their collaboration with American, Swedish, and other partners. It was through such collaborations that state enterprises were able to learn capitalist-like business practices and probe the limits of the socialist economy long before it was dismantled.

## Beyond the 1970s: Concluding Remarks

The developments of the 1970s provided ideal conditions in which the comic book could prosper in Poland. The ensuing economic recession of the 1980s, coupled with shortages of paper, meant that much of the projected growth of comic book culture did not materialize. Following the imposition of martial law in 1981, censorship was tightened and many of the major figures behind the comics scene left the country. The native industry adapted, nonetheless, and new initiatives began springing up already in 1982, when martial law was still in place.[14] The early 1980s saw a gradual emergence of the underground comic scene, linked to *samizdat* publishing. Two works, in particular, were representative of the period. One was *Solidarność—500 pierwszych dni* (*Solidarity: The First 500 Days;* 1984), a comic book on the history of the Polish trade union movement, illustrated by Jacek Federowicz and written by Jan Owsiński. The other was an adaptation of Orwell's *Animal Farm* by Robert Śnieciński and Fernando Molina, published in 1985 (see Puźniak 71–74). Despite being described by scholars as ineptly drawn and largely amateurish, the two comics constituted important outposts of Polish dissent of the

---

13. For a discussion of the attempts to modernize the motor industry in the early 1970s through links with the Italian Fiat, see Lesiakowski.

14. One such initiative was the monthly *Fantastyka,* a sci-fi magazine, which also published comics. See Siuda 194.

mid-1980s (Puźniak 75). Other works, such as *Wampiurs Wars* by Jan Plata-Przechlewski, too, took on the task of criticizing contemporary realities in ways that were infused with allusion and double speech (Puźniak 75–77). Even the usually regime-friendly series *Tytus, Romek i A'Tomek*, published in state-sponsored magazines, became critical of the contemporary situation, which some have interpreted as presaging the "agony of the [Communist] system" (Grzegorzewski 175–78). As the 1980s were drawing to a close and the ailing socialist economy was in urgent need of reform, a new period of hope ensued. This, as the next chapter will show, was quickly replaced with an overwhelming sense of disillusionment and a fear of the free-market economy.

# CHAPTER 4

# THE FOREIGN INVASION

Comics and the Free-Market Economy in the 1990s

Following more than four decades of state-mandated culture in socialist Poland, the 1990s came to be perceived as a decade of change and possibility, not least where popular culture was concerned. This period of "opening up" coincided with economic reform that entailed the transition to a market economy and other changes aimed at regulating the supply of previously unavailable goods. Private publishers that focused exclusively on comics were mushrooming (Zapała 209–15). Foreign genres, such as manga, arrived on the Polish market (E. Witkowska). Comic book festivals were being set up and fan culture grew exponentially.[1] This was a time when the history of comics, unaffected by the constraints of state control, was to begin afresh. Looking back at that decade nearly twenty years later, comic book publisher Szymon Holcman described the 1990s as "the most creative and varied period in the history of Polish comic art" (Woynarowski 179). Reflecting on Holcman's diagnosis in 2017, Jerzy Szyłak con-

---

1. For a discussion on the International Festival of Comics and Games in Łódź, which was inaugurated in 1991, see Tomaszewski.

curred but admitted that the transformations of the 1990s had not yet been sufficiently understood ("Komiks" 158, 162). This remains the case, five years later.

The aim of this chapter is to contribute to our understanding of that period. I explore major developments in the Polish comics culture of the 1990s while discussing the associated ideas of the transition from Communism to democracy, and from command to market economy. My particular focus is on the idea of "foreign invasion" (be it in the cultural or publishing sphere) and the associated influx of foreign comics series. The chapter addresses a series of interrelated questions: What aspects of political and economic transition were being negotiated through public discussions about the comic book? To what extent did artists, journalists, and publishers see comics as a barometer with which to measure the social, cultural, and economic transformation of the time? More importantly, how did they conceive the foreign influences vis-à-vis the necessity of stimulating home-grown comics culture in post-socialist Poland?

## A Recipe for Success

As I have shown earlier, the 1970s have often been described as the time of slow "opening" to foreign comics, including foreign models of comic book production, reception, and distribution. In contrast, the decade from the late 1980s onward was often labeled as a period of "invasion." In the late 1980s and early 1990s, the metaphor of culture "under attack" quickly gained currency in public debates surrounding comics. Many of the foreign imports were seen as an alien element that either needed to be expunged from, or assimilated into, Polish culture. The transition to a market economy and the associated influx of foreign titles also brought about the necessity of rethinking Poland's cultural offerings. Various contributions by the advocates and opponents of comics made for a colorful discussion that spoke volumes about the changing status of the medium in Poland. As we will see below, already in the late 1980s comments on the "comics madness" that was said to have erupted in the US and elsewhere became more pronounced in the Polish press. As in the previous decades, these reflections were intertwined with a discussion on children and youth, including their upbringing and reading habits.

Unlike earlier, however, they were also interspersed with commentaries on the publishing sector and the economic implications of the popularity of comics.

Initially, prior to 1989, much of this reflection concerned solely the situation on the other side of the Iron Curtain, predominantly in the US and Western Europe. In an article "Cywilizacja obrazkowa atakuje" ("The Pictorial Civilization Attacks") published in the daily *Życie Warszawy* in 1987, journalist Wiktor Weggi summarized those changes in the following way:

> Illustrated stories launched another attack on children, young people and adults in the West. After the "golden" forties, comics began losing to film and television. Now they are clearly gaining a foothold again. They have appeared in the majority of eminent dailies in the US, Britain, France, Italy and Spain. Well-known publicists as well as business and bank owners see to it that their articles and advertisements are placed in the vicinity of picture stories because there is a greater chance they will be noticed and read.

Weggi went on to marvel at a high number of comics titles published in the US each year, citing as many as 250 new publications in 1986 only (all of which purportedly sold a total number of 150 million copies). Indeed, a large part of his article was devoted to the accomplishments of enterprising publishers in America and France, including Marvel and DC Comics, and Dupuis and Dargaud, respectively. In Weggi's words, those businesses managed to expand their distribution to such an extent that their merchandise became available in thousands of different locations, from supermarkets and shopping centers to specialist bookshops. Weggi was not mistaken. Toward the end of the 1980s, there were 4,000 comic book stores in the US only and as many as 400 in the UK (Sabin, *Comics* 157; Gabilliet, *Of Comics* 152).

Weggi was not the only one to incorporate economic thinking in his reporting on comics. Toward the end of the 1980s, there were several other commentators who did just that. Admittedly, much of this coverage was drawn from American publications, which were translated, edited, and reprinted in Polish newspapers and cultural magazines. In one reprint of a *Newsweek* article, written by authors based in Brazil, Japan, and Mexico, comics were presented as a recipe for an instant commercial success. As the Polish version put it: "Here is an advice to anyone who has an ambition to become a mass media magnate. It is enough to remember one word; this is a recipe for success: COMICS" ("Zap!"; "Fenomen"). Using West German, Japanese, North American, and South American examples, the authors argued that to publish comics one did not need "big money" but only some imagination and a "child-like sense of unlimited possibilities" (Zap!"). More importantly, the authors applauded publishers in both Americas, Western Europe, and Asia for being able to find new uses for comics, including educational work, political campaigning, and advertising.

As comics historian Jean-Paul Gabilliet has shown, the reality on the ground was not as rosy. Between 1983 and 1988, publishers in the US suffered serious financial loses, stemming from an overabundance of the product and an uneven demand. Even as the market continued to grow throughout the late 1980s and early 1990s (largely due to conscious sales-enhancement strategies and a focus on specialist fan audiences), a disaster was looming.[2] Between 1993 and 1996, decreasing sales numbers brought about a crisis that engulfed numerous retailers and small to midsize publishers (Gabilliet, *Of Comics* 148–51). Of course, those considerations were not relevant to Polish entrepreneurs just yet, but in the atmosphere of economic reform and wider political changes on the horizon, the above-mentioned foreign articles offered a useful glimpse of a Western economy that was largely a mystery to a nonspecialist reader.

An article by Mariusz Piotrowski, the only comprehensive overview of the comics scene in Poland on the eve of transition, shows that this kind of "economic thinking" about comics was beginning to penetrate into the discourse about the Polish publishing market, too. Comparing the domestic situation to Japan, France, Belgium, and the US, Piotrowski fretted over the persisting suspiciousness of local publishers toward the medium. He argued that, despite some recognition achieved by Polish artists abroad and their gradual activization as a group of professionals at home, the situation was still a far cry from that in the above-mentioned countries. "There are considerably more comics [than before]," argued Piotrowski, "but most of them are still unworthy of attention. The somewhat primitive plots,

---

2. Although the number of comics readers in the US was dropping (in the mid-1980s this constituted approximately 20 million Americans), the majority of readers consumed more issues and were prepared to pay more for them than ever (see Wright 280).

narrated through rather poor drawings, are conquering the market simply because they exist. It is hard to talk about competition yet." Piotrowski attributed these shortcomings to the still-negative view of the medium. Comics artists were said to be poorly paid while finding themselves in a disadvantaged position when talking to publishers. This was to be expected, he argued, since comics were not being taken seriously in Poland, unlike elsewhere where they were considered art and an important sector of the economy.

Comments such as those, although still few and far between, were a tacit call for economic restructuring, expressed in the spirit of burgeoning *glasnost* and *perestroika* emanating from Gorbachev's reforms in the Soviet Union. As they described the deficiencies of the Polish publishing market and marveled at the successes of French, Belgian, Japanese, and American publishing tycoons, cultural editors in Poland were well aware that the transformation they wished to see could not happen within the existing economic system. State ownership of publishing houses and distribution channels, as well as the centrally planned publishing program, precluded the successful scenario seen in the countries operating on the basis of a market economy.

As scholars researching the publishing market in the USSR and the Soviet bloc have posited, already in the mid-1980s "the gap between what was offered by publishing houses and public demand had become self-evident" (Dreimane 58). I would argue that this gap was visible to the socialist reader much earlier. As I have shown in the previous chapters, the readers of *Sztandar młodych* welcomed enthusiastically the appearance of *Lucky Luke* episodes already in the 1960s. One decade later, *Relax* audiences repeatedly asked the editors that the then inaccessible American and Franco-Belgian comics be reprinted in the magazine. It was clear that throughout much of the socialist period, the centrally planned economy was not meeting the needs of local readers.

The abolition of censorship in April 1990, the end of state control over the supply of paper, and the departure from centrally planned publishing programs provided ample space for new entrepreneurial ideas and developments to emerge (Żuliński 115). The need for change was so urgent that it is perhaps not entirely surprising that, to quote one scholar,

publishers emerged as the most active group of entrepreneurs in the shift from the centrally planned to the market economy. In 1989,

Poland had 36 state-owned publishing houses, 12 owned by cooperatives, religious denominations and other groups and 36 publishing houses at state universities, social organizations, etc. In 1993, the National Library registered 2273 publishers. (Kołodziejska 51)

The rapid pace with which publishers adapted to economic transition was aided by a growing demand for certain products, popular literature being one of them. This gap in the market was quickly recognized by individual entrepreneurs who forged links with Western publishing houses that catered to specific audiences, from the enthusiasts of romance novels to comics fans, with a view to setting up branch offices in Eastern Europe. According to Waldemar Tevnell, a Polish-Swedish businessman and cofounder of Poland's first specialized comics publishing house, TM-Semic, 1990 was a year of immense opportunity.[3] Tevnell's example powerfully shows that the market was open to any enterprising individual who was able to fill the gap in the various sectors that, up until then, were either centrally controlled or nonexistent.

Tevnell himself had an unusual trajectory. He was born in Poland but had lived in Sweden since he was eleven. Having graduated in economics from Lund University, he worked at a computer company before taking up appointments at the Swedish Post and Volvo, both of which involved corporate management. As he candidly admitted, he had never intended to return to his birth country. But the economic transition in Eastern Europe offered a promise of quick success. In cooperation with the Swedish Semic, then Europe's larger comics publisher, Tevnell devised a publishing plan fit for the Polish market. Already in June 1990, he was able to publish the first issues of *Spiderman* and *Punisher,* only three months after his initial talks with the international director of Semic. The financial gratification was instant. In his own words, "in 1990, comics sold like hotcakes" (Tevnell 25). Tevnell gained the title of *polski król komiksu* (the Polish king of comics) and, in 1993, could pride himself on selling twenty different titles, with a cumulative number of 800,000 copies per month (Tevnell).

In the first few years after the transition, the comics publishing market abounded with ephemeral private publishers. New systems of book and magazine distribution sprang up, including "street ven-

---

3. TM-Semic was initially founded as TM-System Supergruppen Codem. In 1991, the name was changed to TM-Semic. The other founders were Stanisław Dudzik and Amine Murour.

dors, stalls at markets, bazaars and fares [sic], travelling salesmen, [and] subscription sales," which were aimed at enlarging the reader base and maximizing profits (Kołodziejska 51). Soon after the transition, between 1992 until 1999, a clear duopoly emerged. The comics market came to be dominated by TM-Semic and Egmont Polska, the latter of which was an offshoot of another Scandinavian company: Danish publishing giant Egmont. Although the two publishers operated independently of each other, the division of labor was clear. The former focused largely on superhero albums, drawn from the offerings of DC Comics and Marvel, while the latter published predominantly Walt Disney stories addressed to the youngest readers (*Donald Duck* and *Mickey Mouse* in particular) as well as *Asterix*. Even though TM-Semic was initially a leader in terms of the number of publications (877 titles in 1990–1999), Egmont (544 titles in the same period) proved to be more resilient to the ebbs and flows of the market (Zapała 210–11). As of today, Egmont is the only comics publisher that has been in continuous operation since 1990. TM-Semic did not survive beyond 2003.

Scholars argue that TM-Semic's demise was caused by the unstable situation in the American comics market in the 1990s and the appearance of competition, notably Egmont Publishing (Kowalczuk 101–3).[4] Others posit that the publisher's eventual closure was to do with its slapdash publishing, in particular low-quality paper and careless translation (Frąckiewicz, "Komiks" 13). While there is no clear data regarding this, it is also possible that, like many other popular publishers at the time, TM-Semic suffered from overproduction. The surplus of supply over demand was typical for many Polish publishers in the early 1990s, often veering from 50 percent to 300 percent, which increased storage costs exponentially (Klukowski and Tobera 179). As we have seen, this was not that different from the American comic book industry in the 1980s, which often produced more than could be absorbed (see Gabilliet, *Of Comics* 147).

According to scholar Jerzy Szyłak, in the early 1990s the publishing of comics was easier than ever. Declining state enterprises, such as Krajowa Agencja Wydawnicza, and newly emerging private publishers saw the medium as the ticket to instant commercial success (Szyłak, "Komiks w czasach" 159). Scholars estimate that in the

---

4. For a discussion of other (smaller) publishers that emerged in the 2000s or later, and focused predominantly on Marvel Comics titles, see Chudoba, "Komiksy."

early 1990s there were as many as 100 professional and semiprofessional publishers that sold comics, doing so, in most cases, without any clear business strategy (Zapała 209). Szyłak described those early publishing practices as "the reconnaissance through battle," based on the idea that "in order to establish whether a [comics] title (a magazine or series) could be profitable one needed to publish it" (Szyłak, *Komiks* 169). It is likely that publishers specializing in other genres engaged in similar practices. This would explain why the industry kept on expanding, at least in the first two years after the transition. It is estimated that in 1991, the turnover in the book market, in general, grew by 82 percent in comparison with the previous year (Tobera, "Rynek" 238). Foreign titles led the way, most notably Harlequin publications, which sold romance and "women's fiction." Harlequin made skillful use of advertising. Unlike the two Scandinavian publishers of comics, which limited themselves to advertising in youth magazines, Harlequin introduced an active publicity campaign that included not only television spots but also "small acts of goodwill," such as donating an ambulance car to a children's hospital or supporting young people from dysfunctional families.[5]

Thus, sister companies of large international publishing groups, such as TM-Semic, Egmont, and Harlequin, existed side by side with small one-person enterprises established by the enthusiasts of a specific genre. The latter catered to smaller and more specialized reader communities. This is precisely how the first manga publisher was established in 1996 in the provincial town of Olecko. Japonica Polonica Fantastica was a brainchild of Shin Yasuda, a Japanese man who had been living in Poland for several years. Drawing on the success of Japanese anime series in the early 1990s, Yasuda brought titles such as *Sailor Moon, Akira,* and *Dr. Slump* closer to the Polish reader. His enterprise was soon followed by two manga and anime magazines, *Kawaii* and *Animegaido.* Three years later, Waneko, another manga publisher, based in Warsaw, was established by the Polish-Japanese trio of Aleksandra Watanuki, Martyna Taniguchi, and Kenichiro Watanuki (Ostrowska 78; Maciakiewicz 164–65). Unlike TM-Semic, which saw a decrease in sales toward the end of the 1990s and was eventually forced to close, both Japonica Polonica Fantas-

---

5. TM-Semic, for example, announced the publication of its first albums in the May issue of *Świat Młodych.* The advertisement was simple: "American comics in Polish! Beginning in June!" See P. Mazur. For a discussion of Harlequin's arrival in Poland, see Tobera, "Początki" 298–300.

tica and Waneko have been clear success stories. Both of them created a stable reader base and managed to survive the vicissitudes of the 1990s. They are operating until this day.

Although many of these enterprises were initially profit-oriented and thus hardly concerned with the advancing of the Polish comics scene (which echoes Gabilliet's observation that "publishers have always been more interested in selling copies of their publications than in advancing the status of comics as an art form" [*Of Comics* 134]), they created a lively environment in which the various types of comics could be accessed and enjoyed. As we have seen, however, this reinvigoration of the publishing market was largely limited to foreign and popular titles. In the early years of the transition, Polish comics artists were forced underground and resorted to publishing in fanzines. It was only later, toward the end of the 1990s, mostly due to the newly established magazine *Świat komiksu* (*The World of Comics*), that they were able to enter mainstream publishing. The early 1990s were thus marked by the ascendancy of foreign over domestic products.

As the freshly minted publishers were rubbing their hands in anticipation of growing profits, and as comics fans reveled in imported titles, there were also others who were far from feeling enthused. Some public figures framed the early 1990s as a period of an unstoppable attack on "true culture." As a result of this attack, they argued, moral and cultural values were coming under threat. According to some commentators, the Communist ideology came to be replaced with a whole different set of pressures, not least the perceived pressure to commodify culture and, by the same token, to resist that commodification.

## Flooded with "Junk"

The perception of the free market as a battlefield, flooded with (and at times even invaded by) foreign products, ideas, and moral codes, was fairly widespread in the immediate post-1989 period. Irrespective of ideological persuasion, many intellectuals feared that the freedoms that came with the political and economic transition were polluting Poland's cultural landscape. The supposed commodification of culture and the associated influx of popular cultural products were seen as decidedly corrupting influences. The opinion below, voiced in 1990 by publisher and former dissident Grzegorz Boguta, is an apt illustration of the conflicting emotions experienced by those who had contributed to the political transformation and who worked hard to refashion the publishing sector afterward. Although extensive, the statement is representative of the uneasy temper of the times and, as such, deserves to be cited in full:

> Poland is a unique country now. Its uniqueness stems primarily from the fact that Poland was the first country in the communist bloc to have broken off from the repressive political and economic system. A huge price was paid for this, however. As you know, the Polish economy has been drastically affected; severe and immediate economic hardship has been created on the way to hoped-for free market system. The impact that this has had on Polish culture is enormous. The demand for books is decreasing; the distribution system is collapsing; all of the publishing houses are firing employees, minimizing printing costs, and calling off earlier signed contracts with authors, simply in order to survive. We find more and more publishing houses making money on printing only popular works and pornography. The more ambitious books . . . are under threat of vanishing from the market. It looks like extinction, as in the dark Stalin ages. Under Stalin, however, art suffered by being made subservient to communist ideology. It was primarily under the control of the Communist Party and the Secret Police. Today we are going through the hard times of wild capitalism. We are quickly becoming the victims of the free market. . . . Our greatest problem is that we don't know how to save ourselves from the commercialization of culture. (51–52)

Boguta's analysis of the decline in the publishing sector was, of course, restricted to the so-called elite literature. Terms such as "threat," "extinction," and "collapse" penetrated his vision of the "wild capitalism" to the core, standing in sharp contrast with the triumphal pronouncements of success voiced by the likes of king of comics Waldemar Tevnell. To Tevnell and others who sold popular foreign titles, the free market provided a window of opportunity. To Boguta, one of the people behind Nowa, the first and largest publishing house for *samizdat,* established in 1977 and transformed in 1989 into a private enterprise, SuperNowa, the free-market economy meant making concessions and taking commercially minded decisions. Possibly, it also meant departing from the traditional model of national culture.

It would be no exaggeration to describe Boguta as a traditionalist distrustful of economic modernization. Such views were not new in history; neither were they exclusive to Poland. Writing about attitudes toward mass culture in twentieth-century Italy, scholars David Forgacs and Stephen Gundle contended that, both during the fascist and postwar periods, hostility toward modern commercial culture was not necessarily a reflection of one's ideological views but rather echoed one's stance on free trade, economic reform, and, more generally, cultural progress. Thus, proponents of cultural autarky and professed defenders of national identity (be they fascists, Communists, or church representatives) were typically inimical to foreign influence and protective of traditional culture. Those who supported the modernizing drive advocated a greater opening and encouraged economic models that others might have viewed as culturally invasive (Forgacs and Gundle 96).

There was more to Boguta's statement, however. Implicit in his reflection was a realization that in order for the "endangered" national culture to flourish, a powerful patron was needed. Scholar Jadwiga Kołodziejska, who wrote about the book industry in 1995, and who identified similar dilemmas ("the principles of the free market when applied to the cultural sphere do not necessarily produce a cultured people; indeed, they may even pose a barricade to their development" [56]), saw the state as that patron. But the distrust of ideological influence was ever present, and new institutions and practices needed to be devised in order to prevent state intervention. According to Kołodziejska:

> The maintenance of a cultural policy by a central government does not have to involve interference and control over artistic creation and its distribution. Many democracies support the preservation of traditional cultural values at the same time as they let mass culture thrive. But traditional culture is not, like mass culture, self-supporting, and private philanthropy in Poland is as yet undeveloped. The central state budget remains the main source of cultural support besides the local governments. To ensure that the flow of state funds to cultural institutions is not accompanied by ideological pressure, various intermediary institutions must be developed

to act as watchdogs. The organization of these institutions would in itself be helpful in socializing national cultural policy in that they would involve wider circles in the discussion of cultural policy goals. (56–57)

Despite being largely dependent on external funding, the publishers of highbrow literature were reluctant to see the state as a sole provider of financial support. Monopolization, in any aspect of publishing, was associated with the socialist period, and as such, many newly emerged entrepreneurs initially chose to diversify their strategies of production and distribution. This led to absurd situations whereby one publisher would be using hundreds of distributors in order to avoid excessive reliance on just one. This, in turn, increased the cost of delivery and bookkeeping, among other things (Marecki and Sasin 112–13).

That chaotic atmosphere of the first few years of the market economy was experienced in a very similar way by artists. In that respect, the sentiments they expressed about the economic transformation of 1989 brought them closer to the publishers of "ambitious literature" (as Boguta described it) than to the booming commercial comics outlets. Like their publisher colleagues, many established comics illustrators were alarmed by the rapid economic transformation and the associated influx of foreign titles. Importantly, they saw the changes of the early 1990s as detrimental to their professional standing. Often, they blamed popular publishers, such as TM-Semic, for remaining blind to the problems of the local comics community (Chudoba, "Sentymentalna historia" 410). As foreign superhero stories flooded the market, Polish comics were said to remain marginalized, devoid of support, and absent from bookshops. A bitter statement from 1994 by Janusz Christa, the celebrated creator of the 1970s and 1980s classic *Kajko i Kokosz*, was illustrative of that standpoint:

The market is flooded with foreign comics. They are mainly comics that were created several decades ago, most of them in the USA, as a result of which the rights to print them cost literally pennies. After all, the costs of "making" them are non-existent. In addition, [in the West] they are already timeworn. We are a wonderful market, because until recently they were unattainable here. Often, their content is embarrassing, which for us—[comics] creators—is particularly sad. "Junk" would perhaps be a good word to describe it. (Christa, "Kapitan")

Christa's observation is important for several reasons. Other than reinforcing the traditional anti-Americanism and dislike of mass American culture, his idea of the Polish market as an outlet for outdated and worthless products imported from the West is particularly interesting. As Kevin Patrick shows, American syndicates exported backdated stories abroad for a fraction of the original price already in the 1930s, and in that respect, Christa was not saying anything new (see Patrick 66). But his attempt to disassociate the domestic comics production from the American imports, most likely the best-selling products of Marvel and DC Comics, deserves more attention. More specifically, Christa infers here that the Polish comics community was united in their dissatisfaction with the canny publishers who were unwilling to contribute to the making of local comic art. He was right perhaps in suggesting that what he described as the spent and hackneyed "junk" could not be more damaging to the popular perception of his profession as well as purportedly ruining the domestic comics industry. This shows that already then Polish comics artists tried to position themselves as the creators of elite culture that stood in sharp contrast with the mass culture imported from across the ocean.

This idea was well summarized by literary critics Jakub Banasiak and Sebastian Frąckiewicz, who, nearly twenty years later, argued that describing Polish comics as a product of pop culture was not entirely accurate. They maintained that to do so was to copy the Japanese or American model of comics creation, distribution, and readership, which could not be more distant from Polish realities. Even though the two referred to low circulation figures in Poland, often below 1,000 copies per title (which de facto placed Polish comics side by side with highbrow fiction), their message was clear. Polish comic art was not a mass phenomenon, and as such, it would have been simplistic to compare it to American superhero stories and Japanese manga (Banasiak and Frąckiewicz 10–11). And yet, one cannot help but think that both Christa's embarrassment about the popular offerings of the 1990s and the two journalists' distancing from mass culture, expressed in 2012, were underpinned by a fairly narrow understanding of what constituted American comics. If one were to limit that definition to the publications of Marvel and DC Comics, whose products were the only American titles available in Poland on a mass scale, then indeed, admitting that Polish comics shared the same origins as the superhero stories would be incorrect.

If anything, the disparagement of worn-out superhero narratives by Polish comics artists of the 1990s brought them closer to the members of the US underground comix movement who, already in the 1960s and 1970s, voiced similar concerns. Those artists, too, protested the flooding of the market with banal "kids' stuff," and some of their work, most notably Gilbert Shelton's *Wonder Wart-Hog* (1962), was a parody of the superhero genre (Estren 193). Discussing the comix movement in 1975, sociologist Clinton R. Sanders argued that underground artists had a clear advantage over commercial comics, that is, the ability to respond to the social, political, and personal concerns of a growing number of young people. In a similar vein to Christa, he posited that the commercial titles were "simply getting old" (840). To make things worse, the quality of those mass publications was said to be "rapidly declining," while their story lines, drawing styles, and topics were "monotonously similar" (840). As a result, Sanders maintained, "new young artists are no longer willing to be hacks for the large comic firms, preferring artistic freedom to economic security" (840).

Indeed, by choosing to work outside the system, underground artists in the US defied the official comics establishment and resisted the monopoly of DC Comics and Marvel. By refusing to draw comics for either of the publishing giants, they were free to disobey the restrictive Comics Code of 1954, too, which remained in place until the early 2000s and which many of them saw as an assault on free speech. More importantly, they were alternative in every sense of the word: critical of the excesses of capitalism, derisive of (white) middle-class values, and strongly opposed to the government (Rosenkranz 48, 75, 221).

Some of those characteristics, particularly the criticism of traditional values, would become defining for the latter-day underground movement in Poland. Unlike their American counterparts, however, young artists who emerged in Eastern Europe in the 1990s saw the artistic underground as a necessity rather than a choice. This was true not only for Poland but also for other former socialist states (Puźniak 55). Even though the antecedents of the Polish underground comics movement have been traced by scholars to the 1980s, specifically to the fanzines published by the nationwide Club of Fantasy Enthusiasts (Klub Miłośników Fantastyki), its true beginnings are normally

associated with the early 1990s (Szyłak, *Komiks* 170). Krzysztof Owedyk and Dariusz Palinowski, both members of the punk rock scene,
are seen as the pioneers of the movement, while their fanzines *Zaka-
zany owoc* (*The Forbidden Fruit*) and *Prosiacek* (*Piggy*), respectively, are
considered classics of the genre. Like their American predecessors,
the two artists have prided themselves in being antiestablishment
and alternative. Their early works criticized the bigotry and hypocrisy of Polish society, as well as being overtly obscene, anti-clerical,
anti-skinhead, and anti-Nazi, among other things (Owedyk; Gizicki).
One could argue perhaps that the "foreign attack" of the 1990s ener-
gized the comics community and led to an emergence of artists who
would have otherwise remained unknown. But it is also true that due
to its ephemeral character and strong grassroots component, much of
this early work has most likely been lost and will be difficult to map
out by historians of the medium (Szyłak, *Komiks* 171).

Polish comics were to remain underground until the end of the
1990s. Meanwhile, as the free market continued to grow, the purported invasion of foreign comics continued. As one journalist wryly
put it, *buble* (Polish for "poor quality goods") from the West became
Poland's daily reality. Printed on a mediocre quality of paper, American comics were said to be "cast out" to the people (the way one
casts out rubbish) by commercial comics publishers who continued
to fill their pockets (see Chęcińska). Soon enough, the Polish market
came to be presented as a battlefield on which American, European,
and Japanese comics competed and fought for ascendancy (Paluszkiewicz). But this, as some have pointed out, was not an exclusively
Polish problem. As one journalist reported in the mid-1990s, France
was struggling to contain a similar "invasion," specifically the invasion of the "army of yellow dragons"—the Japanese manga. Quoting French dailies, the journalist argued that in France manga was
seen as threatening the domestic *bande dessinée* and corrupting the
French youth. Parents were said to be alarmed by its excessive brutality and sexual content, while teams of psychiatrists were employed
by French publishers to censor the original content of the albums
(Sieczkowski). Even if excessively protectionist, the French way of
dealing with this purported "invasion" was closely observed, and at
times even admired, in Poland. Artist Janusz Christa, who, like many
other established Polish comics illustrators, looked up to the French,
argued that the Polish government should emulate them by introducing quotas on imported foreign comic books (and other popular cul-

tural products, including music). "They are defending themselves," Christa said; "we aren't" (Christa, "Kapitan").[6]

That final constatation could be seen as a wider reflection on the cultural policy of the state and the resulting status of the comic book in Poland. While many artists wished that domestic comics would gain the same status as *bande dessinée* has in France—namely as an important part of the national heritage—they were also hoping to see a greater involvement from the state that would elevate the medium to that position. Like some of the earlier-mentioned scholars and noncommercial publishers, comic book artists felt that in order to protect and nurture cultural production at home, a proper cultural policy was necessary. Such a policy would ideally support private sector cultural industries, including small independent publishers, and promote local cultural production over foreign ones.

Despite those calls from the literary community, in the early years of transition, many in the higher echelons of power assumed that "no cultural policy was the best policy" (Krzysztofek 269). To policy makers, the idea of introducing a cultural policy in a state that was both democratic and operating on the principles of the market economy was illogical, while any form of centralized administration was seen as reminiscent of the socialist system (Gierat-Bieroń 24–25). The first official document that dealt with those issues, entitled *Polityka kulturalna państwa. Założenia* (*The Principles of State Cultural Policy*), was published on August 10, 1993. Policy makers behind the document emphasized their reticence toward a model of culture that profited from state tutelage and made it clear that official intervention in culture was a thing of the past (3).

Book culture and readership assumed a special importance in that document as one of the "protected areas" of culture. Still, the official program made it more than clear that state involvement would be noninterventionist and largely limited to financial support. Even more so, the document implied that applying the principles of the market economy to culture as well as a "moderate commodification" of the publishing sector were not necessarily detrimental to the development of a "thinking society" (*Polityka kulturalna* 7). All in all, however, scholars agree that the political elites of the early 1990s spent

---

6. Already in 1949, a law was passed in France that controlled the influx of foreign comics. This was strengthened by an additional decree passed in 1958 and aimed at protecting the local market. See Reitberger and Fuchs 185.

little time thinking about culture and discussing the need to regulate it with a deliberate policy (Golka 26–28).

Even though Christa's appeal was not necessarily a lone voice in the wilderness, it did fall on deaf ears. Soon enough, like his beloved France, Poland too would see the invasion of the "army of yellow dragons."

## Manga Attacks

In 2003, one of the major newspapers in Poland, *Gazeta Wyborcza,* published an article entitled "Silny znaczy dobry" ("Strong Means Good"), which discussed the impact of Japanese manga on the reso- cialization of Polish prisoners. Focusing on one particular facility in the Upper Silesian city of Gliwice, the article posited that manga pro- vided positive role models with which many prisoners were able to identify. The prison library shelf where manga titles were stacked was said to be always empty, while inmates were impatient to get hold of new albums. In the words of the prison warden, manga glori- fied physical strength, which his charges found appealing, and often conflated it with positive character traits. More importantly, it did so in ways that were subtle and convincing, rather than overly didac- tic. Reading was said to have a visible influence on the behavior of young offenders too. "At least when they are absorbed in [reading] manga," the warden maintained, "they don't beat up and rape other prisoners. I suspect that prison is the only place in which they [have taken up] read[ing]" (Goślińska).

Despite proving to be successful, such experiments with manga were rare in Poland and the governor was isolated in expressing his praise for the genre. And yet the experiences of his charges reflected a wider European trend. In the early 2000s, in Italy, Germany, France, and Switzerland, among other places, manga fandom was growing rapidly. The genre was reported to offer escape to its audiences, fos- ter reflection on important social issues, and promote personal quali- ties to which the readers were said to aspire (Bouissou et al. 261). In the same vein, in the countries of East Asia, audiences saw Japanese popular culture as creative, interesting, funny, and artistically stimu- lating (Otmazgin, "Meta-Narratives" 87). In many of these settings, the success of manga was attributed to savvy publishers who knew how to meet the demands of their audiences by offering products

that were both affordable and that catered to various tastes and interests (Bouissou et al. 262–63).

Like elsewhere, also in Poland, Japanese animation films preceded the arrival of manga by more than two decades.[7] Following the
screening of *Puss 'n Boots* at the International Film Festival in Mos-
cow in 1970, the animation was released in Polish cinemas in 1972
with a Polish-language dubbed version (E. Witkowska 27). This was
followed by further cinema releases of *Puss in Boots: An Adventure
around the World in 80 Days* in 1977 and *Animal Treasure Island* in 1979.
Numerous Japanese TV series were also shown on Polish national
television throughout the 1970s and 1980s, for example the much-
loved *Maya the Honey Bee, Arabian Nights: Sinbad's Adventures,* and
*The Wonderful Adventures of Nils* (Bolałek 6). Dubbed by well-known
Polish actors and singers, the animations were rarely associated with
Japan, all the more because many of the productions were imported
from Europe and the US in their already Occidentalized formats (E.
Witkowska 27). The American adaptation of *Science Ninja Team Gat-
chaman,* known as *Battle of the Planets* (1978), shown on Polish national
television as *Załoga G* (*Team G*) in 1979 and 1980 was a representative example. The American censors shortened the film by almost a
fifth, made changes to the plot, and removed all the elements that
would suggest the Japanese provenance of the series. For example,
the original soundtrack was replaced with a newly composed musical score, and the original names of all the characters were changed
and replaced with local equivalents. It was this already Westernized
version that served as the basis for the Polish adaptation (Siuda and
Koralewska 66–67).

Although fairly frequent, these early encounters with Japanese
films and TV series were thus rarely associated with Japan. After
all, some of the films mentioned above originated from well-known
fairy tales and stories that had been part of European heritage for
centuries; others had textual antecedents in the form of twentieth-
century novels by celebrated European writers.[8] As such, many of
the Japanese animations were seen as typically "Western" products,

---

7. This was also the case with the Soviet Union. See Alaniz, *Komiks* 120.

8. The first group of works includes *Puss in Boots,* of which versions existed
in several European countries, including a sixteenth-century Italian version by
Giovanni Francesco Straparola and a seventeenth-century French one by Charles
Perrault, and the *Sindbad the Sailor* stories of the much-loved *Arabian Nights,* which,
although non-European in its origins, has been present in Europe since at least the

as was often the case with the TV series *Maya the Bee,* which some have incorrectly credited with West German origins (despite it being a Japanese-German-Austrian coproduction).[9]

It was only in the 1990s that "typically Japanese" animation titles were to appear on commercial television channels. Those were based almost exclusively on manga. For example, from 1993 the TV Polonia channel began to show *Tiger Mask* (*Tygrysia Maska*), *Sally the Witch* (*Czarodziejka Sally*), *Captain Tsubasa* (*Kapitan Jastrząb*), and *Yattāman,* among others. Two years later, TV Polsat presented *Sailor Moon* (*Czarodziejka z Księżyca*), and it was this series that supposedly spawned manga and anime fandom in Poland (Bazylewicz 114).

That is not to say that manga was absent from Poland prior to the 1990s. The very first reprint of a Japanese manga appeared already in 1986 in the fanzine *SFera,* published by the Polish Association of Fantasy Enthusiasts (Polskie Stowarzyszenie Miłośników Fantastyki) between 1984 and 1988. The comic series *Black Knight Batto* by Buichi Tarasawa was met with much enthusiasm, but due to the ephemeral character of *SFera,* only six episodes were published (Nowakowski). It was now down to the newly emerging manga publishers, Japonica Polonica Fantastica (1996) and Waneko (1999), to bring the genre closer to the Polish reader with titles such as *Sailor Moon, Neon Genesis Evangelion, Oh My Goddess, Akira,* and *Hello Harinezumi* and *Chōjin Rokku,* respectively (Bazylewicz 115–16).

By the late 1990s and early 2000s, manga became integrated into the Polish cultural fold, even if its assimilation was not always enthusiastic. In that sense, Polish attitudes toward manga mirrored, in many ways, those existing in other European states. On the one hand, there was a growing fan community, enchanted by the "magic" and "fantasy" of the medium.[10] On the other hand, the received view of the genre was infused with prejudice and, at times, even fear. This was no different in France or Italy. According to a survey conducted by the European Manga Network in 2006, a large percentage of French and Italian respondents at the time rated the presence of Japanese popular culture in their countries rather unfavorably. This was

---

eighteenth century. The second group comprises the well-known novel *The Wonderful Adventures of Nils* by Swedish writer Selma Lagerlöf.

9. For a short memoir of a Communist childhood, in which this claim is made, see Kamusella 758.

10. For interviews with Polish fans of Japan and Japanese culture who remember growing up when anime and manga became popular in Poland, see Shibata 625.

all the more puzzling given the fact that both France and Italy were the largest European markets for manga (Bouissou, "Popular Culture" 50). In Poland, too, manga has been met with a mixed response since its arrival in the mid-1990s. Although the two Polish manga publishers, Japonica Polonica Fantastica and Waneko, have been doing an excellent job of attracting a variety of readers, the widespread misconception of the genre as contaminated with brutality and pornography also detracted potential audiences (Musiałowski). In that respect, the supposed role of manga as a tool of soft power, hailed by some Japanese politicians as a cure to Japan's temporary economic downturn and seen as an instrument to increase its appeal abroad, has been fairly problematic where Polish audiences are concerned.[11]

Press reporting from the late 1990s is representative of those contradictory views on manga. According to Tomasz Bazylewicz, in the decade after the systemic transition, the mainstream media revealed a conspicuous lack of understanding of what manga was. On the one hand, they were said to praise the visual qualities and the variety of the genre. On the other hand, they criticized its presumed infantilism, its simplistic dichotomy of good and evil, and its apparent ability to trigger immoral behaviors among young readers (117–18). A closer look at media debates from the late 1990s confirms that manga, indeed, attracted some criticism, particularly from right-wing conservatives. But there were also positive reactions to the new genre. Many press commentaries revealed undisguised curiosity about manga and its emerging fan culture, teaching their readers about *otaku* (manga fans), the difference between *shoujo* and *shounen* manga (publications aimed at young female and male readership, respectively), and the first uses of the term "Man-Ga" (which roughly translates as "unrestrained images") by the nineteenth-century artist Hokusai (see, e.g., "Komiks po japońsku"; Buszman). They talked about how manga creators had to fight the influx of American comics in the 1930s and how, following World War II, the genre solidified its position on the Asian market (Gołębiewski). They also devoted attention to individuals who contributed to the popularization of manga, both in Japan

---

11. Scholars have shown that the soft power discourse has been fairly popular among Japanese political elites in the past two decades, whereby popular culture has been seen as an instrument of boosting Japan's image abroad and kick-starting its economy. See, for example, Otmazgin, "Japan Imagined"; Bouissou, "Pourquoi aimons-nous le manga?"

and in the wider world, including the Japanese writer and columnist Akio Nakamori (e.g., Dziatkiewicz).

Many Polish weeklies and daily newspapers attempted to provide informed discussions of what manga was and how it functioned in Japan, often based on interviews with local manga experts. In one article, published in the popular weekly magazine *Wprost,* the head of publishing house Japonica Polonica Fantastica, Shin Yasuda, explained to readers that "manga is a recipe for life. A Japanese housewife buys a culinary manga instead of a new cook book, and a fan of automotive industry—comics about cars rather than a photo-album" (Kostyła). Elsewhere journalist and manga advocate Robert Korzeniowski spoke of how manga was a useful medium with which to transfer all kinds of knowledge, from banking to stock market news (Janowski). In yet another interview, an informed manga aficio-nado expounded that in Japan, "manga could be placed somewhere in-between a newspaper and a book. *Shonen jump* [a best-selling manga magazine] is as thick as a phone book of a big city (around 800 pages) and is published every week in 5 million copies" (Góra). In a similar vein, the editor-in-chief of Poland's first manga maga-zine, *Kawaii,* Paweł Musiałowski, discussed the supposed differences between Polish and Japanese visual traditions. He admitted rather apologetically that

> it is no secret that our culture is different. They [the Japanese] are not shocked by naked bodies or by death, even the most violent one. . . . After all, every samurai was taught how to commit hara-kiri. Japan was [never] a peaceful country. Wars, invasions and battles between clans were something normal. Today Japan has a techno-logical advantage in comparison to the rest of the world; electronic and information systems as well as artificial intelligence are at a much higher level there than in Poland. This must create fear of the future. (Kaczorowska)

Musiałowski argued that manga was a way of coping with histori-cal traumas (including the bombing of Hiroshima) and tackling the isolation that came with technological progress. Addressing common points of criticism, manga's use of violence in particular, his was a tacit defense of the genre and a preemptive response to its critics.

Being one of the main proponents of manga in Poland, Musia-łowski was right to anticipate criticism and to try to shield the genre from putative attacks. By the end of the 1990s, only several years into the publication of the first manga in Poland, there was already a great deal of skepticism surrounding the genre. An analysis of newspaper headings from the late 1990s demonstrates the journalists' misgivings about manga's present and future in Poland, irrespective of their own enthusiasm for the genre. Their telling choice of words points to some of the common sentiments that emerged around manga during that decade, the fear of foreign influence (influence that could potentially be corrupting) being most prominent. In "Kto się boi mangi?" ("Who Is Afraid of Manga?"), columnist Paulina Kępczyńska attempted to rehabilitate manga by exploring its supposed penchant for brutality and sex. While arguing that many of those influences were a result of an increased Americanization and cultural polluting of manga, Kępczyńska pondered whether the genre could ever be absorbed into the Polish readership culture. In "Niebezpieczny konwent?" ("A Dangerous Convention?"), Anna Rojek reported on how a manga convention in the city of Łódź was canceled by venue providers, supposedly due to rumors that the local manga association, which organized the event, was a satanic sect. While the real reasons for the cancellation turned out to be related to an administrative glitch, the initial rumors spoke volumes about the perceived "foreignness" of the genre and the threat it was seen to pose to traditional values (Reczulski and Gamus 38). Even press commentaries that seemingly were sympathetic to Japan's popular culture rehearsed some of the common stereotypes voiced by its opponents. Young fans who fervently declared that "manga changed their life" were often presented as submitting to a strange affectation (Zduńczyk). Teenage girls, in particular, who gave in to *mangamania,* were portrayed as infantile and unreasonable (see MM). Also their interest in costly manga-themed gadgets, some of which were only available on the British market, puzzled journalists (Minorczyk-Cichy).

But none of these fairly agreeable and mildly spoken commentaries expressed the fears of "foreign attack" and "cultural invasion" as clearly and as forcefully as one article published by *Nasz Dziennik* (*Our Daily*), a radical conservative Roman Catholic daily from Warsaw, in August 2000. The main message of the article was well summarized in its heading, placed above the title, which read: "Japanese comics and animations are full of violence and brutality as well as models that are alien to Polish culture" (Leśniak 13). It was precisely a critique of those "alien models" that formed the crux of the author's argument. The author focused on three issues that he saw as potentially threatening the morals of contemporary youth. First was manga's frequent use of the term "energy" (the Japanese *chi*); this energy was said to come from within and be easily converted into a tangible human-generated force that could subsequently be used as a weapon. Second was the genre's religious syncretism, which was said to blend kabbalah, Christianity, Hinduism, and "Chinese legends." Third was its purported rooting in the beliefs of the New Age movement, as exemplified by manga's apparent fascination with occultism, demonology, and "strange amulets and talismans" (Leśniak 13). Irrespective of the accuracy of some of these points, many of them hinted, of course, at the Ten Commandments and equated reading manga with the sin of idolatry—that is, the worship of idols, images, polytheistic gods, and created things (such as trees, stones, rocks, and animals, among others). More importantly, the author left no doubt as to his assessment of Japanese comics vis-à-vis the American ones, whereby the Asian imports were said to be so violent that they could not even be compared with comics from the United States. Nonetheless, both influences were proclaimed to be a sure path to the "degeneration of children" (*degeneracja dzieci*) (Leśniak 13).

Scholars have long criticized such literal interpretations of manga, including those that have been filtered through one's ideological and religious lens. According to manga scholar Jolyon Baraka Thomas, reading the genre in such a way can lead to an "overemphasis on formal religious doctrine, thereby downplaying the fact that religious activity is often provisional or playful and that religious content is malleable. Additionally, such an approach can place undue emphasis on denominational distinctions, which may not be important or interesting for people involved in the production or consumption of a specific story" (8). As though responding to the *Nasz Dziennik* editor, Thomas argued further that an excessive focus on clear-cut religious denominations "occurs at the expense of understanding religious innovation, which may include the proactive poaching of religious imagery or content, the fusion of previously discrete doctrines, and parodic or irreverent portrayals of saints and saviors" (8). In other words, Thomas was a firm advocate of artistic license, whereby the creative process superseded specific denominational loyalties and divisions. The reader, too, was free to choose their own interpretation of the presented worldview, without attempting to adhere to one particular doctrine. Manga's syncretism could, then, be seen as an advantage rather than a drawback.

There is no denying that should the two authors ever have happened to meet, their opinions would have never been reconciled, not only for ideological reasons. Theirs were two radically different receptions of manga and of comics, more generally. The *Nasz Dziennik* editor represented, no doubt, the conservative position on comics as useful didactic tools that should be edifying and instructional, and placed in the service of the educational intentions of their producers. As a scholar, Thomas believed that manga, like literature, film, and other forms of artistic expression, should not be subservient to such considerations.

And yet, the criticism voiced by the former author is hardly surprising. In France and Italy, in particular, the arrival of manga was met with similar distrust (Bouissou et al. 259). Concerned parents and educators bemoaned its "vulgarity" and "dangerous content" in the same way their predecessors protested the influx of American comics in the 1940s and the 1950s. It could be said, then, that for conservative readers, manga became the new benchmark with which to measure which influences were to be perceived as corrupting and which ones were not. Once more the comic genre became a platform through which the ideas of cultural foreignness were negotiated and local values reflected upon. The upbringing of contemporary youth became one such value. Like in many other contexts, in these discussions, too, the child became the "perpetual horizon" and the "fantasmatic beneficiary," to use Lee Edelman's words, of such (anti-manga) interventions (3). It was the future of Polish child that, once more, was said to be at stake.

Rewind to 1995, when manga was only beginning to be noticed by non-fans in Poland. One of the country's major newspapers, *Rzeczpospolita,* publishes an article entitled "Armia żółtych smoków" ("The Army of Yellow Dragons"). In it, journalist Grzegorz Sieczkowski describes the ongoing "invasion" of manga in France, the fears expressed by parents, and the alarm raised by local comics publishers, who are afraid that domestic production will soon be flooded and taken over by Japanese imported products. Bringing to mind racist color metaphors, the "yellow dragons," whether invented by the journalist himself or lifted from French newspapers, were undoubtedly a nod to the nineteenth-century idea of the "yellow peril" coined by German Kaiser Wilhelm II in 1895. Both then and later, the concept encapsulated wider fears, including a growing immigration of East Asians into the West, a supposed military threat (be it Chinese or Japanese), economic competition, and moral degeneration (Keevak 126–27). Also here, the latter two are strongly present. Yet, little does Sieczkowski know that only five years later, when manga becomes absorbed into the Polish publishing market, similar points will be raised in his home country. Poland, too, would come to be perceived as undergoing an invasion of Japanese popular culture.

## Conclusion

The notion that the 1990s constituted a "difficult transition," as well as being a period of violent cultural and economic invasion from abroad, was not exclusive to the debates about comic books. More than ten years after the transformation of 1989, Polish fiction, too, was to yield similar observations. In the early 2000s, a new generation of writers, including Dawid Bieńkowski, Sławomir Shuty, and Dorota Masłowska, explored the impact of political and economic transformation on the individual and her or his sense of self. In particular, these authors discussed the disillusionment and isolation that came with rampant consumerism, the so-called rat race, and the market economy, more generally. Analyzing the works of those writers, notably that of Bieńkowski, literary scholar Aleksander Fiut caustically remarked that, not unlike Polish prose under socialism, contemporary fiction also involved a gross oversimplification of economic and political realities, presenting a world that was predictably dichotomous. Contemporary writers, he contended, saw the economic changes as conflicting with basic moral principles, while placing the sources of that "evil" outside the national borders. In doing so, they were said to replicate the binary worldview of the socialist era whereby once more the "other" was the West (or the capitalist world more generally), which was "attempting a political and economic conquest of the impoverished Poland" (Fiut 233).

Fiut's observations also ring true where the comics community is concerned. The rapidly changing publishing scene of the 1990s revived some of the deeply ingrained fears of both the West and the comics medium. The anxieties surrounding the medium were by no means exclusive to Poland, and neither were they restricted to the twentieth century. According to comics historian Christina Meyer, such reactions to pictorial stories were present already in late nineteenth-century America, emerging around familiar serial characters such as the Yellow Kid. Those fears stemmed from the "uncontrollable proliferations," "uncontainable energies," and "unprecedented reach" of such narratives, reflecting uncertainty about the rapid social change and the possible effects of mass culture (*Producing* 187). The Polish responses to the economic and cultural transformation of the early 1990s are tinged with similar insecurities.

To some extent, the 1990s also triggered nostalgia for the socialist welfare state, and the top-down control over the influx of foreign cultural products, even if many authors and intellectuals were reticent to admit it. And yet, although many in Poland compared the economic transformation to an invasion by foreign goods, there was a section of society that experienced those changes differently. A new generation of "free-market readers" emerged in the 1990s and made the best of what was on offer. This was, after all, a period of burgeoning comics and manga fan culture, a period in which comics festivals, conventions, and exhibitions were springing up across the country, and young library readers were eagerly making use of the new offerings (see Tkaczyk, "Od piktogramu"; BET; Olszewska; K. M.). This was also a time of renewed interest in other comics markets, most notably France, spearheaded by the activity of foreign cultural institutions, such as Institut Français (Kałużyński, "Dajcie"; "Kraków bliżej"). These efforts and initiatives would bear fruit in the decades to come. The Polish public would eventually warm up to comics.

# CHAPTER 5

# COMICS AFTER 2000

Between Individual and Collective Memory

Writing about Polish comic art in 2012, Jakub Banasiak and Sebastian Frąckiewicz argued it was hidden behind an invisible wall. The invisible wall, they maintained, separated comic books from other art forms. To remove that imaginary barrier, the two continued, comics needed to be seen "as an immanent and indispensable element of Polish culture, on par with film, literature and the visual arts" (9). Calls for the recognition of comics as a legitimate art form have been heard for decades, both in Poland and elsewhere. Over the years, it has become something of a cliché in the field of comic book studies to debate the dismissive treatment of the medium. Scholars all over the world have bewailed the common association of the comic book with "uneducated" or "unsophisticated" readers (be it children or the working class), while citing endless arguments for the worthiness of the medium (see, e.g., Ziolkowska and Howard 163). More recent work in the field critically reassesses the various attempts toward the legitimization of comics, both in scholarship and comic art itself (Ahmed and Tilleuil 30–32). In post-1989 Poland, Polish academics too have tried to demonstrate the "true value" of the medium and rescue it from obscurity (see esp. K. T. Toeplitz; Szyłak, *Komiks w szponach miernoty*). And yet, years after the long-awaited economic and political transformation, which was meant to improve the standing of the medium, commentators are still adamant that the Polish comic book is suffering from a crisis of popularity (see Chełminiak).

These pronouncements are only partly accurate. It is true that even award-winning authors can hardly support themselves from comics and that the sector is severely underfunded (see, e.g., Frąś, "Cudze"). And yet, in the past two decades, the native market has grown both in breadth and depth. With the surfacing of autobiographical graphic narratives, such as Michał Śledziński's *Na szybko spisane* (*Quickly Written*; 2007–2017), Marzena Sowa's *Marzi* (2007; written originally in French), and Agata Wawryniuk's *Rozmówki polsko-angielskie* (*The Polish-English Phrasebook*; 2013), comics began to attract different types of readers. Today, the Polish comic book means many things. It serves a variety of ideological, political, and personal interests too, some of which are not that different from those we saw under state socialism. However, the common denominator of this recent body of work is a distinct plurality of genres, catering to more varied audiences and tastes.

This chapter focuses on two specific case studies that point to the opposite ends of the spectrum. On the one hand, it examines contemporary graphic memoirs written by women that record personal experiences and build on autobiographical modes of writing and drawing developed in the West. On the other hand, it investigates state-funded historical works, many of which are aimed at serving an educational function, a genre that has a fairly long tradition in Poland. In exploring the former, I show how the current trends build on the earlier traditions of "borrowing" foreign models (be it from Denmark in the interwar period, France and Belgium under socialism, and the United States at different points of the twentieth century) and infusing them with distinct Polish experiences. The latter case study demonstrates how the revival of patriotic and nationally minded pictorial narratives, which have existed in Poland since the interbellum, goes hand in hand with the official politics of memory but does little to advance the standing of the comic medium.

## Graphic Memoir: The Individual Perspective

Although the origins of autobiographical comics date back to the underground comix scene in the early 1970s US, it is in the course of the past twenty years that the graphic memoir has become one of the most popular and best-selling comic genres in the world. Marjane Satrapi's highly acclaimed *Persepolis: The Story of a Childhood* (2000) sold more than half a million copies in France and over a million worldwide, winning several prizes and being made into a film in 2007. Praised for its accessible representation of Iranian culture and history told from the perspective of a child, the memoir is also a salient commentary on exile and displacement (Constantino 432). Together with other graphic autobiographies, such as Craig Thomson's *Blankets* (2003) and Alison Bechdel's *Fun Home* (2006), *Persepolis* paved the way for new coming-of-age stories. To quote Bart Beaty, "The wide exposure of her work, and its warm reception beyond the confines of the traditional comics reading public, has served to reinforce the association between serious subjects in contemporary comics and autobiography" ("Autobiography" 232).

In the Polish context, *Marzi,* scripted by Marzena Sowa and illustrated by Sylvain Savoia, builds on the success of Satrapi's work, being one of the first examples of graphic memoirs dealing with Eastern European topics. Originally written in French and published in six volumes by the Belgian publisher Dupuis between 2005 and 2011, the story constitutes a chronicle of growing up in Stalowa Wola, a small town in southeastern Poland. Just like *Persepolis,* the memoir was written in exile, albeit a self-imposed one, in France and Belgium. In a similar manner to Satrapi, Sowa creates her literary alter ego, Marzi, in an attempt to revisit her childhood, lived against the backdrop of momentous historical changes. Born in 1979, she was an only child in a working-class family witnessing her country extricate itself from Communism. In her own words, national history was of no personal significance to her. Rather, hers was an attempt to tell a life-affirming story of growing up behind the Iron Curtain, where personal values and human relationships were not that different from those in the West (Sowa ii). Despite her attempts to detach herself from the vicissitudes of history, her script shows an acute awareness of the complex intertwining of her family life and the life of her nation under Communism, on the brink of independence, and post-1989. As such, alongside telling her deeply personal story, Sowa provides a sensitive portrayal of Polish realities of the 1980s and early 1990s.[1]

---

1. For a longer discussion of Sowa's memoir, see, for example, Mihăilescu.

Unlike Sowa's memoir, most of the other recent graphic novels by women have consisted of short-form works, sparsely scripted and minimalistic in their use of imagery. For example, Katarzyna Kaczor's novella *Powroty* (*Returns*; 2013), comprising twenty-four pages of black-and-white images, tells an understated story about love, longing, and loneliness as the main character spends fleeting moments with a long-distance partner, witnesses his departure, and once more awaits his return. Agata Bara's *Ogród* (*The Garden*; 2012) narrates a wartime secret that affects the life of a family and divides the local community. Drawn in sepia tones and employing hardly any script, the novella (not unlike Kaczor's work) shows clear reticence to combine word and image. This can be explained by the authors' backgrounds as illustrators and graphic artists working in other sectors, such as advertising (as is the case with Bara), rather than as comic book artists per se (Frąckiewicz, "Panie"). This is not unusual; some artists admit that they work between design and comic book art (see, e.g., Nowicka 72). Inevitably, this results in a dearth of relevant experience with the medium that is apparent in many contemporary works. Until recently, there has been a shortage of homegrown models that could teach the artists the possibilities of the medium. In that sense, many of the works mentioned above were a way of testing the ground and learning how to make a contemporary comic book, particularly the kind that represents "everyday experience."

Other publications, including Olga Wróbel's *Ciemna strona księżyca* (*The Dark Side of the Moon*; 2014), come close to what can be described as a full-fledged graphic memoir. They also offer a more thoughtful representation of the female experience than mainstream comics. Wróbel's work documents the author's pregnancy and, as such, follows into the footsteps of other female artists who chose to use graphic narrative to explore that very same experience, most notably A. K. Summers in *Pregnant Butch* (2012).[2] The book also speaks to the centrality of the body in the graphic memoir, a trend that has been visible from the beginnings of the genre in the early 1970s (El Refaie

---

2. In Poland, Agata "Endo" Nowicka's *Projekt: człowiek* (*Project Human*; 2006) is the first such work. Here Nowicka uses her signature pixel art, developed over the years on her Komix Blog, to document the nine months of her pregnancy. The story had been originally serialized in *Wysokie Obcasy*, the women's weekend magazine of newspaper *Gazeta Wyborcza*, and was only later published as an album. Another work on a similar topic is Dominika Węcławek's *Czwórka na pokładzie* (*Four on Board*; 2010).

51). Wróbel's aim was to show pregnancy not merely as the blessed state that, according to popular perception, makes women blossom and turns them into saintly figures, but rather as "nine months of ordinary life, of going to work, where no one cares that I feel sick and sleepy, of arguments with a husband who doesn't necessarily feel like worshipping me or guessing my wishes all the time, of cooking food which you won't feel like eating anyway and of occasional fantasies about a thunderbolt striking your house at night" (Wróbel, "Posłowie"). In that sense, Wróbel breaks the common trend of romanticizing pregnancy and motherhood, and speaks honestly about both the positive and negative aspects of her domestic life.

Polish female graphic novelists do not only focus on intimate themes. They also tackle other important experiences that have wider generational and social resonance. Agata Wawryniuk, for example, looks at Polish migration to Western Europe. In her *Rozmówki polsko-angielskie* (2013), she records the opening up of the British job market to Eastern European migrants after the first eastern expansion of the European Union in 2004. Hers is a telling portrayal of the time when cross-border mobility became a daily experience for millions of young Poles departing for the old member states in search of work and adventure.[3]

Correspondingly, it is impossible to speak about the female perspective without discussing how women function as part of the wider comic book scene in Poland. For decades, much of the scene was dominated by male artists, an undisputable legacy of the twentieth century. Several Polish scholars point out that this contributed to the rise of common representations of women as sex objects, which meant that credible and psychologically complex female characters were absent, at least before 2000 (Szafrańska 63; Serkowska 5).[4] Speaking of her early days in the comic book scene of the late 2000s, artist Olga Wróbel says that there were very few women visible at the time. But this also distinguished her from other artists and made her debut easier (Wróbel, "Dwie" 57). A similar point is made by Maria Rostocka, the author of *Niedźwiedź, kot i królik* (*Bear, Cat and a Rabbit*; 2012), who finds it surprising how easy it was to get recognition in

---

3. I look at this comic book in more detail in Nappi and Stańczyk. For another study of Wawryniuk's memoir in the context of the wider representations of economic migration in Polish literature, see Van Heuckelom.

4. For a detailed discussion of the eroticization of women in Polish comic books, see Szyłak, *Komiks i okolice pornografii*.

the comic book world. "Although there is a lot of talk that the scene is dominated by men," she notes, "I don't think this is the case. The art world is much more sexist" (Frąckiewicz, "Panie" 93). The anthology *Polski komiks kobiecy* (*Polish Women's Comics*; 2012) gives weight to those voices and shows that there is a strong group of female authors emerging on the Polish comic book scene. The anthology, which has also been translated into English, presents more than forty young artists, both those mentioned above and others, such as Joanna Karpowicz, Sylwia Restecka, and Dagmara Matuszak, and represents a diversity of topics and drawing styles. As the editor of the anthology argues, all of those works are unified by a conscious and systematic preoccupation with female concerns and a desire to make female artists more visible (Kuczyńska 62).

A more recent publication, *Totalnie nie nostalgia. Memuar* (*Totally Not Nostalgic: A Memoir*), published in 2017, has been lauded as the country's first graphic memoir. Conceived by a male-female duo—illustrator Jacek Frąś and scriptwriter Wanda Hagedorn—the book can be placed within the wider American tradition of graphic memoir, including the early examples such as Justin Green's *Binky Brown* (1972), which tackled growing up in an oppressive Roman Catholic setting. According to comics scholar Jared Gardner, Green's work "opened up the graphic narrative medium to a powerful wave of autography, one that would be mined and developed over the coming decades" (132). Providing an incisive portrayal of growing up in the oppressive patriarchal society of 1960s Poland, *Totalnie nie nostalgia* derives from this wave, tackling abusive child-parent relationships and exploring the issues of gender, religion, politics, and Polishness. As I argue here, the work provides a powerful critique of Polish patriarchy that is undertaken not only at the thematic level but also through intertextual references that reject Polish culture and build upon an intricate network of texts, images, and associations that are transcultural and detached from Eastern European tradition. My argument is that the patriarchal and the national become conflated here into one category that is symbolically purged and destroyed, both personally and culturally, as the main character severs the relationship with her abusive father and her country of origin.

Illustrated by Jacek Frąś, an accomplished artist known for such works as *Glinno* (2004) and *Stan* (2006), and written by newcomer Wanda Hagedorn, *Totalnie nie nostalgia* offers a distinct female voice. The memoir blends the aesthetics of the Bildungsroman with a story of emancipation and, eventually, permanent migration. Over the course of the narrative, the protagonist comes of age, questions established social norms, undergoes a sentimental and intellectual education, and leaves her home country. In the process, she becomes a liberated woman as well.

Wanda Hagedorn, the author of the script, is not the typical cartoonist: She is neither an illustrator nor a full-time writer. Rather, she is an individual on a journey of self-discovery and healing, undertaken through writing, reading, and reminiscing. Some of the time, this is a lonely journey; at other times, her mother and three sisters join in, contributing their own memories and, most importantly, talking to Wanda about her writing process and her attempts at "getting even" with their abusive father (Hagedorn and Frąś 11). Frąś, whose excellent drawings bring the story to life, is absent from the narrative. We find out very little about the collaboration between the two and the painstaking effort of making Hagedorn's narrative into a graphic memoir. As such, the authors make a clear statement from the start: This is exclusively Wanda's story.

The memoir begins in the early 1960s in the town of Szczecin, incorporated into Poland following the border shifts of 1945 when the former German lands of Silesia, Pomerania, and Warmia-Masuria became part of the newly established Polish state. In Hagedorn's own words, this was a typical Polish childhood, characterized by Catholic, patriarchal, and socialist "oppression, repression, and depression" (17). Written from the temporal and geographical safety of her Australian adult life, *Totalnie nie nostalgia* is a way of "collecting scraps of memories and recreating a childhood which is recognizable by many Polish women who grew up in the shadow of patriarchy. . . . Hagedorn talks about that childhood and about the ways of overcoming patriarchy" (Domagalska 18). Working through her memories and putting them on paper over the course of four years, Hagedorn-the-author explains how she came to a decision to sever the connection with her abusive father. Before revealing this to the reader in the very last splash page, which depicts the father tending to his apple trees, she reflects on her family relationships and interpersonal problems. One is her parents' dysfunctional marriage, the leitmotif of the story that shows the disquiet, confusion, and volatility of the home environment. This is juxtaposed with the more positive relationship that young Wanda shares with her grandmother Helena. These two narrative strands recur throughout the plot, shaping the protagonist as a person and structuring her storytelling as a writer. As comics scholar Hillary Chute put it, the comics medium lends itself well to such narratives; it "can express life stories, especially traumatic ones, powerfully because it makes literal the presence of the past by disrupting spatial and temporal conventions to overlay or palimpsest past and present" ("Comics Form" 109).

Wanda's story also records her intellectual education, one that happens predominantly through reading. In that sense, Hagedorn's narrative can be compared to Alison Bechdel's *Fun Home* (2006), whose references to Joyce, Proust, Camus, Fitzgerald, and others inform Bechdel's own coming of age. In *Totalnie nie nostalgia*, too, we are shown how both young and adult Wanda draw comfort from reading. As she attempts to verbalize her childhood experiences, the adult author delves into feminist writing (names such as bell hooks, Nancy Friday, and Carol Hanisch come up at different points in the memoir) and explores the work of Freud, whose discussion of narcissism proves a fruitful way of understanding Wanda's abusive father. The latter, in particular, is accompanied by masterful drawings from Frąś, as the father's image multiplies on the page, alluding to his egotism and self-absorption (Hagedorn and Frąś 154). According to feminist writer and scholar Inga Iwasiów, it is this theoretical scaffolding that gives the memoir depth and distinguishes it from many other coming-of-age stories (103). But reading is also a formative part of Wanda's childhood. People, events, emotions, and experiences are often associated in her memory with particular books and stories. For example, her grandmother Helena introduces her to erotic novels by the French writer Colette when sharing her own stories of initiation. Helena goes against the grain, ignoring the sanctimonious and patriarchal environment of 1960s Poland, and encouraging her granddaughter to be a self-assured and well-informed young woman. The close, loving, and stimulating relationship the two share brings to mind similar intergenerational bonds in other graphic memoirs by women, such as Marjane Satrapi's highly acclaimed *Persepolis* and the more recent *Flying Couch* by Amy Kurzweil (2016).

As we look at the young Wanda reading Colette with her grandmother and sharing moments of familial love, we are once more transported to 1960s Poland by Frąś's illustrations. The two women delight in *ptyś*, a typical Polish cake modeled on the French *chou à la crème*, resting proudly on a dessert plate (Hagedorn and Frąś 98). Literature is also used to comment on Helena's aging and her progressing Alzheimer's disease. As we see the grandmother wander aimlessly through the park, Hagedorn recalls Simone de Beauvoir's 1970 essay *La Vieillesse* (*Ageing*), about the dismissive treatment of the elderly and their marginalization in society (138). Reading literature and, more importantly, writing about literature becomes the cure for the author of *Totalnie nie nostalgia*. As she reminisces about and recalls famous works, Hagedorn regains her equilibrium. This is not an unusual strategy in graphic memoirs, particularly those that deal with suppressed childhood traumas. As Diederik Oostdijk shows in his analysis of Miriam Katin's work on overcoming painful experiences of World War II, "multimodal creativity" (be it reading, writing, drawing, or even listening to music) is "essential to Katin's finding a hidden wholeness inside herself" (89). In Hagedorn's case, too, literary references enable the author to articulate her experience and find sense in what initially seems like a confusing puzzle.

And yet, her frame of reference is almost exclusively non-Polish, showing her detachment from the *fatherland*. I argue that those omissions are not coincidental. Rather, they are aimed at emphasizing the author's conscious rejection of what she sees as that which stymies her growth as a person: Polishness, patriarchy, and the associated repression. Frąś's drawings further accentuate Wanda's attempts at refuting those influences. If visual allusions to Polish literature or culture ever appear in the memoir, those are usually pushed to the background, becoming part of the scenery, rather than being internalized as an inherent element of Wanda's mental and intellectual milieu. At times, those references serve as the backdrop for painful memories of physical abuse. For example, a poster advertising a 1965 film adaptation of Stefan Żeromski's novel *Popioły* (*Ashes*; 1902), compulsory reading in the school curriculum, is pinned to the wall of the young girl's bedroom. However, one might easily miss the poster in the background, as the image of Wanda's father smashing her head on the desk takes center stage in the panel (Hagedorn and Frąś 163). This, as the author tells us, is punishment for receiving a B in math.

As Hagedorn eliminates Polish cultural references from her narrative, Frąś makes skillful use of period stories and sources to bring the spirit and material culture of the time closer to the reader. This is a result of countless hours of visual research by the illustrator (Frąś, "Cudze"). Thus, Wanda's coming-of-age narrative is often interspersed with renditions of authentic documents and newspaper clippings. One such source is an inventory of German furniture and appliances purchased by the girl's grandfather from the so-called liquidation commission, which had confiscated property from the local Germans expelled in the immediate aftermath of World War II (Hagedorn and Frąś 34). Another is a leaflet warning the citizens of the invasion of Colorado beetles, an alleged American plot aimed at destroying the socialist economy (46). There is also an article from a children's magazine about Yuri Gagarin, a Soviet cosmonaut and the first man in space, which praises his achievements and aims to instill pride in the triumphs of the Soviet Union (62). In addition to redrawing period documents, Frąś based many of the panels in the book on old family photographs to add color and credence to the story (Frąś, "Afterlives" 77).

In the words of scholar Elisabeth El Refaie, such artifacts are ubiquitous in graphic memoirs and "have a key role to play in persuading readers of the authenticity of a particular work" (158). According to Hillary Chute, reinscribing period documents, letters, and photographs is also a deeply embodied process for the artist. Redrawing the sources with their own hand enables the artist not only to "fruitfully repurpose archives" but also to inhabit the past ("Comics Form" 113). In the case of Frąś, this process is invested with additional meaning. Aside from gaining insight into the past of his female coauthor (a life that had not been lived by him) and "reliving" that past through the comics medium, Frąś is also able to creatively reinvent that past. His renditions of period sources, in particular, give at times a lighter tinge to the memoir, which is otherwise somber in tone. Still, his illustrations do not invalidate the seriousness of Hagedorn's disturbing revelations.

As the memoir progresses, the female author divulges new details about her past. Some of those revelations concern Wanda's younger sister, Ania. At one point we find out that Ania was sexually abused by a local priest while preparing for her first communion. One year later, at the age of nine, she was molested by her step-grandfather. Both confessions are prompted by Hagedorn's work on the memoir (Hagedorn and Frąś 57, 174). Other painful recollections (and the graphic portrayals thereof) concern the sustained domestic abuse experienced by Wanda, her mother, and her sisters. Stories of brutal beatings and persistent bruising are Kafkaesque in their visual rendition, referencing *Metamorphosis*, as Wanda turns into a giant insect savaged by her father with a blizzard of red apples (224–27). She also represents certain collective memories common to her whole generation, for instance, the memory of films about extermination camps with recurring images of stacks of naked corpses that haunted her as a child (89). These undesirable memories slip into Wanda's consciousness as she tries to work through and disconnect from her childhood. But traumatic memories keep reoccurring, lingering on, reminding her of the uncomfortable, the unwanted, and the repressed aspects of her personal history.

Hillary Chute shows that the comic book lends itself well to "the movement of memory" or the "excavation of childhood memories," and indeed, many artists have done just that (*Graphic* 4). The abusive parent-child relationship, in particular, recurs in many other autobiographical works, from Kominsky-Crumb's *Need More Love* (2007) to Bechdel's *Are You My Mother?* (2012). Like many of these other women, Wanda refuses to be defeated by her past. Instead, she puts the past on trial and brings justice to herself, her mother, and her sisters. By revealing the deeply abusive patriarchal and Catholic environment in which she grew up, the author strikes a familiar chord with many Polish readers. This echoes Gardner's point that graphic memoirs have the power of forging "meaningful connections with others, opening up a dialogue with audiences and a sense of communal experience and release" (132). Although the scenes of domestic and institutional violence are shocking, all the more so for their banality and cruel repetitiveness, Wanda is not after retribution, despite her initial claims that this is the case. Rather, she understands her memoir as a restorative act. Enabling the victim to speak, *Totalnie nie nostalgia* is as much about finger-pointing as it is about healing through writing and visualizing painful experiences, for herself and, possibly, for others.

Wanda's Australian life, away from her country of origin and her abusive father, is part of the cure. Here she feels fulfilled and liberated, and unburdened by the national-conservative mythology of her birth country. Her active lifestyle and engagement in women's empowerment projects brings a sense of purpose and direction to her life. And while the memory of her father does not leave her until the very end of the story, the Australian Wanda cannot be further from the young Polish girl we see earlier in the memoir. She becomes the woman her grandmother wanted her to be: strong, independent, intelligent, and self-assured.

Local commentators described *Totalnie nie nostalgia* as a milestone in Polish women's comics writing (Wróbel, "Z szuflady" 105). It certainly stands out among other Polish graphic memoirs written by women: Not only does it present as painfully honest in a way that makes the reader feel both uncomfortable and deeply moved, but it is also beautifully drawn and scripted. It is hopeful, too, as Wanda and her sisters triumph over the domineering father by excluding him from their lives. Despite the demoralizing history of abuse, the four women manage to sustain the love and affection they had for each other as children. Their sisterly bonds endure time and geographical distance, growing stronger over the course of Hagedorn's memoir. As the women talk, reveal uncomfortable truths, and publicly share their girlhood secrets, the memoir becomes a thoughtful rejection of the hypocrisy and philistinism in which the young Wanda and her sisters grew up. Here those qualities have a distinctly patriarchal, Catholic, and socialist face—the three pillars of repression that need to be rejected and rhetorically destroyed in order to attain closure. Once more, the view of the ocean and Wanda's safe Australian life bring her peace and enable her to regain equilibrium after the mentally exhausting process of writing. Although the ghost of the father has been (seemingly) expunged, in the end the last ironic splash page is still devoted to him: The abuser becomes a tree hugger, tending lovingly to his fruit trees, vegetable patches, and flowers.

## Historical Comics: In Search of Collective Identity

Scholars have noted that recent historical comics are an important medium with which to explore the history of war, ethnic conflict, and genocide (see, e.g., Chute, *Disaster*; Aarons). Such works are said to mark and gauge political transformation, too, particularly a transformation from dictatorship to democracy (Catalá Carrasco et al. 15). According to Hillary Chute, comics that "draw history" can be considered a "visual-verbal narrative documentary form" that makes the past tangible on the page and "gives it corporeality, a physical shape" (*Disaster* 14, 27). In the words of Victoria Aarons: "The interplay of distinct moments in history and the reach of the imagination unrestricted by temporal, spatial, and geographical boundaries create urgency and immediacy" (4).

It is perhaps that said ability of graphic stories to render the past corporeal and urgent that inspired policy makers and publishers to consider the comic book a useful vehicle for various identity projects, from national to supranational ones. For example, political geographer Jason Dittmer proposes to employ graphic narratives to inform about Europe and spread European soft power. He maintains that, if paired with European subsidies for multilingual translations and supported by established cultural institutions, new narratives that describe "everyday life in Europe" could easily reach a transnational reader and "advance the European project both with 'domestic' populations and those beyond the border" (Dittmer 136). As Dittmer's proposal shows, also nowadays, the medium can be viewed as a powerful instrument of persuasion. Even if employed in supposedly innocuous identity projects, such as the European one, the ability of comics to entice the young mind and exert politically minded content should not be underestimated.

In what follows, I discuss state-sponsored historical comics in Poland, which are based on a similar principle. Since the early 2000s, several state institutions have used the medium to pursue state-sponsored politics of memory and respond to the immediate needs of nation building. While exploiting the ability of comics to provide a documentary-like record of the past, including the "canonical" events of national history, these narratives have also been promoted as useful educational resources. This is not a new strategy. Scholars working in a variety of national contexts show how at different points of the twentieth century, regimes used ideologically charged narratives to cultivate a particular type of young citizens, incite patriotic sentiment, and shape specific visions of the past, among other things (see, e.g., Eedy, "Four Colour Anti-Fascism" and *Four Color Communism*; Scholz, "The First" and "Images").

Since the late 1990s, Poland has seen an evolution of comics publishing presses toward more specialist content, aimed at a younger readership. Zin Zin Press has dominated the market of custom-made historical books, some of which have been commissioned by state institutions. The press has been present on the Polish market since 1997, initially producing one of the first comics magazines, *AQQ* (now discontinued). Since the early 2000s, Zin Zin became a chief publisher of historical comic books. To date it has produced nearly twenty albums on various topics dealing predominantly with twentieth-century Polish history. Works on the Second World War have focused on a wide variety of issues and events, including the Battle of Westerplatte and the defense of the Polish Post Office in Danzig in September 1939, and the Katyń massacre. There are also comics devoted to the underground freedom fighters, such as Witold Pilecki and the "cursed soldier" Józef Franczak. Equally well represented have been albums on the Communist period, some of which commemorate important anniversaries related to workers' strikes and trade unions, for example the twenty-fifth anniversary of Solidarity (1980) and of the massacre at the Wujek coal mine by the police and army (1981), as well as the fiftieth anniversary of the 1956 workers' revolt in Poznań. Alongside these examples, two narratives emphasizing the role of the Catholic Church in the dissident movement and in sustaining the national spirit under Communism deserve to be mentioned, one of them recalling the first Polish pilgrimage of Polish-born Pope John Paul II in 1979, and another telling the story of the murder of Jerzy Popiełuszko, the Catholic priest killed by Security Service officers in 1984.

These works derive largely from the official discourse of Poland's nationalist-conservative circles, such as the ruling Law and Justice Party. Here, two dominant narratives of the national past can be identified. First is the narrative of martyrdom and victimhood, associated with Poland's forced submission to its powerful neighbors and the ensuing tragic events: the Katyń massacre of 1940, where an estimated 20,000 Polish officers and civilians were killed by the NKVD; the anti-German Warsaw Uprising of 1944, in which many young people perished; and the post–World War II subjugation to the Soviet Union. Second and closely intertwined is the narrative of Polish heroism and resistance in the face of foreign oppression.[5] Memories that contradict these visions of Polishness have often been viewed as unpatriotic and, as such, refused legitimacy. For example, debates on Polish anti-Semitism and pogroms during and after the war, initiated by Jan T. Gross's *Neighbors,* caused an uproar in Poland and led to a renewed soul-searching concerning Poland's "dark past" (Polonsky and Michlic, Introduction 1). Equally, discussions surrounding the expulsions of Germans from western territories after World War II suggest that accounts of the wartime suffering of other nations, especially those whose stereotypical role was that of perpetrator, tend to be seen in Poland as an attempt to falsify history and undermine the extent of Polish suffering (Lutomski 452). It is this very model of collective memory that has had the greatest impact on historical Polish

---

5. For a more detailed discussion of these narratives in the public discourse, see, for example, Ochman 29–32.

comic books of the last decade. Not only does this status quo hamper the development of new pictorial narratives on the national past, but it also relegates historical topics to publications that are by nature prescriptive and one-dimensional.

While tackling themes that were either suppressed or distorted prior to the fall of Communism, these graphic narratives are aimed predominantly at educating young people about national history. More specifically, they are addressed to readers "who were lucky enough to have been born in free Poland" (Wałęsa 3). In the words of Witold Tkaczyk, head of the publishing house, the albums are meant to appeal to a wide readership (Tkaczyk, "Wyjść" 44). To attract the popular reader, the authors behind Zin Zin Press have set great store by exploiting the educational potential of these narratives. The didactic purpose of the comics is often made explicit, emphasized in either the works' forewords or jacket blurbs. For instance, *1956: Poznański Czerwiec* (*Poznań: June 1956*) praised the accessible format of the medium. In a similar way, *Pierwsi w boju* (*First in Battle*) limits its target readership from the very outset; the authors explicitly state that "as befits the medium used, the book is aimed primarily at the young reader" (Jasiński et al., *1956* front cover flap; Wójtowicz-Podhorski and Przybylski 3). To some extent, these remarks reiterate the stereotypical perception of the medium as appealing only to children and adolescents, along with the suggestion that the comic is a convenient vehicle with which to convey complex subject matter in a clear and comprehensible manner.

The educational function of the publications is underpinned by solid historical research. Lengthy bibliographical references are often listed, including accounts by eyewitnesses such as diaries and life stories (Wójtowicz-Podhorski and Przybylski 4). In some cases, almost entire scripts are built on personal narratives, for example *1940 Katyń: zbrodnia na nieludzkiej ziemi* (*Katyń 1940: Crime in the Inhuman Land*), which draws on memoirs of Starobilsk camp survivor Józef Czapski. The scripts' strict adherence to scholarly sources and eyewitness testimonies is meant to create an appearance of "objective" historical knowledge that is free from constraints imposed by political influence. As such, the books are presented as trustworthy educational material. Further, most albums are supplemented with articles or epilogues providing additional background information on the events they represent. Some of these sources contain archival photographs and images of weapons used by Polish soldiers, as in

*Pierwsi w boju*; annotations and a timeline of events, as exemplified by *1956: Poznański Czerwiec*; and drawings of military uniforms, for example in *1940 Katyń* (T. Nowak et al.).

Such narratives and the associated formats are not exclusive to contemporary Poland, and neither are they solely used by actors pursuing conservative political agendas. Jorge Santos shows that also recent civil rights comics in the US, which have a clear pedagogical focus (being aimed at primary- and secondary-school audiences) tend to uncritically adhere to a largely prescriptive "consensus-memory frame" (6). Exploring the biographies of celebrated icons of the civil rights movement, such as Martin Luther King and Rosa Parks, these works rarely go beyond the traditional narratives of martyrdom; neither do they expand the conventional understandings of the persons and events in question. This is despite the fact that, like the Polish examples discussed above, the comics pride themselves in being thoroughly researched, pointing audiences to background reading and providing additional information, including glossaries, bibliographies, and web links (6).

The prescriptiveness of such narratives can be explained, to some extent, by the funding strategies in place. In Poland, the majority of those publications have been funded by various state institutions and other official actors of memory. One of the subsidies came from the program "The Patriotism of Tomorrow," overseen by the Polish History Museum. This is how the then minister of culture, Kazimierz Ujazdowski, defined the aims of the program in a foreword to the comic on the 1956 workers' protest in Poznań:

> This is a new program supporting initiatives that promote history in modern and communicative ways. Historical comics are one of them. As the Minister of Culture and a father of two school-age boys, I am in favor of such projects. Together we should look for fresh and light formats that will restore the positive and happy character of [Polish] patriotism. (Ujazdowski 3)

Aside from replicating the formulaic definition of comics as a "light format" written for schoolchildren, Ujazdowski's statement projects a far more optimistic vision of Polish patriotism than the graphic narrative he introduces. In fact, both this and many of the other historical albums produced by Zin Zin Press seem to fit into a quite different national discourse, one that is firmly grounded in the idea of Poland as the "Christ of Nations," torn by powerful enemies and sacrificing itself for other countries.[6] According to Dieter De Bruyn, who analyzed other state-funded comics, "this new tendency in comic art . . . threatens to reinvigorate the 'typically' Polish martyrological messianistic mythology of suffering," and as the traumatic historical "events are increasingly claimed as the sacrosanct landmarks of the newly forged Polish identity, they may themselves start to take on an ideological and even propagandistic guise" (50–51).

Some scholars proclaim that today seemingly "anything can be adapted and translated to the sequential art form" (Weiner and Syma 3). They could not be more correct. Nonetheless, despite the spread of such publications, both in Poland and elsewhere, some educators continue to be skeptical about using historical comics in the classroom. According to one teacher, "comics must not be overly serious or didactic in their approach to national history" or they risk becoming textbooks (Howell 30). Students, too, are said to voice concerns about such material, describing it as "frivolous" and failing to advance the ultimate goal of exam preparation (Howell 30). More importantly, like historical textbooks, state-sponsored comic books, too, are subject to the ebbs and flows of educational policy, reflecting the official preoccupation with specific national figures, events, and narratives (see Howell 3).

Investing state funds into such narratives might also result in siphoning off subsidies from other comics projects that are less focused on advancing the political agenda of the state. Polish scholar Michał Słomka echoes this, claiming that the recent historical turn in comics has led to the deterioration of the medium, hampering the growth of original graphic narratives. He also notes that some of these comic books revive the strategies used in Communist-era publications, including one-dimensional characters, conventional representation of specific themes, arbitrary choice of topics, and unnatural dialogues (80–81). Słomka certainly has a point. It is all the more relevant since throughout the 2000s there was a proliferation of publishers like Zin Zin Press. Public institutions, such as the Museum of the Warsaw Rising, the Institute of National Remembrance, and the Auschwitz Museum, started their own series aimed at supporting

---

6. The idea of Poland as the "Christ of Nations" or the rampart of Christian Europe is a fifteenth-century invention that was revived in the nineteenth century and often linked with the Polish opposition movement under Communism. See Wagner 202–5; Zubrzycki 68–69.

educational activities. However, unlike Zin Zin Press, which focuses on high-profile historical events, many of these outlets opt for lesser-known stories. At the same time, they strive to create narratives with a high level of factual content and realism that would be accessible and appealing to adolescents.

The multilingual series *Epizody z Auschwitz* (*Scenes from Auschwitz*), devised by the Auschwitz Museum in cooperation with K&L Press, is one case in point. Despite selecting unconventional plotlines, with the first album recalling a true story of an Auschwitz love affair between a Jewish woman and a Polish man, the stories can disappoint at times. In their attempt to offer a reliable portrayal of historical events, many of these stories overemphasize "historical objectivity" and the ability of comics to provide an "accurate" portrayal of the past (see, e.g., Gałek and Nowakowski 39). Issues that might be unclear or considered problematic by the reader are explained in both the introduction and the afterword, as is the case with the third album in the series, recalling the story of the "saint of Auschwitz," Father Maksymilian Kolbe, who sacrificed himself for another prisoner selected to die of starvation. As the editors rightly point out, Kolbe's prewar "journalism is criticized at times as antisemitic" (Gałek and Poller 39). They argue, however, that his criticism of Jews should not be viewed as racially motivated but rather as an outcome of the specific socioeconomic climate of the time, including the economic recession of the 1930s (39). The comic itself presupposes, nonetheless, that the Franciscan's views originated in his reading of *The Protocols of the Elders of Zion,* a fraudulent text describing the alleged Jewish plans to dominate the world, which lies at the basis of twentieth-century anti-Semitism (Gałek and Poller 11). To balance this representation, the album gives examples of the monk's compassion toward his Jewish fellow prisoners at Auschwitz (26). While it is clear that the scriptwriter attempts to present a judicious portrayal of this sensitive issue, the brevity, simplicity, and educational function of the comic render it impossible to provide a convincing argument.

The whitewashing of Kolbe's anti-Jewish statements is by no means limited to this particular comic book. As Paolino Nappi shows in his discussion of Italian comics on Kolbe, produced by the Catholic Church in the 1970s and 1980s, the monk featured prominently in narratives that were aimed at claiming Auschwitz as an important site of Christian martyrdom (53–54). This "de-Judification" of the Shoah, as I have called it elsewhere, is typical also for other Polish comics on Auschwitz, whereby it is the Christian victims of Nazi extermination camps that often take center stage in those narratives (see Stańczyk).

The cover of the Polish comic on Kolbe seems to echo that point. It portrays a hand of an Auschwitz prisoner praying the rosary. His striped pyjamas, which have by now become almost synonymous with Jewish victims, are visible in the top corner of the image. The juxtaposition of this particular symbol of Auschwitz with the Christian rosary (and the Christian identity of the prisoner) brings to mind the public discussions of the 1990s, including the so-called war of the crosses, which placed the former extermination camp at the heart of wider attempts to redefine the nation in the aftermath of political transformation (figure 5.1). As a contested site of "competitive suffering," Auschwitz featured powerfully in the ongoing discussions on Polish victimhood (see Zubrzycki). The cover harks back to that narrative, granting primacy to Christian suffering, and using Kolbe to embody the "Christian sacrifice" in Auschwitz. According to Nappi, such "quasi-educational hagiographies for youngsters skew and distort historical realities . . . to fit in with the Catholic ethos of sacrifice," while calling "the didactic value of the stories into question" (54).

In post-2000 Poland, governed by the free-market economy, publishers and creators of comic books have tried to capitalize on the recent "historical turn." The history of World War II and Communism have become the main focus of these attempts. These developments have been bound up inextricably with the redefinition of national identity and the shifting of the cultural economy following the collapse of Communism. Consequently, the production of historical comic albums has become largely subservient to mirroring dominant narratives of Poland's traumatic past. Graphic accounts adhering to such a vision of history have been mushrooming in Poland, particularly in the last fifteen years. Stimulated by generous state funding, annual comic competitions organized by state institutions, and the growing importance of certain publishing outlets, such as Zin Zin Press, these publications have dominated the perceived view of historical comics. This trend has been succinctly described by journalist Sebastian Frąckiewicz, who said that such works contained "Za dużo Polski, za mało autora" (too much of Poland, too little of the author). In other words, Frąckiewicz claims that the excessive focus on national history has hampered the individuality and originality of comics creators in favor of nationalistically minded narratives (Frąckiewicz, "Za dużo" 82–83).

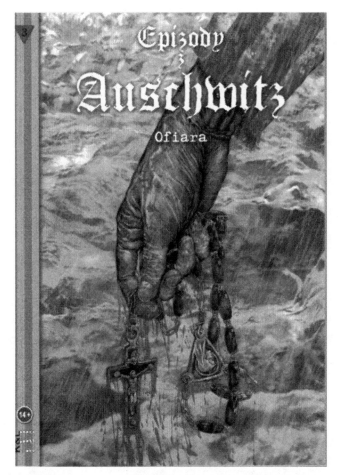

**FIGURE 5.1.** Cover image, *Epizody z Auschwitz: Ofiara* (K&L Press, 2009)

Alternative projects exploring fictionalized stories of the past have been less fortunate in attracting government subsidies and not as vital in shaping the popular view of the past.[7] Rather, once more, the state-funded stories turned comics into powerful tools of ideological struggle. Enforcing fact-based plotlines that were meant to run counter to the propagandistic and supposedly distorted stories of the Communist era, many of these publications fell into the trap of repeating some of the models developed by state-funded publishers under Communism.

---

7. Two stories that deserve particular attention are Jacek Frąś's *Kaczka* (*The Duck*) and *Stan* (*The State*).

Such narratives are inevitably prone to reflecting various ideological tensions. Discussing the American context, Jorge Santos shows that even the liberal civil rights comics that attempt to expand the readers' understanding of the movement are still bound to succumb to certain prescribed narratives of memory, which, in this case, call for themes of "nonviolence, integration, and martyrdom" (10). Understandably, such works stand little chance of providing a powerful counternarrative of the past. It remains to be seen how the funding strategies will develop in Poland and to what extent they will continue to support new nationally minded stories. The slowing down of the educational comics market, visible in the past few years, could herald a gradual departure from such narratives. In order for this to happen, the cultural policy might need to move away from the past and focus on the present. This would possibly mean realizing some of the appeals from the 1990s, such as investing in local talent and supporting original narratives.

## Conclusion

One hundred years after the emergence of comics in Poland, contemporary graphic narratives continue to be shaped by some of the same forces as their antecedents under Communism and earlier. These include funding sources and the associated pressures, the continued interaction between native and foreign fashions, and political influences of all kinds. Despite these similarities, the two trends discussed in this chapter merit discrete attention and close analysis. Both trends are illustrative of the continued reckoning with the past that has been happening in Poland since the 1990s. This process, as we have seen, has had individual and collective dimensions. The autobiographical trend, exemplified by *Totalnie nie nostalgia*, is representative of a wider turn toward a social history of Communism, visible both in the cultural production and the historiography of the past twenty years. Women's voices, in particular, became more prominent in such narratives.[8] Everyday life under Communism has featured in a variety of comics from the region, offering insight into the private sphere in the Eastern Bloc. Representative examples include the works of Marzena Sowa, mentioned above, and Romanian Andreea Chirică (e.g.,

---

8. For recent work in the social history of Poland, see, for example, Fidelis; Mazurek, "Keeping" and "Dishonest."

*The Year of the Pioneer*; 2011), in addition to others.[9] The second trend, represented by Zin Zin Press and other state-funded publications, speaks to the official efforts to gain control over the national past. This has been particularly prominent since 2001, when the Law and Justice Party emerged as the leading actor in national-conservative memory-making.

Even if distinct in terms of themes, publishers, and creators, the two trends are part of a broader discussion on the limits of representation, particularly where portrayals of the past are concerned (see, e.g., Frey and Noys 258–59). Comics and graphic novels from other countries, which tackle painful history and explore the possibility of healing through creative activity, show that this has been a prominent theme in the past few decades. In particular, we have seen such themes explored by a variety of graphic narratives by child survivors of the Holocaust as well as second- and third-generation authors, to mention the work of Miriam Katin, Art Spiegelman, Bernice Eisenstein, Amy Kurzweil, and others.[10] The preoccupation with memory (be it personal or collective) is, of course, pervasive in most societies today, as the works of countless scholars, such as Pierre Norra, Maurice Halbwachs, Aleida Assman, Jeffrey K. Olick, and many others, have shown.[11] It is only fitting, then, that memory has found its way into comics too.

The works discussed in this chapter provide a fitting end to this book too. Published nearly 100 years after *Szczutek's Ogniem i mieczem, czyli Przygody szalonego Grzesia* (1919), the story of a patriotic Pole fighting on several fronts to consolidate Poland's porous state borders, these narratives speak to the continuities and ruptures in Polish comics. Those have largely mirrored the vicissitudes of national history, the shifts between sovereignty and conquest, between "us" and "them," and between "then" and "now." It is fair to say that the authors' continued preoccupation with the nation and the persistent fascination with the West have both run consistently through the history of comics in Poland. It is somewhat striking, however, that such defining features of Polish national identity have been so central to a medium that, for decades, has been seen as inept, unsophisticated, and fundamentally alien to the homegrown culture.

---

9. For a discussion of the Romanian comic book, see Precup.

10. There is an extensive scholarly literature covering these works. For a most recent and comprehensive publication, see Aarons.

11. Memory studies is a continuously growing field of study. For a recent comprehensive collection of studies in the field, see, for example, Tota and Hagen.

# CONCLUSION

Poland might not be the first country that comes to mind when one thinks of comics. Why study Polish comics, then? Even more so, what do we learn from examining the impact of global comic culture on Poland? As I have shown in the course of this book, Polish readers, critics, and artists have been passionate consumers and producers of comics for at least one century now. During this time, comics (both native and foreign) have been central to the redefinition of Polish culture and Poland's place in the wider world. Comics and debates surrounding comics have featured prominently in the reconfiguration of the nation as, respectively, modern, socialist, European, and post-Communist. The interrelated categories of citizenship, state building, and personal/collective identity have all played a role in these processes. Comics' producers, consumers, and uninvolved observers have used the medium to examine and respond to wider political, social, cultural, and economic changes. It has been those various actors, be it comics' advocates or adversaries, who have contributed to the creation of the Polish comic culture.

As we have seen in the course of this book, comics gained traction around important moments of transformation, be it the establishment of the Polish state in 1918, the consolidation of Communist power in the late 1940s, the gradual opening to the West in the 1970s, and the transition to a free-market economy in the 1990s and later. Chapter 1 showed how comics and the attendant products of American and European popular culture allowed for the reconfiguration of Poland's symbolic cultural geographies, partaking in the transition from the imperial period to an independent state and, ultimately, supporting the consolidation of that nascent state. Chapter 2 demonstrated how the ferocious anti-comics/anti-American campaign, undertaken despite an absence of comics, fueled socialist state building and signaled growing Cold War rivalries. Chapter 3 focused on the supposed *cud gospodarczy* (economic miracle) of Gierek's Poland, whereby increased consumption of comics became part of the "propaganda of success." This was eventually stalled by the stagnation of the late 1970s and the clamping down on the previously instituted freedoms, culminating in the imposition of martial law in 1981. Chapter 4 discussed how the long-awaited transition to democracy brought about both a mass influx of substandard products of foreign popular culture and a general disillusionment with Western-style capitalism. Chapter 5 showed how comics came to be used to comprehend the new political reality that emerged in Poland in the early 2000s, facilitating the authors' efforts to shed the vestiges of authoritarian legacies and "move on," both as individuals and as a nation.

For nearly one century now, the production, reception, and consumption of comics in Poland has been a subtle balancing act between homegrown, European, American, and, more recently, Japanese influences. Polish journalists, artists, intellectuals, and readers alike have employed comics (and discussions around comics) to negotiate these various attachments. At different points in Polish history, comics have been a moniker for the "colorful" American mass media, a byword for all that was wrong with the "imperialist" enemy, and a bitter symbol of the capitalist dream gone wrong. How did Europe fit into these dynamics? In the 1970s, Polish commentators envisioned Europe as the eternal horizon of their cultural and intellectual pursuits, while Europe was an aspiration that could not (yet) be fully realized. Later on, in the 1990s, Europe became a long-lost ally who shared the burden of American-style mass consumerism and bore the brunt of the "invasion" of other foreign fashions, including Japanese manga and anime. The homegrown comics were imagined alternately as a medium that still needed to mature in order to reach its full potential, a medium that was distinctly alien to Polish culture, a medium that has been misused by those in power, and a medium that could serve both individual and collective interests.

From the moment comics appeared in Poland, illustrators and readers alike embraced their intrinsically malleable nature. Acculturation, syncretism, hybridization, and mimicry have all been part of the package. Foreign comics have thus been adapted and manipulated to charm local audiences; stories were altered and names Polonized, as the interwar renderings of *Pat and Patachon, Superman, Adamson,* and other graphic narratives demonstrate. New stories were modeled on famous foreign series, too, to mention Drozdowski's famous spin-off *Wicek i Wacek.* This pliability of the medium was exploited in socialist Poland, too, where issues surrounding intellectual property were, to put it mildly, occasionally flouted. *Kajko i Kokosz* and *Binio Bill,* the Polish knockoffs of *Asterix and Obelix* and *Lucky Luke,* respectively, were representative of these practices. At different points of the past century, comics were conflated with other media and their sororal links emphasized, for a variety of reasons, publicity being one of them. For example, in the interbellum comics were inosculated with film, Disney animations in particular. In the 1960s and 1970s, television series, specifically *Stawka większa niż życie,* were used as a springboard for comic adaptations, which were also exported abroad. We saw a reversal of these practices in the 1990s, when the popularity of Japanese anime spurred interest in the manga series that preceded it, to mention the example of *Sailor Moon.*

It is fair to say that it was through comics and the associated print media that Polish readers were able to partake in a truly global visual culture already in the interwar period. Although the knowledge of being part of that global community was largely suppressed through the early decades of Communist Poland, the glimmers of that exposure could be felt again in the 1970s. This is when state censorship allowed cultural editors and commentators to acknowledge the participation of Polish readers in that rich interwar tradition, as some of the press articles discussed in this book showed. It is no wonder, then, that many readers, critics, and illustrators in socialist Poland felt they were forcibly removed from that global milieu and longed to be part of it again. Once global popular culture arrived in Poland in the 1990s, many felt indignant that this was not what they had longed for.

The comic has thus been a highly emotive site that allowed for the processing of collective affects, be it those constructed by political elites, intellectuals, readers, or comic book creators. From the fascination with American mass media in the interbellum, to the state-enforced sense of threat around the corrupting effects of comics in the 1950s, to the yearning for foreign comics by intellectuals and readers in the 1970s, to a feeling of being overrun by imported "junk" in the 1990s, for nearly one century, the medium has been an important site of affective and imaginative attachment.

While some scholars tend to disregard the Cold War criticism of comics as ideological and, thus, somewhat aberrant, I would argue it tells us as much about the emotional community that formed around the medium as the (supposedly unpoliticized) voices of its exponents. Even if happening in different historical periods and having distinctive focal points, not one of the debates discussed in this book happened in a void. The proponents and opponents of the medium have always been inadvertent partners in an ongoing dialogue, both with each other and with global players in the field. Even at the height of Stalinism, Wertham's voice was heard loud and clear in Poland, and was embraced as representing universal moral codes, despite the ideological divide enforced by the Cold War.

Now that the comic has been seemingly nativized, and the access to global production is no longer restricted, the medium has lost much of that affective power. While scholars, journalists, and fans still like to debate the comic, trying to break that "invisible wall" that supposedly separates it from other art forms, the medium has now been largely freed from the rhetorical fold it had inhabited for so long. The comic—as a discursive construct—is no longer a vessel waiting to be filled with new political, social, and cultural meanings. It is a medium that has been adopted as part of the everyday life in Poland, one that is no longer feared or disregarded. Comics— the artistic products—are once more works in their own right. They are used to speak about individual and collective experiences. They tackle both the grand narratives promoted by the government and the deeply personal stories of individual artists. Like their interwar and socialist-era predecessors, contemporary comics, too, portray gallant freedom fighters sitting atop tanks and barricades. Unlike the earlier works, however, they have also developed the autobiographical idiom, which bears the imprint of the social and political emancipation of the past few decades. Comics in Poland have diversified beyond recognition and continue to do so.

At the same time, the comic in Poland is not, and is unlikely ever to become, a product of mass culture. The sale figures are low, rarely above 1,000 copies per title. Publishing houses specializing in the medium tend to be small enterprises, consisting of one or two employees. Accomplished artists are often underfunded and forced to combine creative work with commissioned projects. But the future of Polish comics is not all that bleak. Since the early 1990s, we have seen an unparalleled growth of fan culture, as exemplified by the International Festival of Comics and Games, held annually in Łódź. In the past thirty years, several important exhibitions have been held in Poland that have told the history of homegrown comics. Artists are increasingly drawn to the medium, too, viewing it as an attractive and challenging format with which to address contemporary audiences. More and more, both veterans and newcomers to the scene tend to turn to familiar themes that speak to local sensitivities and capture the flavors of the Polish province, urban lifestyles, and contemporary identities. The present-day comic book in Poland is absorbing the best foreign models and shedding those influences that are detrimental to its growth. This is still a largely uncharted territory, one that deserves a more sustained analysis and, perhaps, even a separate book.

# BIBLIOGRAPHY

"10 tys. listów do kpt. Żbika." *Kurier Polski,* 4 July 1973.

"23rd Ball to Aid Kosciuszko Fund." *New York Times,* 18 March 1956.

"320 tys. zwiedzających na wystawie 'Oto Ameryka.'" *Życie Warszawy,* 13 February 1953, p. 4.

"5,000 Youths Attend St. Patrick's Mass." *New York Times,* 12 November 1950.

"700 Attend a Gala of Kosciuszko Fund." *New York Times,* 23 January 1966.

A. L. "O komiksach i ich brodatej historii." *Express Ilustrowany,* 1 October 1976, p. 8.

Aarons, Victoria. *Holocaust Graphic Narratives: Generation, Trauma, and Memory.* Rutgers UP, 2019.

Adams, Mary Louise. "Youth, Corruptibility, and English-Canadian Postwar Campaigns against Indecency, 1948–1955." *Journal of the History of Sexuality,* vol. 6, 1995, pp. 89–117.

Advertisement for bibs "St 2369." *Przegląd Mody,* vol. 9, no. 15, 1937, p. 36.

Ahmed, Maaheen, and Jean-Louis Tilleuil. Introduction. *Le statut culturel de la bande dessinée—Ambiguïtés et évolutions,* edited by Maaheen Ahmed, Stéphanie Delneste, and Jean-Louis Tilleuil, Academia—L'Harmattan, 2016, pp. 23–36.

Ahrens, Jörn, and Arno Meteling. Introduction. *Comics and the City: Urban Space in Print, Picture and Sequence,* Continuum, 2010, pp. 1–16.

Alaniz, José. "Eastern/Central European Comics." *The Routledge Companion to Comics,* edited by Frank Bramlett, Roy T. Cook, and Aaron Meskin, Routledge, 2017, pp. 98–105.

——. *Komiks: Comic Art in Russia.* U of Mississippi P, 2010.

"Aleksander Hertz, Author, 87; Studied Sociology of Theater" (Obituary). *New York Times,* 18 May 1983.

Allen, Debra J. *The Oder-Neisse Line: The United States, Poland, and Germany in the Cold War.* Praeger, 2003.

"Anioł pod szminką," "Jedynaczka króla nafty," and "'Roxy' w warszawskim Teatrze Małym." *Ilustrowany Kuryer Codzienny,* 18 July 1931.

Arct., Michał. "Myszka Miki." *Małe Pisemko,* 25 June 1932, p. 1.

Arski, Stefan. "Superman i powrotny analfabetyzm." *Nowa Kultura,* vol. 2, no. 94, 1952, p. 2.

Assouline, Pierre. *Hergé: The Man Who Created Tintin.* Translated by Charles Ruas, Oxford UP, 2009.

"Astérix i Obélix rozśmieszają Francuzów." *Tygodnik Kulturalny,* 23 January 1977, p. 12.

"Atomowe 'comicsy.'" *Słowo Ludu,* 4–5 May 1954, p. 2.

Bainbridge, Jason, and Craig Norris. "Hybrid Manga: Implications for the Global Knowledge Economy." *Manga: An Anthology of Global and Cultural Perspectives,* edited by Toni Johnson-Woods, Continuum, 2010, pp. 235–52.

"Baj i Disney." *Czas,* 9 October 1938, p. 11.

Banach, Andrzej. "Mała historia komiksów." *Projekt,* vol. 3, no. 42, 1964, pp. 16–21.

Banasiak, Jakub, and Sebastian Frąckiewicz. "W tym szczególnym momencie. Polski komiks u progu drugiej dekady XXI wieku." *Wyjście z getta. Rozmowy o kulturze komiksowej w Polsce,* edited by in Sebastian Frąckiewicz, Stowarzyszenie 4000 malarzy, 2012, pp. 7–17.

Bańdo, Adam. "'Ilustrowany Kurier Codzienny' w dziewięćdziesiątą rocznicę powstania (1910–2000)." *Annales Academiae Paedagogicae Cracoviensis. Studia Ad Bibliothecarum Scientiam Pertinentia,* vol. 9, no. 2, 2003, pp. 119–44.

Barańczak, Stanisław. "Blurp!" *Książki najgorsze i parę innych ekscesów krytyczno-literackich 1974–1980 i 1993,* Wydawnictwo Znak, 2009, pp. 94–105.

——. "Kapitan Żbik w świetle najnowszych ustaleń historii sztuki europejskiej." *Książki najgorsze i parę innych ekscesów krytyczno-literackich 1974–1980 i 1993,* Wydawnictwo Znak, 2009, pp. 40–41.

Barker, Martin. *A Haunt of Fears: The Strange History of the British Horror Comics Campaign.* UP of Mississippi, 1992.

Barrier, Michael. *Hollywood Cartoons: American Animation in Its Golden Age.* Oxford UP, 1999.

Baudry, Julien, and Marie-Pierre Litaudon. "Hachette entre héritage et renouvellement (1920–1960): comment 'faire collection' face au défi des albums 'transmédiatiques'?" *Strenæ: Recherches sur les livres et objets culturels de l'enfance,* vol. 11, 2016, pp. 1–29.

Bazylewicz, Tomasz. "Transfer of Japanese Culture Patterns on the Example of Comic Book: How Manga Conquered the World and Became an Integral Part of the Polish Publishing Market." *Studia Historiae Oeconomicae,* vol. 36, 2018, pp. 105–23.

Beaty, Bart. "Autobiography as Authenticity." *A Comics Studies Reader,* edited by Jeet Heer and Kent Worcester, UP of Mississippi, 2009, pp. 226–35.

———. *Fredric Wertham and the Critique of Mass Culture.* UP of Mississippi, 2005.

Becattini, Alberto. *Disney Comics: The Whole Story.* Theme Park Press, 2016.

Bellido, Jose, and Kathy Bowrey. "Disney in Spain (1930–1935)." *Business History,* vol. 60, no. 8, 2018, pp. 1277–307.

BET. "Komiksowo." *Gazeta Wyborcza,* 11 March 1999.

"Bezrobotny Froncek na dożynkach w Wodzisławiu." *Siedem Groszy,* 25 August 1935, p. 2.

"Bezrobotny Froncek w kinie 'Apollo' w Rybniku." *Siedem Groszy,* 29 April 1936, p. 2.

"Bezrobotny Froncek z Mikołajem wciąż jeżdżą po Śląsku." *Siedem Groszy,* 10 December 1938, p. 2.

"Biblia w comicsach." *Życie Warszawy,* 26 September 1953, p. 2.

Bidwell, George. *Ani chwili nudy.* Wydawnictwo Śląskie, 1976.

———. "Ponury import z USA." *Dziennik Łódzki,* 24–26 December 1952, p. 2.

Bieloch, Katharina, and Sharif Bitar. "Batman Goes Transnational: The Global Appropriation and Distribution of an American Hero." *Transnational Perspectives on Graphic Narratives: Comics at the Crossroads,* edited by Shane Denson, Christina Meyer, and Daniel Stein, Bloomsbury, 2013, pp. 113–26.

Birek, Wojciech. "Od Żbika do Thorgala." *Rzeczpospolita,* 8 March 2003, p. A12.

Blaustein, George. *Nightmare Envy and Other Stories: American Culture and European Reconstruction.* Oxford UP, 2018.

Boguszewska, Anna. "Ilustratorzy wybranych baśni polskich." *Annales Universitatis Mariae Curie-Skłodowska. Sectio L. Artes,* vol. 3, no. 4, 2005/2006, pp. 79–92.

Boguta, Grzegorz. "From the Surveillance of the Secret Police to the 'Free Market': Publishing in Poland Today." *Agni,* vol. 31, no. 32, 1990, pp. 50–52.

Bolałek, Radosław. "Trzy pokolenia fanów mangi." *Zeszyty Komiksowe,* vol. 13, 2012, pp. 4–9.

Borkowska, Anna. "Superman Żbik." *Perspektywy,* 13 May 1977, p. 28.

Borowkin, Stanisław. "'Gazetka Miki' (1938–1939)." *Kwartalnik Historii Prasy Polskiej,* vol. 27, no. 1, 1988, pp. 39–49.

Bouissou, Jean-Marie. "Popular Culture as a Tool for Japanese 'Soft Power': Myth or Reality? Manga in Four European Countries." *Popular Culture and the State in East and Southeast Asia,* edited by in Nissim Otmazgin and Eyal Ben-Ari, Routledge, 2011, pp. 46–64.

———. "Pourquoi aimons-nous le manga? Une approche économique du nouveau soft power japonais." *Cités,* vol. 27, no. 3, 2006, pp. 71–84.

Bouissou, Jean-Marie, Marco Pellitteri, and Bernd Dolle-Weinkauff, with Ariane Beldi. "Manga in Europe: A Short Study of Market and Fandom." *Manga: An Anthology of Global and Cultural Perspectives,* edited by Toni Johnson-Woods, Continuum, 2010, pp. 253–66.

Brannigan, Augustine. "Delinquency, Comics and Legislative Reactions: An Analysis of Obscenity Law Reform in Post-war Canada and Victoria." *Australian-Canadian Studies,* vol. 3, 1985, pp. 53–69.

Bren, Paulina, and Mary Neuburger. Introduction. *Communism Unwrapped: Consumption in Cold War Eastern Europe,* edited by Paulina Bren and Mary Neuburger, Oxford UP, 2012, pp. 3–17.

Bromke, Adam. "La nouvelle élite politique en Pologne." *Revue de l'Est,* vol. 5, no. 3, 1974, pp. 7–18.

Bryan, Julien. "Documentary Record of the Last Days of Once Proud Warsaw." *Life,* 23 October 1939, pp. 73–77.

Buszman, Łukasz. "Niepohamowane obrazy." *Dziennik Zachodni,* 26 February 2000.

Campbell, Bruce. ¡*Viva la historieta!: Mexican comics, NAFTA, and the Politics of Globalization.* UP of Mississippi, 2009.

Catalá Carrasco, Jorge, Paulo Drinot, and James Scorer. Introduction. *Comics and Memory in Latin America,* U of Pittsburgh P, 2017, pp. 3–32.

Central Intelligence Agency (CIA) Archive. CIA-RDP85T00875R001100130078–7, "Gierek's Poland: A Mandate for Change (Intelligence Memorandum)." 17 May 1972.

———. General CIA Records, CIA-RDP82–00046R000300050010–2, "Poland: Popular Attitudes." 17 December 1953.

Chaciński, Bartłomiej. "Antypolska 'Mysz'?" *Życie,* 11–12 October 1997.

Chęcińska, Elżbieta. "Niełatwe życie komiksu." *Głos Pomorza,* 23 August 1990.

Chełminiak, Wiesław. "Smutek dymków." *Życie Warszawy,* 11 June 2005.

"Chickie idzie w świat." *Ilustrowany Kuryer Codzienny,* 17 May 1932.

Chioni Moore, David. "Is the Post- in Postcolonial the Post- in Post-Soviet? Toward a Global Postcolonial Critique." *PMLA,* vol. 116, no. 1, 2001, pp. 111–28.

Chmielewski, Henryk Jerzy. "Nasycony komiksami." Interview by Piotr Kitrasiewicz, *Gazeta Współczesna. Tele-Program,* 5–7 April 2002.

———. *Urodziłem się w Barbakanie.* Prószyński i S-ka, 1999.

Christa, Janusz. "Kajtek Majtek." *Dookoła świata,* 17 October 1971, p. 2.

———. "Kapitan Żbik powróci?" Interview by Paweł Bieńka, *Słowo Ludu,* 3–4 December 1994.

Chudoba, Marcin. "Komiksy wydawnictwa Marvel Comics na polskim rynku wydawniczym w latach 2012–2016 (publikacje zwarte)." *Annales Universitatis Paedagogicae Cracoviensis. Studia ad Bibliothecarum Scientiam Pertinentia,* vol. 15, 2017, pp. 268–85.

———. "Sentymentalna historia oficyny TM-Semic (uwagi nad książką Łukasza Kowalczuka TM-Semic: największe komiksowe wydawnictwo lat dziewięćdziesiątych w Polsce)." *Annales Universitatis Paedagogicae Cracoviensis. Studia ad Bibliothecarum Scientiam Pertinentia,* vol. 15, 2017, pp. 408–11.

Chute, Hillary. "Comics Form and Narrating Lives." *Profession,* 2011, pp. 107–17.

———. *Disaster Drawn: Visual Witness, Comics, and Documentary Form.* Harvard UP, 2016.

———. *Graphic Women. Life Narrative & Contemporary Comics.* Columbia UP, 2002.

Ciborska, Elżbieta. *Leksykon polskiego dziennikarstwa.* Dom Wydawniczy Elipsa, 2000.

Clark, Emily. "Of Catholics, Commies, and the Anti-Christ: Mapping American Social Borders through Cold War Comic Books." *Journal of Religion and Popular Culture,* vol. 21, no. 3, 2009, pp. 1–42.

"'Comicsy' i wolność." *Życie Warszawy,* 31 May 1955, p. 3.

"Comicsy, pasja współczesności." *Życie Literackie,* vol. 27, no. 7, 1967, p. 11.

Constantino, Manuela. "Marji: Popular Commix Heroine Breathing Life into the Writing History." *Canadian Review of American Studies/Revue canadienne d'études américaines*, vol. 38, 2008, pp. 429–47.

Conway, Christopher, and Antoinette Sol. "Introduction: The Globalization of the Comic Book Western." *The Comic Book Western: New Perspectives on a Global Genre*, edited by Christopher Conway and Antoinette Sol, U of Nebraska P, 2022, pp. 1–34.

Cook, Roy T. "Underground and Alternative Comics." *The Routledge Companion to Comics*, edited by Frank Bramlett, Roy T. Cook, and Aaron Meskin, Routledge, 2017, pp. 34–43.

Cortsen, Rikke Platz, Erin La Cour, and Anne Magnussen. Introduction. *Comics and Power: Representing and Questioning Culture, Subjects, and Communities*, edited by Rikke Platz Cortsen, Erin La Cour, and Anne Magnussen, Cambridge Scholars Publishing, 2015, pp. xvii–xxv.

Costigliola, Frank. "American Foreign Policy in the 'Nut Cracker': The United States and Poland in the 1920s." *Pacific Historical Review*, vol. 48, no. 1, 1979, pp. 85–105.

Cowan, Michael. "Learning to Love the Movies: Puzzles, Participation, and Cinephilia in Interwar European Film Magazines." *Film History*, vol. 27, no. 4, 2015, pp. 1–45.

Crist, Judith. "Horror in the Nursery." *Collier's*, 27 March 1948, pp. 22–23, 95–97.

Crowley, David. *Warsaw*. Reaktion Books, 2003.

Cybulski, Władysław. "Wystawa w Muzeum Narodowym 'Oto Ameryka.'" *Dziennik Polski*, 5 March 1954, p. 4.

Czaja, Justyna. *Historia Polski w komiksowych kadrach*. PTPN, 2010.

Czaja, Justyna, and Michał Traczyk, editors. *Komiks. Wokół warstwy wizualnej*. Instytut Kultury Popularnej, Biblioteka Uniwersytecka w Poznaniu, 2016.

Czeszko, Bohdan. "Komiksy po polsku." *Nowe Książki*, 30 June 1978, pp. 42–44.

Dajnowicz, Małgorzata. "'Walka o pokój' w wypowiedziach propagandowych publikowanych na łamach 'Naszej Pracy'—biuletynie Ligi Kobiet (1947–1953)." *Bezpieczeństwo Europy—bezpieczeństwo Polski*, vol. 5, edited by Ewa Maj, Wojciech Sokół, Anna Szwed-Walczak, and Łukasz Jędrzejski, Wydawnictwo UMCS, 2017, pp. 409–21.

Davé, Shilpa. "Spider-Man India: Comic Books and the Translating/Transcreating of American Cultural Narratives." *Transnational Perspectives on Graphic Narratives: Comics at the Crossroads*, edited by Shane Denson, Christina Meyer, and Daniel Stein, Bloomsbury, 2013, pp. 127–43.

David-Fox, Michael. "The Iron Curtain as Semipermeable Membrane: Origins and Demise of the Stalinist Superiority Complex." *Cold War Crossings: International Travel and Exchange across the Soviet Bloc, 1940s–1960s*, edited by Patryk Babiracki and Kenyon Zimmer, Texas A&M UP, 2014, pp. 14–39.

De Bruyn, Dieter. "Patriotism of Tomorrow? The Commemoration and Popularization of the Warsaw Rising through Comics." *Slovo*, vol. 22, 2010, pp. 46–65.

Delaney, Kate, and Andrzej Antoszek. "Americanization and Anti-Americanism in Poland: A Case Study, 1945–2006." *Global Perspectives on the United States: Pro-Americanism, Anti-Americanism, and the Discourses Between*, edited by Virginia R. Domínguez and Jane C. Desmond, U of Illinois P, 2017, pp. 73–91.

Denson, Shane, Christina Meyer, and Daniel Stein. "Introducing Transnational Perspectives on Graphic Narratives: Comics at the Crossroads." *Transnational Perspectives on Graphic Narratives: Comics at the Crossroads*, edited by Shane Denson, Christina Meyer, and Daniel Stein, Bloomsbury, 2013, pp. 1–14.

Dittmer, Jason. "Towards New (Graphic) Narratives of Europe." *International Journal of Cultural Policy*, vol. 20, no. 2, 2014, pp. 119–38.

"Dla dzieci i niepiśmiennych." *Perspektywy*, 24 June 1974.

Domagalska, Paulina. "Świetny komiks 'Totalnie nie nostalgia': PRL bez złudzeń, ale—niestety—z ojcem." *Gazeta Wyborcza*, 27 January 2017, p. 18.

Dorfman, Ariel. "Introduction to the Fourth Edition." *How to Read Donald Duck: Imperialist Ideology in the Disney Comic*, by Ariel Dorfman and Armand Mattelart, translated by David Kunzle, Pluto Press, 2019, pp. v–xii.

Dreimane, Jana. "Authors, Publishers and Readers of Popular Literature in Latvia in the Late 1980s and Early 1990s." *Interlitteraria*, vol. 20, no. 2, 2015, pp. 56–70.

*Drugi powszechny spis ludności z dn. 9. XII. 1931 r.* Główny Urząd Statystyczny Rzeczypospolitej Polskiej, 1938.

Dunin, Janusz. "Prolegomena do 'komiksologii.'" *Literatura Ludowa*, vol. 6, 1972, pp. 3–18.

Dziatkiewicz, Łukasz. "Japończycy robią duże oczy." *Przekrój*, 22 November 1998.

"Dziwne tropy kapitana Żbika." *Trybuna Ludu*, 25 March 1973.

Edelman, Lee. *No Future: Queer Theory and the Death Drive*. Duke UP, 2004.

Eedy, Sean. "Co-Opting Childhood and Obscuring Ideology in Mosaik von Hannes Hegen, 1959–1974." *Comics of the New Europe: Reflections and Intersections*, edited by Martha Kuhlman and José Alaniz, Leuven UP, 2020, pp. 143–57.

——. "Four Colour Anti-Fascism: Postwar Narratives and the Obfuscation of the Holocaust in East German Comics." *Journal of Modern Jewish Studies*, vol. 17, no. 1, 2018, pp. 24–35.

——. *Four-Color Communism. Comic Books and Contested Power in the German Democratic Republic*. Berghahn Books, 2021.

Ehrenburg, Ilya. "Odwrócimy wyloty dział od piersi człowieka. W tym naszym dążeniu jesteśmy jednomyślni. Przemówienie Ilii Erenburga na Kongresie w dniu 18 listopada br." *Dziennik Łódzki*, 19 November 1950, p. 2.

Ellwood, David W. *The Shock of America: Europe and the Challenge of the Century*. Oxford UP, 2012.

El Refaie, Elisabeth. *Autobiographical Comics: Life Writing in Pictures*. UP of Mississippi, 2012.

Estren, Mark James. *A History of Underground Comics: 20th Anniversary Edition*. Ronin Publishing, 2012.

Etty, John. *Graphic Satire in the Soviet Union: Krokodil's Political Cartoons*. UP of Mississippi, 2019.

Faber-Chojnacka, Anna. *Czasopisma krakowskie dla dzieci i młodzieży w dwudziestoleciu międzywojennym*. Wydawnictwo Naukowe WSP, 1995.

"Fenomen komiksu." *Głos Robotniczy*, 8–9 October 1988.

Fidelis, Małgorzata. *Women, Communism, and Industrialization in Postwar Poland*. Cambridge UP, 2010.

Fiut, Aleksander. *Spotkania z innym.* Wydawnictwo Literackie, 2006.

Forgacs, David, and Stephen Gundle. *Mass Culture and Italian Society from Fascism to the Cold War.* Indiana UP, 2007.

Frąckiewicz, Sebastian. "Komiks w polskiej komunikacji społecznej po 1989 roku." Unpublished MA Thesis, U of Poznań, 2006.

———. "Panie przodem." *Polityka,* 13 March 2013.

———. "Za dużo Polski, za mało autora." *Zeszyty Komiksowe,* vol. 12, 2011, pp. 82–83.

Frąś, Jacek. "Afterlives of Photographs: The Artist's Point of View." *Slavic Review,* vol. 76, no. 1, 2017, pp. 72–79.

———. "Cudze wspomnienia." Interview by Tomasz Pstrągowski, *Dwutygodnik.com,* https://www.dwutygodnik.com/artykul/6983-cudze-wspomnienia.html. Accessed 22 September 2020.

Freeman, Matthew. "Branding Consumerism: Crossmedia Characters and Storyworlds at the Turn of the 20th Century." *International Journal of Cultural Studies,* vol. 18, no. 6, 2015, pp. 629–44.

Frey, Hugo, and Benjamin Noys. "Editorial: History in the Graphic Novel." *Rethinking History,* vol. 6, 2002, pp. 255–60.

Friedman, Max Paul. "The Specter Haunting Europe." *Rethinking Anti-Americanism: The History of an Exceptional Concept in American Foreign Relations.* Cambridge UP, 2012, pp. 87–122.

Gabilliet, Jean-Paul. "C'était demain: 'Is This Tomorrow? America under Communism.'" *Culture américaine,* 30 July 2011.

———. "A Disappointing Crossing: The North American Reception of Asterix and Tintin." *Transnational Perspectives on Graphic Narratives: Comics at the Crossroads,* edited by Shane Denson, Christina Meyer, and Daniel Stein. Bloomsbury, 2013, pp. 257–70.

———. *Of Comics and Men: A Cultural History of American Comic Books.* Translated by Bart Beaty and Nick Nguyen, UP of Mississippi, 2014.

Gałek, Michał, and Marcin Nowakowski. *Epizody z Auschwitz: miłość w cieniu zagłady.* K&L Press, 2009.

Gałek, Michał, and Michał Poller. *Epizody z Auschwitz: ofiara.* K&L Press, 2009.

Gardner, Jared. *Projections: Comics and the History of Twenty-First-Century Storytelling.* Stanford UP, 2012.

Garnysz, Maria. "Osoba czy product? Nowa technika i nowe sytuacje." *Znak,* vol. 10, no. 7, 1958, pp. 796–814.

Gassert, Philipp. "With America against America: Anti-Americanism in West Germany." *The United States and Germany in the Era of the Cold War, 1945–1990,* edited by Detlef Junker, Cambridge UP, 2004, pp. 502–9.

Gębski, Józef. "Pif-paf! Pluuum plouff! Ooj . . . Comics!!!" *Magazyn filmowo-telewizyjny,* vol. 1, 1972, pp. 98–103.

Gierat-Bieroń, Bożena. "Kultura kontraktowa. Izabella Cywińska (12 września 1989–14 grudnia 1990)." *Ministrowie kultury doby transformacji, 1989–2005: Wywiady,* edited by Bożena Gierat-Bieroń, Universitas, 2009, pp. 19–32.

Gizicki, Daniel. "Polska rzeczywistość w polskim komiksie undergroundowym." *Zeszyty Komiksowe,* vol. 2, no. 10, 2004, p. 37.

Gmyz, Cezary. "Fipcio, Hipcio, Żbik i Tytus." *Życie,* 10–11 November 2001.

Golka, Marian. *Transformacja systemowa a kultura w Polsce po 1989 roku. Studia i szkice.* Instytut Kultury, 1997.

Gołębiewski, Łukasz. "Japoński komiks zdobywa Europę." *Rzeczpospolita,* 2 July 1997.

Góra, Anna. "Manga—niepohamowane obrazy." *Trybuna Śląska,* 12 November 1999.

Gordon, Ian. *Comic Strips and Consumer Culture 1890–1945.* Smithsonian Institution Press, 1998.

Górny, Alfred. "O komiksach i potędze futbolu." Interview by Jacek Semkowicz, *Perspektywy,* 29 November 1974, p. 36.

Górski, Artur. "Jak ze złego snu." *Polityka,* 20 December 1997.

Goscinny, René. "Goscinny o sobie i o komiksach." *Przekrój,* vol. 34, no. 1533, 1974, pp. 16–17.

Goscinny, René, and Sempé. "Rekreacje Mikołajka. O szkole na wesoło." *Przekrój,* vol. 34, no. 1533, 1974, p. 16.

Goślińska, Małgorzata. "Silny znaczy dobry." *Gazeta Wyborcza,* 11 December 2003.

Grącka, Monika. "Z historii polskiej animacji okresu międzywojennego." *Artyści sceny i ekranu dwudziestolecia międzywojennego Europy Środkowo-Wschodniej w ujęciu semiotyki antropologicznej,* edited by Robert Boroch and Yelena Karetina, Wydawnictwo Naukowe Instytutu Komunikacji Specjalistycznej i Interkulturowej Uniwersytet Warszawski, 2017, pp. 96–104.

Grodzicki, August. "Żoliborski Broadway." *Życie Warszawy,* 25 September 1957, p. 6.

Gross, Jan Tomasz. *Sąsiedzi: Historia zagłady żydowskiego miasteczka.* Fundacja Pogranicze, 2000.

Grove, Laurence. *Comics in French: The European Bande Dessinée in Context.* Berghahn Books, 2010.

Grzegorzewski, Krzysztof. "Obraz wartości PRL w komiksie Henryka Jerzego Chmielewskiego Tytus, Romek i A'Tomek (analiza ksiąg z lat 1966–1987)." *Acta Universitatis Lodziensis. Folia Litteraria Polonica,* vol. 3, no. 41, 2017, pp. 159–80.

Grzelecki, Stanisław. "Mały uciekinier." *Życie Warszawy,* 24 August 1955, p. 4.

Guentcheva, Rossitza. "Images of the West in Bulgarian Travel Writing during Socialism (1945–1989)." *Under Eastern Eyes: A Comparative Introduction to East European Travel Writing on Europe,* edited by Wendy Bracewell and Alex Drace-Francis, CEU Press, 2008, pp. 355–78.

Hagedorn, Wanda, and Jacek Frąś. *Totalnie nie nostalgia. Memuar.* Wydawnictwo Komiksowe, Kultura Gniewu, 2017.

Hajdu, David. *The Ten-Cent Plague: The Great Comic-Book Scare and How It Changed America.* Farrar, Straus and Giroux, 2009.

Hajduk-Gawron, Wioletta. "Komiks w kształceniu polonistycznym obcokrajowców." *Acta Universitatis Lodziensis,* vol. 17, 2010, pp. 351–58.

Hertz, Aleksander. "Amerykańskie klechdy obrazkowe." *Kuźnica,* vol. 34, 1947, pp. 4–5.

——. "Amerykańskie klechdy obrazkowe II." *Kuźnica,* vol. 35, 1947, p. 4.

——. "Czym jest kultura amerykańska?" *Kultura,* vol. 1, no. 51, 1952, pp. 21–32.

——. "Refleksje amerykańskie." *Kultura,* vol. 11, no. 97, 1955, pp. 35–60.

Hilbish, Melissa. "Advancing in Another Direction. The Comic Book and the Korean War." *War, Literature & the Arts: An International Journal of the Humanities*, vol. 11, no. 1, 1999, pp. 209–27.

Honsza, Norbert. "Nobilitacja komiksów." *Życie Literackie*, vol. 15, 1976, p. 7.

Howell, Jennifer. *The Algerian War in French-Language Comics: Postcolonial Memory, History, and Subjectivity*. Lexington Books, 2015.

Hunt, Nancy Rose. "Tintin and the Interruptions of Congolese Comics." *Images and Empires: Visuality in Colonial and Postcolonial Africa*, edited by Paul Landau and Deborah Kaspin, U of California P, 2002, pp. 90–123.

Isaak, Zbigniew. "Na tropach Chińszczyzny." *Dookoła świata*, 10 July 1960, pp. 12–13.

Isernia, Pierangelo. "Anti-Americanism in Europe during the Cold War." *Anti-Americanism in World Politics*, edited by Peter J. Katzenstein and Robert O. Keohane, Cornell UP, 2011, pp. 57–92.

Iwasiów, Inga. "Sok malinowy." *Znak*, vol. 743, 2017, pp. 100–103.

"Jak mała myszka Miki zdobyła świat." *Dzień dobry!*, 17 January 1938, p. 4.

Janicki, Bartłomiej. *Dydaktyczny potencjał komiksu historycznego*. Zin Zin Press, 2016.

——. "Rzetelność treści i obudowy dydaktycznej polskich komiksów historycznych (lata 1945–1991)." *Zeszyty Komiksowe. Komiks Historyczny*, vol. 12, 2011, pp. 30–35.

Janowski, Michał. "Naśladowanie mistrza." *Rzeczpospolita*, 7 February 1997.

Jasiński, Maciej. *Jerzy Wróblewski okiem współczesnych artystów komiksowych*. Ongrys, 2016.

Jasiński, Maciej, et al. *1956: Poznański Czerwiec*. Zin Zin Press, 2006.

——. *Solidarność: 25 lat. Nadzieja zwykłych ludzi*. Zin Zin Press, 2005.

Jaszuński, Grzegorz. "'Kultura' po amerykańsku. Miliony analfabetów—Brak szkół— Nie ma teatrów." *Życie Warszawy*, 6 May 1951, p. 5.

——. "Poważnie o 'comicsach.'" *Życie Warszawy*, 24–26 December 1954, p. 4.

Jaworski, Marcin. "'Obrócić się przeciw czasowi.' Opowieści alternatywne a wzorcowe wizje przeszłości historycznej na przykładzie wybranych komiksów polskich okresu PRL-u." *Creatio Fantastica*, vol. 2, no. 60, 2019, pp. 127–47.

——. *Urodzony, żeby rysować. Twórczość komiksowa Jerzego Wróblewskiego*. Wydawnictwo Naukowe Uniwersytetu Mikołaja Kopernika, 2016.

"Jeden rozwód co 55 minut." *Ilustrowany Kuryer Codzienny. Kuryer Kobiecy*, 23 July 1931.

Jensen, Helle Strandgaard. "Why Batman Was Bad: A Scandinavian Debate about Children's Consumption of Comics and Literature in the 1950s." *Barn*, vol. 28, 2010, pp. 47–70.

Jobs, Richard Ivan. "Tarzan under Attack: Youth, Comics, and Cultural Reconstruction in Postwar France." *Global Perspectives on Tarzan: From King of the Jungle to International Icon*, edited by Annette Wannamaker and Michelle Ann Abate, Routledge, 2015, pp. 73–106.

Jovanovic, Goran, and Ulrich Koch. "The Comics Debate in Germany: Against Dirt and Rubbish, Pictorial Idiotism, and Cultural Analphabetism." *Pulp Demons: International Dimensions of the Postwar Anti-Comics Campaign*, edited by John A. Lent, Fairleigh Dickinson UP, 1999, pp. 93–128.

Kaczorowska, Katarzyna. "Mangowy szał." *Gazeta Wrocławska,* 18 June 1999.

Kaider, W. "Wydawnictwa na eksport." *Echo Krakowa,* 9 May 1957, p. 3.

Kałucki, Jerzy. "Przygody Kajtka Majtka." *Dookoła świata,* 19 September 1971.

Kałużyński, Zygmunt. "Dajcie nam komiks." *Polityka,* 2 March 2002.

———. "Polak nie pasuje do komiksów." *Polityka,* 16 November 1985.

Kamusella, Tomasz. "Crocodile Skin, or the Fraternal Curtain." *The Antioch Review,* vol. 70, no. 4, 2012, pp. 742–59.

"Karol Ferster." *Przekrój,* vol. 48, no. 3515, 2012, p. 83.

Kauranen, Ralf. "Transnationalism in the Finnish 1950s Debate on Comics." *Comics and Power: Representing and Questioning Culture, Subjects, and Communities,* edited by Rikke Platz Cortsen, Erin La Cour, and Anne Magnussen, Cambridge Scholars Publishing, 2015, pp. 218–43.

K. C. K. "Adamson by Oscar Jacobsson." *Books Abroad,* vol. 4, no. 4, 1930, p. 363.

Keevak, Michael. *Becoming Yellow: A Short History of Racial Thinking.* Princeton UP, 2011.

Kępczyńska, Paulina. "Kto się boi mangi?" *Gazeta Poznańska,* 14–15 August 1997.

"Kilka słów o Baśce." *Wiosenka,* 30 May 1937, p. 1.

Klukowski, Bogdan, and Marek Tobera. *W tym niezwykłym czasie. Początki transformacji polskiego rynku książki (1989–1995).* Wydawnictwo Akademickie Sedno, 2013.

K. M. "Asteriks ulubieńcem dzieci." *Rzeczpospolita,* 30 July 1997.

Knight, Claire. "Enemy Films on Soviet Screens: Trophy Films during the Early Cold War, 1947–52." *Kritika,* vol. 18, no. 1, 2017, pp. 125–49.

Kobylański, Władysław. "Niektóre zagadnienia psychologii społecznej a badania prasoznawcze." *Prasa Współczesna i Dawna,* vol. 1, 1958, pp. 39–60.

Kochan, Marek. "Kapitan Żbik głosuje na Platformę, czyli komiks w służbie reklamy politycznej (analiza przypadku)." *Zeszyty Prasoznawcze,* vol. 44, nos. 3–4, 2001, pp. 37–57.

"Kochane Dzieci!" *Gazetka Miki,* 18 December 1938, p. 2.

"Kochany Miki!" *Gazetka Miki,* 15 January 1939, p. 2.

Kołodziejska, Jadwiga. "Reading and Libraries in Poland Today: Between Romantic Traditionalism and the Free Market." *The International Information & Library Review,* vol. 27, 1995, pp. 47–57.

"Komiks po japońsku." *Wiadomości dnia,* 28 August 1998.

"Komiks po polsku." *Słowo Powszechne,* 23 July 1980.

Konstantynów, Dariusz. "Antysemickie rysunki z prasy polskiej 1919–1939." *Obcy i niemili: antysemickie rysunki z prasy polskiej 1919–1939,* Żydowski Instytut Historyczny, 2013, pp. 35–48.

Kořínek, Pavel. "Self-Regulation and Self-Censorship: Comics Creators in Czechoslovakia and Communist Eastern Bloc." *The Oxford Handbook of Comic Book Studies,* edited by Frederick Luis Aldama, Oxford UP, 2020, pp. 239–55.

Kornbluth, Andrew. *The August Trials: The Holocaust and Postwar Justice in Poland.* Harvard UP, 2021.

Koryga, Magdalena. "Polskie edycje zbiorów baśni Braci Grimm." *Debiuty Bibliologiczno-Informatologiczne*, vol. 2, 2014, pp. 5–19.

"The Kosciuszko Foundation." *New York Times*, 17 October 1955, p. 26.

"The Kościuszko Foundation Exchange Program with Poland for the Academic Year 1988/89." *The Polish Review*, vol. 33, no. 2, 1988, pp. 260–65.

Kossak, Jerzy. "Kariera komiksów." *Kultura*, vol. 28, no. 3, 1965.

Kostyła, Joanna. "Mangamania." *Wprost*, 11 October 1998.

Kothenschulte, Daniel, J. B. Kaufman, David Gerstein, and Anna-Tina Kessler. *Walt Disney's Mickey Mouse: The Ultimate History*. Taschen, 2018.

Kowalczuk, Łukasz. *TM-Semic: największe komiksowe wydawnictwo lat dziewięćdziesiątych w Polsce*. Centrala, 2013.

"Kowboj goni indjanina." *Gazetka Miki*, 19 February 1939, p. 2.

"Kraków bliżej Francji." *Gazeta Krakowska*, 24 April 1999.

Krastev, Ivan. "The Anti-American Century?" *Journal of Democracy*, vol. 15, no. 2, 2004, pp. 5–16.

Kroes, Rob. *If You've Seen One You've Seen the Mall: Europeans and American Mass Culture*. U of Illinois P, 1995.

Krupka, Władysław. "Akuszer Żbika." Interview by Alex Kłoś, *Przekrój*, vol. 19, no. 2968, 2002, pp. 52–55.

Krzanicki, Marcin. *Komiks w PRL, PRL w komiksie*. IPN, 2011.

Krzysztofek, Kazimierz. "Ewolucja założeń i programów polityki kulturalnej w Polsce." *Kultura polska w dekadzie przemian*, edited by Teresa Kostyrko and Marcin Czerwiński, Instytut Kultury, 1999, pp. 267–95.

"'Książki,' których oni nie palą." *Dziennik Bałtycki*, 3 June 1954.

Kuczyńska, Kinga. "Zakończenie." *Polski komiks kobiecy*, edited by Kinga Kuczyńska. Timof i cisi wspólnicy, 2012, pp. 62–63.

Kuhlman, Martha, and José Alaniz. "General Introduction: Comics of the New Europe." *Comics of the New Europe: Reflections and Intersections*, edited by Martha Kuhlman and José Alaniz, Leuven UP, 2020, pp. 7–24.

Kundera, Milan. "The Tragedy of Central Europe." *The New York Review of Books*, vol. 31, no. 7, 1984, pp. 33–38.

Kunicki, Mikołaj. "A Socialist 007: East European Spy Dramas in the Early James Bond Era." *The Cultural Life of James Bond: Specters of 007*, edited by Jaap Verheul, Amsterdam UP, 2020, pp. 41–60.

Kunzle, David. *Father of the Comic Strip: Rodolphe Töpffer*. UP of Mississippi, 2007.

———. *History of the Comic Strip: The Nineteenth Century*. U of California P, 1990.

———. "Introduction to the English Edition." *How to Read Donald Duck: Imperialist Ideology in the Disney Comic*, by Ariel Dorfman and Armand Mattelart, translated by David Kunzle, Pluto Press, 2019, pp. 1–20.

———. "Precursors in American Weeklies to the American Newspaper Comic Strip: A Long Gestation and a Transoceanic Cross-breeding." *Forging a New Medium: The Comic Strip in the Nineteenth Century*, edited by Charles Dierick and Pascal Lefèvre, VUB Press, 1998, pp. 157–85.

Kurta, Henryk. "Bohaterowie." *Relax,* vol. 2, 1977, p. 2.

Landau-Czajka, Anna. *Wielki "Mały Przegląd": społeczeństwo i życie codzienne w II Rzeczypospolitej w oczach korespondentów "Małego Przeglądu."* Żydowski Instytut Historyczny, 2018.

Leinwand, Aleksandra J. "Bolszewicki plakat propagandowy w okresie wojny polsko--sowieckiej 1920 roku." *Studia z Dziejów Rosji i Europy Środkowo-Wschodniej,* vol. 27, 1992, pp. 75–87.

——. "Polski plakat propagandowy w okresie wojny polsko-sowieckiej (1919–1920)." *Studia z Dziejów Rosji i Europy Środkowo-Wschodniej,* vol. 28, 1993, pp. 57–67.

Lent, John A. "The Comics Debates Internationally: Their Genesis, Issues, and Commonalities." *Pulp Demons: International Dimensions of the Postwar Anti-Comics Campaign,* edited by John A. Lent, Fairleigh Dickinson UP, 1999, pp. 9–41.

Lesiakowski, Krzysztof. "'Aby Polska rosła w siłę . . .' Koncepcja unowocześnienia polskiej motoryzacji 1971–1972." *Przegląd Nauk Historycznych,* vol. 2, 2017, pp. 181–204.

Leśniak, Antoni. "Świat mangi." *Nasz Dziennik,* 3 August 2000, pp. 12–13.

Leszczyńska, Cecylia. "Level of Living of Polish Citizens in the Interwar Period, and Its Diversification." *Roczniki Dziejów Społecznych i Gospodarczych,* vol. 76, 2016, pp. 93–120.

Leszczyński, Adam. "Wojna koreańska w propagandzie polskiej od czerwca do grudnia 1950 roku." *Przegląd Historyczny,* vol. 86, no. 1, 1995, pp. 47–66.

Lewis, Flora. "A 10-Year Treaty of Friendship Is Signed by France and Poland." *New York Times,* 7 October 1972.

Leydi, Roberto. "Gdy komiksy kształtują modę." *Forum,* 13 October 1971.

Ligarski, Sebastian. "Polityka władz komunistycznych wobec twórców kultury w latach 1945–1989." *Pamięć i Sprawiedliwość,* vol. 2, 2014, pp. 51–73.

Lipiński, Eryk. *Drzewo Szpilkowe.* Czytelnik, 1976.

——. "Polak w Turcji . . ." *Życie Warszawy,* 3 November 1954, p. 2.

——. *Szpilki, 1935–1965: Coś nam zostało z tych lat . . .* Wydawnictwo Artystyczno-Graficzne RSW "Prasa," 1967.

Lipoński, Wojciech. "Anti-American Propaganda in Poland from 1948 to 1954: A Story of an Ideological Failure." *American Studies International,* vol. 28, no. 2, 1990, pp. 80–92.

"Listy, listy, listy. Trudno dogodzić każdemu." *Relax,* vol. 3, 1979, p. 2.

"Listy, listy, listy." *Relax,* vol. 4, 1978, p. 2.

"Listy, listy, listy." *Relax,* vol. 7, 1977, p. 2.

"Listy, listy. Poszukuję Relaxu." *Relax,* vol. 3, 1978, p. 2.

Loeb, Madeleine. "Anti-Comics Drive Reported Waning." *New York Times,* 21 January 1950.

London, Ivan D., and Oleg Anisimov. "The Soviet Propaganda Image of the West." *Psychological Reports,* vol. 3, 1957, pp. 19–65.

Lovell, Barbara. "O Salonie Komiksu Lucca-12." *Przekrój,* vol. 8, no. 1663, 1977, p. 23.

Lubelski, Kazimierz. "Superman rządzi światem?" *Kierunki,* vol. 32, 1968, p. 12.

Łukasiewicz, Maciej. "Batman, Asterix i inni." *Wiedza i Życie*, vol. 10, 1967, pp. 27–32.

——. "Pismo obrazkowe." *Polityka*, 8 June 1974.

——. "Porucznik Ola i aferzystka Erika." *Wiedza i Życie*, vol. 5, 1971, pp. 6–12.

Lutomski, Paweł. "The Debate about a Center against Expulsions: An Unexpected Crisis in German–Polish Relations?" *German Studies Review*, vol. 27, 2004, pp. 449–68.

Lye, Sian. *The Real Hergé: The Inspiration behind Tintin*. Pen & Sword Books, 2020.

Łysak, Tomasz. "Contemporary Debates on the Holocaust in Poland: The Reception of Art Spiegelman's 'Graphic Novel' Maus." *Polin: Studies in Polish Jewry, Volume 21: 1968, Forty Years After*, edited by Leszek W. Głuchowski and Antony Polonsky, Littman Library of Jewish Civilization, 2009, pp. 469–79.

Łysiak, Waldemar. "Anatomia komiksu." *Perspektywy*, 18–25 December 1970.

——. "Bajthriller." *Literatura*, 3 September 1977.

——. "Monarchia komiksu." *Dookoła świata*, 26 October 1975, pp. 14–15.

——. "Monarchia komiksu II." *Dookoła świata*, 2 November 1975, pp. 12–13.

——. "Przejrzyj się w komiksie." *Polityka*, 23 April 1977.

Maciakiewicz, Katarzyna. "Rynek mangi w Polsce—oferta wydawnicza w latach 1996–2015." *Annales Universitatis Paedagogicae Cracoviensis. Studia ad Bibliothecarum Scientiam Pertinentia*, vol. 16, 2018, pp. 161–76.

Maciejewski, Bogdan. "Comics." *Sztandar Młodych*, 16–17 October 1976, p. 6.

Madsen, Frank, Per Sanderhage, and Niels Roland. *Danish Comics Today*. Danske Tegneserieskabere, 1997.

Mainardi, Patricia. *Another World: Nineteenth-Century Illustrated Print Culture*. Yale UP, 2017.

Małcużyński, Karol. "Włosi mają własne troski. Nie fraternizacja a prostytucja." *Robotnik*, 22 November 1946.

Malinowski, Sławomir W. "Trzydzieści lat—a ciągle młodzi." *Świat młodych*, 10 September 1987, p. 1.

*Mały Rocznik Statystyczny 1931*. Główny Urząd Statystyczny, 1931.

*Mały Rocznik Statystyczny 1937*. Główny Urząd Statystyczny, 1937.

Marciniak, Tomasz. "Koniec świata przygody, czyli Janusz Christa." *Guliwer*, vol. 4, 2008, pp. 31–36.

——. "Śmierć polskiego komiksu dziecięcego?" *Guliwer*, vol. 2, 2005, pp. 28–33.

Marecki, Piotr, and Ewelina Sasin. "'Ciężkie książki' vs. 'lekka i tania informacja.' Warunki produkcji książki w Polsce po 1989 roku." *Przegląd kulturoznawczy*, vol. 2, no. 24, 2015, pp. 108–25.

Mark, James, Artemy M. Kalinovsky, and Steffi Marung. Introduction. *Alternative Globalizations: Eastern Europe and the Postcolonial World*, edited by James Mark, Artemy M. Kalinovsky, and Steffi Marung, Indiana UP, 2020, pp. 1–32.

Mary, Rose. "Od stóp do głowy." *Przegląd Mody*, vol. 12, no. 15, 1937, p. 4.

Matejko, Aleksander. "Odszedł światły człowiek." *Kultura*, vol. 07/08, nos. 430/431, 1983, pp. 173–75.

Matsner Gruenberg, Sidonie. "The Comics as a Social Force." *The Journal of Educational Sociology*, vol. 18, no. 4, 1944, pp. 204–13.

Matusik, Marta Maria. "'Jesteśmy z wami, ludzie walczącej Korei.' Obraz Korei Północnej w Polskiej Kronice Filmowej 1947–1984." *Ogrody Nauk i Sztuk*, vol. 5, 2015, pp. 562–70.

Mazur, Mariusz. *Propagandowy obraz świata. Polityczne kampanie prasowe w PRL (1956–1980). Model analityczno-koncepcyjny.* Trio, 2003.

Mazur, Przemysław. "TM-Semic: historia w dziewięćiuset komiksach zawarta." *Magazyn Miłośników Komiksów KZ*, vol. 51, 2008, https://www.kzet.pl/2008_03/tm_historia.html. Accessed 22 May 2020.

Mazurek, Małgorzata. "Dishonest Saleswomen: On Gendered Politics of Shame and Blame in Polish State-Socialist Trade." *Labor in State Socialist Europe, 1945–1989: Contributions to a Global History of Work*, edited by Marsha Siefert, CEU Press, 2020, pp. 123–44.

——. "Keeping It Close to Home: Resourcefulness and Scarcity in Late Socialist and Post-Socialist Poland." *Communism Unwrapped: Consumption in Cold War Eastern Europe*, edited by Paulina Bren and Mary Neuburger, Oxford UP, 2012, pp. 404–35.

Meda, Juri. *Stelle e strips. La stampa a fumetti italiana tra americanismo e antiamericanismo.* EUM, 2007.

Meier, Stefan. "'Truth, Justice, and the Islamic Way': Conceiving the Cosmopolitan Muslim Superhero in The 99." *Transnational Perspectives on Graphic Narratives: Comics at the Crossroads*, edited by Shane Denson, Christina Meyer, and Daniel Stein, Bloomsbury, 2013, pp. 181–93.

Meneses, Juan. "Reconsidering International Comics: Foreignness, Locality, and the Third Space." *Journal of Graphic Novels and Comics*, vol. 5, no. 1, 2014, pp. 58–69.

Meyer, Christina. "Medial Transgressions: Comics—Sheet Music—Theatre—Toys." *Journal of Graphic Novels and Comics*, vol. 7, no. 3, 2016, pp. 293–305.

——. *Producing Mass Entertainment: The Serial Life of the Yellow Kid.* The Ohio State UP, 2019.

Michnik, Adam. "What Europe Means for Poland." *Journal of Democracy*, vol. 14, no. 4, 2003, pp. 128–36.

"Mickey Mouse zamieszczona w Encyclopaedia Britannica." *Kurjer Wileński*, 16 November 1934, p. 7.

Mihăilescu, Dana. "The Legacy of Communism through a Child's Lens: The Trusts of Emotional Knowledge out of Marzi's Poland." *Literary and Visual Dimensions of Contemporary Graphic Narratives*, edited by Mária Kiššová and Simona Hevešiová, Constantine the Philosopher UP, 2012, pp. 45–75.

Minorczyk-Cichy, Aldona. "Wielkie oczy mangi." *Dziennik Zachodni*, 15 March 1999.

Misiora, Marek. *Bibliografia komiksów wydanych w Polsce w latach 1905 (1858)–1999.* Centrala, 2010.

Mizwa, Stephen P. "The Kosciuszko Foundation Plans." *Bulletin of the Polish Institute of Arts and Sciences in America*, vol. 2, no. 3, 1944, p. 628.

MM. "Tacy piękni chłopcy." *Gazeta Wyborcza*, 12 February 2001.

"Morski komiks." *Morze*, vol. 5, no. 462, 1969.

Musiałowa, Alicja. "Przed Międzynarodową Konferencją w Obronie Dziecka." *Dziennik Łódzki*, 11 April 1952, p. 2.

Musiałowski, Paweł. "Mr Jedi." "Mangowy survival." *Kawaii*, vol. 2–3, 1999, p. 48.

"Myszka Mickey obchodzi we wrześniu 10 rocznicę urodzin." *Mój głosik*, 17 June 1938, p. 1.

"Myszka Miki." *Dziennik Wileński*, 21 April 1935, p. 14.

Nappi, Paolino. "Between Memory, Didacticism and the Jewish Revival: The Holocaust in Italian Comic Books." *Journal of Modern Jewish Studies. Special Issue Beyond Maus: Comic Books, Graphic Novels and the Holocaust*, vol. 17, no. 1, 2018, pp. 51–63.

Nappi, Paolino, and Ewa Stańczyk. "Women Cross Borders: Economic Migration in Contemporary Italian and Polish Comic Books." *Journal of Graphic Novels and Comics*, vol. 6, no. 3, 2015, pp. 230–45.

"Nauka nie idzie w las." *Życie Warszawy*, 15 October 1953, p. 3.

"Nehru przeciw comicsom oraz filmom propagującym wojnę." *Życie Warszawy*, 1 March 1955, p. 2.

North, Sterling. "A National Disgrace and a Challenge to American Parents." *Childhood Education*, vol. 17, no. 2, 1940, p. 56.

Nowak, Barbara A. "Serving Women and the State: The League of Women in Communist Poland." Unpublished PhD Thesis, The Ohio State University, 2004.

Nowak, Tomasz, et al. *1940 Katyń: zbrodnia na nieludzkiej ziemi*. Zin Zin Press, 2010.

Nowakowski, Witold. "Black Knight Batto." *Kawaii*, vol. 11, no. 15, 1998, pp. 48–49.

"Nowa porywająca powieść p.t. Chronometr Grozy." *Ilustrowany Kuryer Codzienny*, 21 July 1931.

"Nowe gwiazdy ekranu" and "Film trójwymiarowy." *Ilustrowany Kuryer Codzienny. Kuryer Filmowy*, 8 April 1931.

"Nowe publikacje Fundacji Kościuszkowskiej." *Dziennik Związkowy: Polish Daily Zgoda*, 15 May 1978.

Nowicka, Agata "Endo." "Mam poczucie totalnego farta. Rozmowa z Agatą 'Endo' Nowicką, ilustratorką i twórczynią komiksów." *Wyjście z getta. Rozmowy o kulturze komiksowej w Polsce*, edited by Sebastian Frąckiewicz, Stowarzyszenie 4000 malarzy, 2012, pp. 70–99.

"NYC-72 December Crypto Message." 15 December 1961. HU OSA 298-1-2-35-1670a; Records of Free Europe Committee: President's Office: Encrypted Telex Communication between FEC New York and RFE Munich; Open Society Archives at Central European University, Budapest.

Nyberg, Amy Kiste. "Comic Book Censorship in the United States." *Pulp Demons: International Dimensions of the Postwar Anti-Comics Campaign*, edited by John A. Lent, Fairleigh Dickinson UP, 1999, pp. 42–68.

———. "The Comics Code." *The Routledge Companion to Comics*, edited by Frank Bramlett, Roy T. Cook, and Aaron Meskin, Routledge, 2017, pp. 25–33.

———. *Seal of Approval: The History of the Comics Code*. UP of Mississippi, 1998.

Obremski, Wojciech. *Krótka historia sztuki komiksu w Polsce: 1945–2003*. Adam Marszałek, 2005.

Ochman, Ewa. *Post-Communist Poland—Contested Pasts and Future Identities*. Routledge, 2013.

Ochocki, Adam. "Jak się narodzili Wicek i Wacek." *Wicek i Wacek*. KAW, 1989.

Olszewska, Ewelina. "80 lat komiksu w Polsce." *Nasz Dziennik*, 15 March 1999.

Oostdijk, Diederik. "'Draw Yourself out of It': Miriam Katin's Graphic Metamorphosis of Trauma." *Journal of Modern Jewish Studies*, vol. 17, no. 1, 2018, pp. 79–92.

Openshaw, Roger, and Roy Shuker. "'Worthless and Indecent Literature': Comics and Moral Panic in Early Post-War New Zealand." *History of Education Review*, vol. 16, 1987, pp. 1–12.

Oppman, Artur, and Saturnin Sikorski, editors. *Albumowy Kalendarz Polski Satyryczny.* Druk Józefa Sikorskiego, 1895.

Ostrowska, Magdalena. "Problemy rynku mangi w Polsce." *Toruńskie Studia Bibliologiczne*, vol. 1, no. 10, 2013, pp. 69–88.

Otmazgin, Nissim. "Japan Imagined: Popular Culture, Soft Power, and Japan's Changing Image in Northeast and Southeast Asia." *Contemporary Japan*, vol. 24, no. 1, 2012, pp. 1–19.

———. "Meta-Narratives of Japanese Popular Culture and of Japan in Different Regional Contexts: Perspectives from East Asia, Western Europe, and the Middle East." *Regioninės studijos*, vol. 7, 2013, pp. 83–94.

"Oto Ameryka." *Dziennik Bałtycki,* 13 July 1953.

"Oto Ameryka." *Trybuna Robotnicza,* 17 July 1953.

"Oto Ameryka." *Życie Warszawy,* 16 December 1952, p. 4.

Owedyk, Krzysztof. "Tęsknota za niematerialnym światem." Interview by Witold Tkaczyk, *AQQ*, vol. 31, no. 1, 2004, pp. 48–49.

Oxoby, Marc. "Comics Code Authority." *St. James Encyclopedia of Popular Culture*, 2nd ed., edited by Thomas Riggs and Jim Cullen, St. James Press, 2013, pp. 667–68.

Paczkowski, Andrzej. *Prasa codzienna Warszawy w latach 1918–1939.* PIW, 1983.

———. "Prasa Drugiej Rzeczypospolitej (1918–1939): ogólna charakterystyka statystyczna." *Rocznik Historii Czasopiśmiennictwa Polskiego*, vol. 11, no. 1, 1972, pp. 49–88.

Paluszkiewicz, Monika. "Tytus dla doroslych." *Wprost*, 21 December 1997.

PAP. "Przeciw 'Mausowi.'" *Gazeta Wyborcza*, 28 May 2001.

Papuzińska, Magda. "Molo trzeszczy w posadach." *Przekrój*, 21 July 2002.

Parks, J. D. *Culture, Conflict, and Coexistence: American-Soviet Cultural Relations, 1917–1958.* MacFarland, 1983.

Parowski, Marciej. "Komiks: Chłopiec do bicia (II)." *Ekran*, 4 September 1977.

Paryz, Marek. "Beyond Parody: Polish Comic Book Westerns from the 1960s through the 2010s." *The Comic Book Western: New Perspectives on a Global Genre*, edited by Christopher Conway and Antoinette Sol, U of Nebraska P, 2022, 119–44.

Patrick, Kevin. *The Phantom Unmasked: America's First Superhero.* U of Iowa P, 2017.

Pawlas, Jerzy. "Trudny powrót komiksu." *Tygodnik Kulturalny*, 29 September 1979.

Piasecki, Władysław. "'American Comics' jako problem bibliotekarzy brytyjskich. Z zagadnień ochrony czytelników przed literaturą szkodliwą." *Przegląd Biblioteczny*, vol. 21, no. 3, 1953, pp. 219–26.

Pieczara, Anna, and Łukasz Dziatkiewicz. "Superman spod Kalisza." *Przekrój*, vol. 43, no. 2940, 2001, pp. 22–23.

*Pierwszy powszechny spis Rzeczypospolitej Polskiej z dnia 30 września 1921 roku.* Główny Urząd Statystyczny Rzeczypospolitej Polskiej, 1927.

Pilot, Marian. "Superman w Wietnamie." *Tygodnik Kulturalny,* 31 January 1971, pp. 5–6.

Piotrowski, Mariusz. "Obrazkomania." *Fakty,* 17 September 1988.

Piotrowski, Piotr. "How to Write a History of East-Central European Art?" *Third Text,* vol. 23, no. 1, 2009, pp. 5–14.

Plach, Eva. *The Clash of Moral Nations: Cultural Politics in Piłsudski's Poland, 1926–1935.* Ohio UP, 2006.

"Podarunki świąteczne Siedmiu Groszy." *Siedem Groszy,* 11 April 1935, p. 2.

"Podręczniki języka polskiego." *Dziennik Związkowy: Polish Daily Zgoda,* 5–6 January 1979.

Pojmann, Wendy. "For Mothers, Peace and Family: International (Non)-Cooperation among Italian Catholic and Communist Women's Organisations during the Early Cold War." *Gender and History,* vol. 23, no. 2, 2011, pp. 415–29.

Pokorna-Ignatowicz, Katarzyna. *Robotnicza Spółdzielnia Wydawnicza "Prasa–Książka–Ruch" w polskim systemie medialnym.* Krakowska Akademia im. Andrzeja Frycza Modrzewskiego, 2016.

Polch, Bogusław, and Władysław Krupka. *Kapitan Żbik 17: "Złoty" Mauritius.* Sport i Turystyka, 1970.

———. *Kapitan Żbik 23: Nocna wizyta.* Sport i Turystyka, 1972.

———. *Kapitan Żbik 32: Niewygodny świadek.* Sport i Turystyka, 1975.

———. Letter to Readers. *Kapitan Żbik 17: "Złoty" Mauritius,* Sport i Turystyka, 1970, p. 3.

———. Letter to Readers. *Kapitan Żbik 23: Nocna wizyta,* Sport i Turystyka, 1972, p. 3.

———. Letter to Readers. *Kapitan Żbik 32: Niewygodny świadek,* Sport i Turystyka, 1975, p. 3.

"Polityczne wychowanie przez apolityczne 'comicsy.'" *Życie Warszawy,* 7 January 1951, p. 3.

*Polityka kulturalna państwa. Założenia.* Ministerstwo Kultury i Sztuki, 1993.

"Polka Ball Aids Kosciuszko Fund." *New York Times,* 27 January 1945.

Polonsky, Antony, and Joanna B. Michlic. Introduction. *The Neighbors Respond: The Controversy over the Jedwabne Massacre in Poland,* edited by Antony Polonsky and Joanna B. Michlic, Princeton UP, 2004, pp. 1–43.

———, editors. *The Neighbors Respond: The Controversy Over the Jedwabne Massacre in Poland.* Princeton UP, 2004.

"Polsko-francuska współpraca przyczyni się do umocnienia pokoju w Europie." *Dziennik Polski,* 7 October 1972.

Precup, Mihaela. "The Autobiographical Mode in Post-Communist Romanian Comics: Everyday Life in Brynjar Åbel Bandlien's Strîmb Living and Andreea Chirică's The Year of the Pioneer." *Comics of the New Europe: Reflections and Intersections,* edited by Martha Kuhlman and José Alaniz, Leuven UP, 2020, pp. 239–59.

"Prowincjonalne zmartwienia." *Ilustrowany Kuryer Codzienny,* 20 July 1931, p. 4.

"Przeciw selekcji i atomówce." *Słowo Ludu,* 8 April 1950, p. 8.

"Przygody bezrobotnego Froncka." *Siedem Groszy,* 8 December 1938, p. 12.

"Przygody Profesora Nimbusa." *Dzień dobry!*, 1 May 1935, p. 6.

"Przyjęcie w bibliotece." *Mój głosik*, 7 July 1939, p. 4.

"Psychiatrist Charges Stalling Tactics on Legislation to Control Comic Books." *New York Times*, 24 January 1950.

Puźniak, Marcin. "Współczesny komiks polski—wersja niezależna." Unpublished MA Thesis, U of Rzeszów, 2005.

Rabiński, Jarosław. "Obraz Stanów Zjednoczonych Ameryki w Polskiej Kronice Filmowej 1948–1953." *Roczniki Humanistyczne*, vol. 2, 2011, pp. 171–96.

Reczulski, Łukasz, and Paula Gamus. "Historia łódzkiego fandomu mangi i anime w latach 1995–2010." *Acta Universitatis Lodziensis. Folia Linbrorum*, vol. 2, no. 21, 2015, pp. 27–50.

Reitberger, Reinhold, and Wolfgang Fuchs. *Comics: Anatomy of a Mass Medium*. Little, Brown and Company, 1972.

Rifas, Leonard. "Korean War Comic Books and the Militarization of US Masculinity." *Positions: East Asia Cultures Critique*, vol. 23, no. 4, 2015, pp. 619–31.

Rogalska, Halina. "Ku czemu zdąża młodzież niemiecka?" *Znak*, vol. 10, no. 6, 1958, pp. 725–28.

Rojek, Anna. "Niebezpieczny konwent?" *Dziennik Łódzki*, 20 November 2000.

Romek, Zbigniew. "Walka z 'amerykańskim zagrożeniem' w okresie stalinowskim." *Polska 1944/1945–1989. Życie codzienne w Polsce 1945–1955. Studia i materiały*, vol. 5, Instytut Historii PAN, 2001, pp. 173–220.

Rosenkranz, Patrick. *Rebel Visions: The Underground Comix Revolution 1963–1975*. Fantagraphics, 2002.

Rosiński, Grzegorz. "Impresjonista." Interview by Wojciech Orliński, *Gazeta Wyborcza*, 14 October 1999.

———. "Komiks spod znaku Erosa." Interview by Jolanta Gajda-Zadworna, *Życie Warszawy*, 20 March 2004.

Rosiński, Grzegorz, and Zbigniew Bryczkowski. "Jak chodzić? Jak jeździć?" *Kapitan Żbik 5: Diadem Tamary*, Sport i Turystyka, 1968, p. 3.

———. *Kapitan Żbik 5: Diadem Tamary*. Sport i Turystyka, 1968.

Rosiński, Grzegorz, Anna Kłodzińska, and Jan Tomaszewski. *Kapitan Żbik 16: Czarna Nefretete*. Sport i Turystyka, 1970.

———. Letter to Readers. *Kapitan Żbik 16: Czarna Nefretete*, Sport i Turystyka, 1970, p. 3.

Rosiński, Grzegorz, and Władysław Krupka. *Kapitan Żbik 10: Zapalniczka z pozytywką*. Sport i Turystyka, 1970.

———. *Kapitan Żbik 11: Spotkanie w "Kukerite."* Sport i Turystyka, 1970.

———. *Kapitan Żbik 13: Porwanie*. Sport i Turystyka, 1970.

———. Letter to Readers. *Kapitan Żbik 10: Zapalniczka z pozytywką*, Sport i Turystyka, 1970, p. 3.

———. Letter to Readers. *Kapitan Żbik 11: "Spotkanie w Kukerite,"* Sport i Turystyka, 1970, p. 3.

———. Letter to Readers. *Kapitan Żbik 13: Porwanie*, Sport i Turystyka, 1970, p. 3.

Rosiński, Grzegorz, and Stanisław Szczepański. *Kapitan Żbik 8: Tajemnica Ikony.* Sport i Turystyka, 1969.

——. "Pamiętaj!" *Kapitan Żbik 8: Tajemnica Ikony,* Sport i Turystyka, 1969, p. 3.

Rowland, Michael. "'Angry Young People': The Representation of Anglo-American Pop-Rock in Przekrój 1964–74." Unpublished BA Thesis, U of Amsterdam, 2020.

"Rozszerza się front pokoju." *Życie Warszawy,* 21 November 1950.

Rubenstein, Anne. *Bad Language, Naked Ladies, and Other Threats to the Nation: A Political History of Comic Books in Mexico.* Duke UP, 1998.

Rubin, Barry, and Judith Colp Rubin. *Hating America: A History.* Oxford UP, 2004.

Rusek, Adam. *Dawny komiks polski. Tom 4: Przygody bezrobotnego Froncka.* Wydawnictwo Komiksowe and Prószyński i S-ka, 2016.

——. "Krótka historia opowieści obrazkowych w Polsce Ludowej." *45–89: Comics behind the Iron Curtain,* edited by Michał Słomka, Centrala, 2009, pp. 31–41.

——. *Leksykon polskich bohaterów i serii komiksowych.* Centrala, 2010.

——. "Magazyn 'Relax' (1976–1981) i jego losy." *Rocznik Historii Prasy Polskiej,* vol. 1, no. 33, 2014, pp. 74–87.

——. "Od 'Grzesia' do 'Gazetki Miki': dzieje czasopism obrazkowych dla młodzieży w II Rzeczypospolitej." *Rocznik Historii Prasy Polskiej,* vol. 12, no. 2, 2009, pp. 57–76.

——. *Od rozrywki do ideowego zaangażowania. Komiksowa rzeczywistość w Polsce w latach 1939–1955.* Biblioteka Narodowa, 2011.

——. "Od szalonego Grzesia do Szninkla: krótka historia samoistnych publikacji komiksowych w Polsce do roku 1989." *Bibliotheca Nostra,* vol. 46, no. 4, 2016, pp. 83–96.

——. *Tarzan, Matołek i inni. Cykliczne historyjki obrazkowe w Polsce w latach 1919–1939.* Biblioteka Narodowa, 2001.

R. W. "Komiksy uczą nie tylko języków obcych." *Kurier Polski,* 22–23 May 1976.

Sabin, Roger. "Ally Sloper: The First Comics Superstar?" *A Comics Studies Reader,* edited by Jeet Heer and Kent Worcester, UP of Mississippi, 2009, pp. 177–89.

——. *Comics, Comix and Graphic Novels.* Phaidon, 1996.

Sanders, Clinton R. "Icons of the Alternative Culture: The Themes and Functions of Underground Comix." *Journal of Popular Culture,* vol. 8, no. 4, 1975, pp. 836–52.

Santos, Jorge. *Graphic Memories of the Civil Rights Movement: Reframing History in Comics.* U of Texas P, 2019.

Schmölzer, Hilde. "O komiksie." *Forum,* 23–29 July 1970.

Scholz, Michael. "'Comics' in der deutschen Zeitungsforschung vor 1945." *Deutsche Comicforschung,* vol. 11, 2015, pp. 59–84.

——. "The First World War and the German Revolution of 1918–1919 in East German Comics." *European Comic Art,* vol. 8, no. 2, 2015, pp. 34–60.

——. "Images of Spies and Counter Spies in East German Comics." *Comics of the New Europe: Reflections and Intersections,* edited by Martha Kuhlman and José Alaniz, Leuven UP, 2020, pp. 159–76.

Semczuk, Przemysław. "Wybrałem Pol(s)kę." *Newsweek,* 29 March 2009.

Serkowska, Danuta. "Kobieta w komiksie. Od Amazonki do . . . jokera." *Zeszyty Komiksowe*, vol. 3, 2005, pp. 5–7.

Sheridan, Martin. *Comics and Their Creators: Life Stories of American Cartoonists.* Luna Press, 1971.

Shibata, Yasuko. "Konsumpcja globalnej kultury japońskiej we współczesnej Polsce." *Przemiany kulturowe we współczesnej Polsce. Ramy, właściwości, epizody,* edited by Joanna Kurczewska, Wydawnictwo IFIS PAN, 2016, pp. 613–39.

Sieczkowski, Grzegorz. "Armia żółtych smoków." *Rzeczpospolita,* 27 October 1995.

"Silly Symphony." *Wiadomości filmowe,* 1 January 1934, p. 14.

Sitkiewicz, Paweł. *Gorączka filmowa. Kinomania w międzywojennej Polsce.* Słowo/obraz terytoria, 2019.

——. *Miki i myszy. Walt Disney i film rysunkowy w przedwojennej Polsce.* Słowo/obraz terytoria, 2012.

——. *Polska szkoła animacji.* Słowo/obraz terytoria, 2011.

"Situation Report: Poland, 12 December 1960." 12 December 1960. HU OSA 300–8–47–124–30; Records of Radio Free Europe/Radio Liberty Research Institute: Publications Department: Situation Reports; Open Society Archives at Central European University, Budapest.

Siuda, Piotr. "In Pursuit of Pop Culture: Reception of Pop Culture in the People's Republic of Poland as Opposition to the Political System—Example of the Science Fiction Fandom." *European Journal of Cultural Studies,* vol. 17, no. 2, 2014, pp. 187–208.

Siuda, Piotr, and Anna Koralewska. *Japonizacja. Anime i jego polscy fani.* Wydawawnictwo Naukowe Katedra, 2014.

Skarżyński, Jerzy. "O Międzynarodowym Salonie Komiksu." *Przekrój,* vol. 1, no. 1604, 1976, p. 22.

——. "Z komiksowego raju." *Przekrój,* vols. 51–53, nos. 1758–60, 1978, p. 39.

Skonka, Czesław. "Cenna inicjatywa Sportu i Turystyki." *Słowo Powszechne,* 10 May 1985, p. 5.

Skwarnicki, Marek. "Nowe języki." *Znak,* vol. 12, no. 4, 1960, pp. 525–32.

Ślęzak, Jolanta. "Karykatura socrealistyczna o wojnie w Korei—na przykładzie wybranych rysunków satyrycznych opublikowanych na łamach 'Trybuny Ludu' w latach 1950–1953." *Res Politicae,* vol. 1, 2011, pp. 253–69.

Słomka, Michał. "Polacy lubią brąz: czyli o heroizacji polskiej historii w komiksie. Zarys zagadnienia." *Komiks a problem kiczu: 9 Sympozjum Komiksologiczne. Antologia Referatów,* edited by Krzysztof Skrzypczyk, Stowarzyszenie Twórców "Contur," 2009, pp. 80–81.

Smolak, Marek. Letter to *Relax. Relax,* vol. 3, 1977, p. 2.

Smolderen, Thierry. *The Origins of Comics: From William Hogarth to Winsor McCay.* Translated by Bart Beaty and Nick Nguyen, UP of Mississippi, 2014.

Sobala, Zbigniew, and Władysław Krupka. *Kapitan Żbik 20: Strzał przed północą.* Sport i Turystyka, 1971.

Sobala, Zbigniew, Anna Kłodzińska, and Jan Tomaszewski. *Kapitan Żbik 9: Kryształowe Okruchy.* Sport i Turystyka, 1970.

——. "Niewypały grożą ci śmiercią! Strzeż się ich!" *Kapitan Żbik 9: Kryształowe Okruchy*, Sport i Turystyka, 1970, p. 3.

Sostaric, Mia. "The American Wartime Propaganda during World War II." *Australasian Journal of American Studies*, vol. 38, no. 1, 2019, pp. 17–43.

Sowa, Marzena. Introduction. *Marzi: A Memoir*, by Sylvain Savoia and Sowa, translated by Anjali Singh, Vertigo, 2011, pp. 1–2.

"Spellman Warns on Communist Rise: 45,000 at Holy Name Service Hear Cardinal Make Plea for Aid to Democracy." *New York Times*, 29 September 1947, p. 12.

Spiegelman, Art. *MetaMAUS: A Look inside a Modern Classic, Maus*. Pantheon Books, 2011.

Śpiewak, Helena. "Obrazek z dymkiem." *Perspektywy*, 27 May 1988, p. 23.

Stańczyk, Ewa. "De-Judaizing the Shoah in Polish Comic Books." *Journal of Modern Jewish Studies. Special Issue beyond Maus: Comic Books, Graphic Novels and the Holocaust*, vol. 17, no. 1, 2018, pp. 36–50.

Stark, Larry. "An Appreciation." *Horror Comics of the 1950's*, edited by Ron Barlow and Bhob Stewart, Nostalgia Press, 1971.

Staroń, Justyna. "Matołek Broda. Przygody twórczo-wydawnicze." *Poznańskie Studia Polonistyczne. Seria Literacka*, vol. 26, 2015, pp. 355–67.

Sterling, Christopher H. "Feature Syndicate." *Encyclopedia of Journalism*, edited by Christopher H. Sterling, SAGE, 2009, pp. 569–71.

Stopnicka Heller, Celia. *On the Edge of Destruction: Jews of Poland between the Two World Wars*. Wayne State UP, 1993.

Strömberg, Fredrik. "Comics Studies in the Nordic Countries—Field or Discipline?" *Journal of Graphic Novels and Comics*, vol. 7, no. 2, 2016, pp. 134–55.

Strzyżewski, Tomasz. *Wielka księga cenzury PRL w dokumentach*. Prohibita, 2015.

Stuart, John. "Amerykanie 'wychowują' dzieci." *Życie Warszawy*, 31 August 1951, p. 3.

——. "Koszmar dzieci amerykańskich." *Dziennik Bałtycki*, 30 August 1951.

"Ś. p. Kamil Mackiewicz" (Obituary). *Dziennik Płocki*, 14 December 1931.

Świątecka, K. "Dwa światy—dwie kultury." *Na Straży Wybrzeża. Gazeta Marynarki Wojennej*, 8 May 1951.

"Święto dzieci w Rybniku." *Siedem Groszy*, 12 June 1935, p. 2.

Szafrańska, Monika. "Kobieta w komiksie—bohater drugiej kategorii." *"Gorsza" kobieta. Dyskursy inności, samotności, szaleństwa*, edited by Daria Adamowicz, Yulia Anisimovets, and Olga Taranek, Sutoris, 2008, pp. 57–63.

Szałek, Jakub. "'I śmiech niekiedy może być nauką.' Polska polityka międzywojenna w czasopiśmie satyrycznym Mucha." *Media—Biznes—Kultura. Dziennikarstwo i komunikacja społeczna*, vol. 4, 2011, pp. 111–26.

Szancer, Jan Marcin. *Curriculum Vitae*. Czytelnik, 1969.

Szczygieł, Mariusz. "Powściągliwie o zbrodni." *100/XX. Antologia polskiego reportażu XX wieku*, Czarne, 2014, p. 610.

Szép, Eszter. "Avatars and Iteration in Contemporary Hungarian Autobiographical Comics." *Comics of the New Europe: Reflections and Intersections*, edited by Martha Kuhlman and José Alaniz, Leuven UP, 2020, pp. 261–75.

"Szkoła młodocianych zbrodniarzy." *Dziennik Bałtycki*, 10 April 1949.

Szlachtycz, Mateusz. *Kapitan Żbik. Portret pamięciowy*. The Facto, 2017.

"Szukajcie bezrobotnego Froncka." *Siedem Groszy*, 23 October 1934, p. 7.

"Szukajcie bezrobotnego Froncka." *Siedem Groszy*, 29 October 1934, p. 8.

"Szukajcie bezrobotnego Froncka." *Siedem Groszy*, 16 April 1935, p. 2.

"Szukajcie bezrobotnego Froncka." *Siedem Groszy*, 3 August 1935, p. 2.

Szyłak, Jerzy. *Komiks*. Wydawnictwo Znak, 2000.

———. *Komiks i okolice kina*. Wydawnictwo Uniwersytetu Gdańskiego, 2000.

———. *Komiks i okolice pornografii: o seksualnych stereotypach w kulturze masowej*. Akia, 1996.

———. *Komiks: świat przerysowany*. Słowo/obraz terytoria, 1998.

———. "Komiks w czasach niekoniecznie normalnych." *Teksty Drugie*, vol. 5, 2017, pp. 147–67.

———. *Komiks w kulturze ikonicznej XX wieku*. Słowo/Obraz Terytoria, 1999.

———. *Komiks w szponach miernoty: rozprawy i szkice*. Timof Comics, 2013.

Teler, Marek. "Królewna Modzelewska i Chór Dana, czyli jak zdubbingowano 'Królewnę Śnieżkę.'" *HistMag*, 6 January 2018, https://histmag.org/Krolewna-Modzelewska-i-Chor-Dana-czyli-jak-zdubbingowano-Krolewne-Sniezke-16211/. Accessed 17 June 2020.

Teneta, Adam. "Gitowiec w internacie." *Dziennik Polski*, 28 February 1975.

Tevnell, Waldemar. "Król komiksu." Interview by Teresa Kokocińska, *Sukces*, September 1993, pp. 24–25.

Thomas, Jolyon Baraka. *Drawing on Tradition: Manga, Anime, and Religion in Contemporary Japan*. U of Hawai'i P, 2012.

Thompson, Kristin. *Exporting Entertainment: America in the World Film Market 1907–1934*. British Film Institute Publishing, 1985.

Tkaczyk, Witold. "Od piktogramu do komiksu." *Życie Warszawy*, 26 February 1995.

———. "Wyjść z komiksem do szerokiego odbiorcy." Interview by Michał Błażejczyk, *Zeszyty komiksowe*, vol. 12, 2011, pp. 44–49.

Tobera, Marek. "Początki transformacji polskiego rynku książki. Rekonstrukcja najważniejszych wydarzeń z lat 1989–1995 (część pierwsza)," *Przegląd Biblioteczny*, vol. 3, 2010, pp. 285–302.

———. "Rynek książki w Polsce (1989–2000)." *Przegląd Biblioteczny*, vol. 3, 2001, pp. 237–41.

Tochman, Wojciech. "Gdzie jesteś, kapitanie." *Gazeta Wyborcza*, 20–21 August 1994, pp. 10–12.

Toeplitz, Jerzy. *Historia filmu polskiego (1930–1939)*. Wydawnictwa Artystyczne i Filmowe, 1988.

Toeplitz, Krzysztof Teodor. *Sztuka komiksu*. Czytelnik, 1985.

Tomaszewski, Tomasz. "Zjawisko komiksologii w optyce twórcy komiksów i organizatora imprez." *10. Sympozjum Komiksologiczne. Komiks a komiksologia*, edited by Krzysztof Skrzypczyk, Łódzki Dom Kultury, 2010, pp. 109–11.

Tota, Lisa, and Trever Hagen, editors. *Routledge International Handbook of Memory Studies*. Routledge, 2016.

Trenkler, Carsten, and Nikolaus Wolf. "Economic Integration across Borders: The Polish Interwar Economy 1921–1937." *European Review of Economic History*, vol. 9, 2005, pp. 199–231.

"Twórca słynnych filmów obrazkowych z Mickey Mouse." *Nasz Przegląd Ilustrowany*, 14 May 1933, p. 6.

Tylicka, Barbara. "Komiksy—sztuka czy szmira?" *Świat młodych*, 1 April 1975.

Ujazdowski, Kazimierz Michał. "Słowo wstępne." *1956: Poznański Czerwiec*. Zin Zin Press, 2006, p. 3.

Untitled drawings by A. Heidrich and others. *Gazetka Miki*, 2 April 1939.

Van Heuckelom, Kris. "Praca fizyczna z różowymi akcentami. Polskie doświadczenie migracyjne w powieści graficznej Rozmówki polsko-angielskie Agaty Wawryniuk." *Teksty Drugie*, vol. 3, 2016, pp. 81–97.

Verdery, Katherine. "The Transition from Socialism: Anthropology and Eastern Europe." *Lewis Henry Morgan Lectures, University of Rochester*. Cambridge UP, 1992.

"W Chorzowie." *Siedem Groszy*, 8 December 1938, p. 8.

Wagner, Gerhard. "Nationalism and Cultural Memory in Poland: The European Union Turns East." *International Journal of Politics, Culture, and Society*, vol. 17, 2003, pp. 191–212.

Wałęsa, Lech. "Wstęp." *Solidarność: 25 lat. Nadzieja zwykłych ludzi*. Zin Zin Press, 2005, p. 3.

Weathersby, Kathryn. "The Soviet Role in the Early Phase of the Korean War: New Documentary Evidence." *Journal of American-East Asian Relations*, vol. 2, no. 4, 1993, pp. 425–58.

Weggi, Wiktor. "Cywilizacja obrazkowa atakuje." *Życie Warszawy*, 30 May 1987.

Weiner, Robert V., and Carrye Kay Syma. Introduction. *Graphic Novels and Comics in the Classroom: Essays on the Educational Power of Sequential Art*, edited by Carrye Kay Syma and Robert V. Weiner, McFarland & Company, 2013, pp. 1–10.

Welt, Jacek. "Od Supermanów do Super-Zbrodniarzy." *Morze*, vol. 12, 1950, pp. 10–11.

Wertham, Fredric. *Seduction of the Innocent*. Rinehart & Company, Inc., 1954.

"'Wesołe książeczki' kardynała Spellmana. O pewnym rodzaju amerykańskiej propagandy." *Słowo Ludu*, 8 April 1950, p. 8.

Whitted, Qiana. *EC Comics: Race, Shock, and Social Protest*. Rutgers UP, 2019.

Wiśniewski, Mieczysław, and Ryszard Doński. *Kapitan Żbik 7: Śledzić Fiata 03–17 WE*. Sport i Turystyka, 1968.

——. "Przestrzeganie przepisów przeciwpożarowych twoim obowiązkiem." *Kapitan Żbik 7: Śledzić Fiata 03–17 WE*, Sport i Turystyka, 1968, p. 3.

Witkowska, Ewa. *Komiks japoński w Polsce. Historia i kontrowersje*. Kirin, 2012.

Witkowska, Joanna. "Creating False Enemies: John Bull and Uncle Sam as Food for Anti-Western Propaganda in Poland." *Journal of Transatlantic Studies*, vol. 6, no. 2, 2008, pp. 123–30.

Witz, Ignacy. "Kazimierz Grus" (Obituary). *Życie Warszawy*, 5 July 1955.

Wojtczuk, Michał. "Kapitan Żbik w żałobie. Zmarł twórca kultowego komiksu." *Gazeta Wyborcza. Warszawa*, 5 September 2019.

Wójtowicz-Podhorski, Mariusz, and Jacek Przybylski. *Pierwsi w boju: obrona Poczty Polskiej w Gdańsku*. Zin Zin Press, 2010.

Wolk, Douglas. *Reading Comics: How Graphic Novels Work and What They Mean*. Da Capo Press, 2007.

Wolski, Tomasz. "Tytus, Kloss i A'Tomuś." *Przekrój*, vol. 43, no. 2940, 2001, p. 16.

Woynarowski, Jakub. "Story art. W poszukiwaniu awangardy polskiego komiksu." *Kultura niezależna w Polsce 1989–2009*, edited by Piotr Marecki, Korporacja Ha!Art, 2010, pp. 171–98.

Wright, Bradford W. *Comic Book Nation: The Transformation of Youth Culture in America*. The Johns Hopkins UP, 2001.

Wróbel, Olga. *Ciemna strona księżyca*. Centrala, 2014.

——. "Dwie rozmowy z Olgą Wróbel: luty 2010 i maj 2012 roku." *Polski komiks kobiecy*, edited by Kinga Kuczyńska, Timof i cisi wspólnicy, 2012, pp. 57–61.

——. "Posłowie." *Ciemna strona księżyca*. Centrala, 2014.

——. "Z szuflady na barykady." *Znak*, vol. 745, 2017, pp. 100–105.

Wróblewski, Jerzy, Wanda Falkowska, and Barbara Seidler. *Kapitan Żbik 39: Wyzwanie dla silniejszego*. Sport i Turystyka, 1975.

Wróblewski, Jerzy, Zbigniew Gabiński, and Jerzy Bednarczyk. *Kapitan Żbik 41: Wodorosty i pasożyty*. Sport i Turystyka, 1976.

——. Letter to Readers. *Kapitan Żbik 41: Wodorosty i pasożyty*, Sport i Turystyka, 1976, p. 3.

Wróblewski, Jerzy, and Władysław Krupka. *Kapitan Żbik 30: Tajemniczy nurek*. Sport i Turystyka, 1973.

——. *Kapitan Żbik 47: Granatowa Cortina*. Sport i Turystyka, 1978.

——. *Kapitan Żbik 50: "St. Marie" wychodzi w morze*. Sport i Turystyka, 1982.

——. *Kapitan Żbik 52: Ślady w lesie*. Sport i Turystyka, 1982.

——. Letter to Readers. *Kapitan Żbik 30: Tajemniczy nurek*, Sport i Turystyka, 1973, p. 3.

——. Letter to Readers. *Kapitan Żbik 47: Granatowa Cortina*, Sport i Turystyka, 1978, p. 3.

——. Letter to Readers. *Kapitan Żbik 50: "St. Marie" wychodzi w morze*, Sport i Turystyka, 1982, p. 3.

——. Letter to Readers. *Kapitan Żbik 52: Ślady w lesie*, Sport i Turystyka, 1982, p. 3.

Wróblewski, Jerzy, and Stanisław Milc. *Kapitan Żbik 22: Jaskinia zbójców*. Sport i Turystyka, 1976.

Wrona, Grażyna. "'Przeciw bezwstydowi w druku i obrazku.' Krakowska cenzura w walce z demoralizacją (1918–1939)." *Klio. Czasopismo poświęcone dziejom Polski i powszechnym*, vol. 2, 2011, pp. 97–112.

Wrona, Katarzyna. "Zmiana formuły 'Przekroju' w latach 2000–2013." *Acta Universitatis Lodziensis. Folia Literaria Polonica*, vol. 2, no. 28, 2015, pp. 221–40.

"Wychowankowie amerykańskiej 'kultury.'" *Życie Warszawy*, 5 October 1954, p. 3.

"Wystawę 'Oto Ameryka' zwiedziło 100 tys. osób." *Echo Krakowskie*, 29 April 1954, p. 3.

Żaglewski, Tomasz. "Białe Orły komiksu. Wokół polskiej specyfiki narracji superbohaterskich." *Teksty Drugie*, vol. 5, 2017, pp. 108–28.

Zajiček, Edward. *Zarys historii gospodarczej kinematografii polskiej. Kinematografia wolnorynkowa 1896–1939*. Wydawnictwo PWSFTviT, 2008.

Zanettin, Federico. "Translation, Censorship and the Development of European Comics Cultures." *Perspectives: Studies in Translation Theory and Practice*, vol. 26, no. 6, 2018, pp. 868–84.

Zapała, Mateusz. "Polski rynek komiksowy w latach 1989–2010." *Zeszyty Prasoznawcze*, vol. 2, no. 214, 2013, pp. 204–37.

"Zap! Crash! Pow! Sigh! Świat zwariował na punkcie komiksów." *Tygodnik kulturalny*, 9 October 1988.

Zdrzynicki, Piotr. "Ciemna strona tuszu." *Dziennik Łódzki*, 27–29 October 1993.

Zduńczyk, Justyna. "Japońskie anime." *Gazeta Wyborcza: Lublin*, 4 December 1997.

Żelazny, Marek. "Antypolonizm literacką fikcją." *Nasz Dziennik*, 14 March 2002, pp. 1–2.

Zhang, Xiaoming. *Red Wings over the Yalu: China, the Soviet Union, and the Air War in Korea*. Texas A&M UP, 2002.

Ziemilski, Andrzej. "Filozofia i obrazki. 24,000,000 komiksów." *Życie Warszawy*, 29 December 1963, p. 5.

Zientek, Jolanta K. "Dlaczego landrynki nie wschodzą, czyli komiks po polsku." *Walka młodych*, 1 August 1976, p. 8.

Ziolkowska, Sarah, and Vivian Howard. "'Forty-One-Year-Old Female Academics Aren't Supposed to Like Comics!': The Value of Comic Books to Adult Readers." *Graphic Novels and Comics in Libraries and Archives: Essays on Readers, Research, History and Cataloging*, edited by Robert G. Weiner, McFarland, 2010, pp. 154–66.

Żółkiewski, Stefan. "Sprostać współczesności." *Polityka*, vol. 46, 1972, p. 6.

Zorbaugh, Harvey. "The Comics—There They Stand!" *The Journal of Educational Sociology*, vol. 18, no. 4, 1944, pp. 196–203.

"Zrobiłem to dla dreszczyku emocji." *Echo Krakowa*, 13 November 1948.

Zubrzycki, Geneviève. *The Crosses of Auschwitz: Nationalism and Religion in Post-Communist Poland*. Chicago UP, 2006.

Żuliński, Leszek. *Foksal 17*. PIW, 2006.

Zwierzchowski, Piotr. "'Comicsy' w służbie imperializmu." *Kultura Popularna*, vol. 1, 2004, pp. 113–18.

"Życie sentymentalne Charlie Chaplina." *Ilustrowany Kuryer Codzienny. Kuryer Filmowy*, 30 June 1931.

Żynda, Marcin. "'Wysoce demoralizująca i pornograficzna' inicjatywa wydawnicza. Obrona moralności publicznej a wolność słowa w międzywojennym Grudziądzu." *Klio. Czasopismo poświęcone dziejom Polski i powszechnym*, vol. 2, 2011, pp. 143–48.

# INDEX

## STUDIES IN COMICS AND CARTOONS

Jared Gardner, Charles Hatfield, and Rebecca Wanzo, Series Editors
Lucy Shelton Caswell, Founding Editor Emerita

Books published in Studies in Comics and Cartoons focus exclusively on comics and graphic literature, highlighting their relation to literary studies. The series includes monographs and edited collections that cover the history of comics and cartoons from the editorial cartoon and early sequential comics of the nineteenth century through webcomics of the twenty-first. Studies that focus on international comics are also considered.